Aboriginal Australia

SECOND EDITION

Aboriginal Australia

An Introductory Reader
in Aboriginal Studies
SECOND EDITION

Edited by Colin Bourke,
Eleanor Bourke and Bill Edwards

University of Queensland Press

First published 1994 by University of Queensland Press
Box 42, St Lucia, Queensland 4067 Australia
Second edition 1998

The typeset text of this book was supplied by the editors in camera-ready form.
Printed in Australia by McPherson's Printing Group, Victoria

Distributed in the USA and Canada by
International Specialized Book Services, Inc.,
5804 N.E. Hassalo Street, Portland, Oregon 97213-3640

Cataloguing in Publication Data
National Library of Australia

Aboriginal Australia: An introductory reader in Aboriginal studies.

New ed.
Bibliography.
Includes index.

[1.] Aborigines, Australian. [2.] Aborigines, Australian —
Ethnic identity. [3.] Aborigines, Australian — Cultural
assimilation. [4.] Aborigines, Australian — Social life and
customs. [5.] Aborigines, Australian — Social conditions.
6. Australia — Race relations — History. I. Bourke, Colin.
II. Bourke, Eleanor. III. Edwards, W.H. (William Howell).

305.89915

ISBN 0 7022 3051 0

Contents

Preface to Second Edition

The chapters in the first edition of this volume published in 1994 were written to accompany the Open Learning Aboriginal Studies course. The material was originally adapted from scripts developed for the 13 television programs presented on ABC TV.

The Open Learning course was prepared soon after the momentous Native Title decision of the High Court overturned the previous concept of *terra nullius*, by recognising pre-colonial occupation of Australia by the indigenous people including property rights.

The use of the first edition has encouraged the University of Queensland Press to publish this second edition. This has provided an opportunity to correct typographical and other errors which were present in the first edition. It has also enabled the authors to bring the content up-to-date, by referring to significant events of the past three years. These include the Wik decision of the High Court which found that the granting of pastoral leases did not necessarily extinguish native title rights, the Stolen Generations Report on the removal of Aboriginal children from their families, the movement towards Reconciliation between Aborigines and other Australians; the rise of conservative movements in reaction to these developments, and the growing concern about continued racism in Australian society.

Each chapter of the volume deals with a specific topic and attempts to introduce readers to the traditional, historical and contemporary aspects of that topic. We trust that this revised edition will increase understanding of indigenous societies in Australia and assist in the process of reconciliation.

The editors thank staff of the University of Queensland Press, including Rosanne Fitzgibbon, for their patient guidance in preparing the manuscript, and also Christine Keen of the Faculty of Aboriginal and Islander Studies for her commitment in preparing the manuscript.

Colin J. Bourke   )
Eleanor Bourke   ) Editors
Bill Edwards   )

The editors wish to thank the authors for their dedication to the cause of presenting, as authentically as possible, these perspectives of indigenous Australia.

About the Authors

Editors

Professor Colin Bourke, MBE, was born in Sunshine, Victoria, in 1936, son of an Aboriginal *Gamilaroi* mother and an Irish Australian father. He grew up at Yarrawonga and, after attending parish Catholic primary schools, he attended Wangaratta High School.

After twenty years as a primary school teacher he has worked in the public service and universities and is currently Professor and Dean, Faculty of Aboriginal and Islander Studies, University of South Australia. Professor Bourke has also worked in an honorary capacity for Aboriginal community organisations involved with education, welfare, race relations and Aboriginal advancement for two decades. He has held a number of advisory positions for Federal and state governments and tertiary organisations.

Eleanor Bourke, a descendant of the Wergaia and Wamba Wamba peoples, was born at Hamilton, Victoria. Eleanor became active in Aboriginal politics in the 1960s through various Aboriginal women's meetings. In the late 1970s Eleanor become the first Victorian woman on the National Aboriginal Education Committee.

In 1979 she was Aboriginal Liaison Officer at the University of Melbourne and has held several senior appointments including Aboriginal Adviser to the Victorian Government, Director of Aboriginal and Torres Strait Islander Services, Commonwealth Department of Social Security and Aboriginal Adviser to the Office of the Status of Women in the Department of the Prime Minister and Cabinet. An Associate Professor at the University of South Australia, Eleanor became Director of the Aboriginal Research Institute in 1989, among her qualifications she holds a Master of Educational Studies from the University of Adelaide. Eleanor is a fluent speaker of Greek, has a Greek Interpreter's Certificate. As Director of the Aboriginal Research Institute she has won many major Commonwealth grants and published extensively.

Bill Edwards is an adjunct lecturer in the Faculty of Aboriginal and Islander Studies, at the University of South Australia and an ordained Minister of The Uniting Church in Australia. A graduate of Arts and Education at the University of Melbourne, he was Superintendent of Ernabella Mission in the far north west of South Australia from 1958 to 1972, Superintendent of Mowanjum Mission in north west Western Australia in 1972-73, and Parish Minister of the Pitjantjatjara Parish of The Uniting Church in Australia in 1973 and from 1976 to 1980.

Bill's teaching and research interests include Pitjantjatjara language, Aboriginal religion and mission history. He is the author of many articles and two books and he interprets for Pitjantjatjara people in hospitals and courts. He has also been involved in cross-cultural awareness training of medical staff and police officers.

Notes on Other Contributors

Franchesca Alberts is Curator in the Division of Anthropology, South Australian Museum in Adelaide. She obtained her degree in Aboriginal Affairs Administration at the University of South Australia in 1991. Franchesca comes originally from Darwin and has curated exhibitions for the World Council of Churches and Tandanya, the National Aboriginal Cultural Institute in Adelaide. She has also worked with the Remote Areas Services Unit of the Department of Social Security in the Northern Territory.

Franchesca's research interests include most aspects of Aboriginal art and culture, but particularly those involving Aboriginal youth and the representation of Aboriginal women in museums and art collections.

Rob Amery has worked in a variety of Aboriginal contexts including Central Australia, north east Arnhem Land and southern South Australia. He has worked in the field, taught linguistics within tertiary institutions and worked on a national curriculum project, the Australian Indigenous Languages Framework (AILF) which introduced Aboriginal and Torres Strait Islander languages into senior secondary schools.

Rob is currently completing a PhD in Linguistics at the University of Adelaide where he is researching efforts to relearn and revive Kaurna, the language of the Adelaide Plains, from nineteenth century sources. In 1997, with the support of the Kaurna people, he introduced a course in Kaurna linguistics at the University of Adelaide.

Christopher Anderson is Director of the South Australian Museum. He obtained a Ph.D in Anthropology from the University of Queensland in 1984. He has worked with Aboriginal people since 1976 in Cape York Peninsula, north Queensland and more recently in Central Australia. His main publications include works on the political economy of Aboriginal Australia, contact history and contemporary Western Desert art. Dr Anderson has curated a number of exhibitions including (with others), 'Dreamings: The Art of Aboriginal Australia', and 'Boomerang'. He has a special interest in the relationship between museums and indigenous peoples and has been instrumental in developing and running the Secret/Sacred Object Custodianship Programme at the South Australian Museum.

Alwin Chong is a Research Associate with the Aboriginal Research Institute (ARI). He previously taught Aboriginal Studies with the School of Aboriginal and Islander Administration at the University of South Australia. He obtained his BA from the University of South Australia in 1991. Born at Mareeba, Queensland and raised in Mt Isa, Alwin travelled extensively before working in the Northern Territory where he has ancestral roots.

Alwin's focus is on Aboriginal enterprise with particular interest in Aboriginal organisations in the regions around Alice Springs and Kalgoorlie.

Helen Cox was originally from the Northern Territory but came to Adelaide to continue her education. The Aboriginal Task Force was her first base for tertiary studies. In the following years she completed a Bachelor of Social Work, an Associate Diploma in Community Development, a Bachelor of Laws (Honours) and a Graduate Diploma in Legal Practice.

Helen has been employed in a variety of areas including research, social work, counselling, legal work and tutoring. She is Administrator/Solicitor for the Norwood Community Legal Service.

Olga Gostin is a Senior Lecturer in The Unaipon School, Faculty of Aboriginal and Islander Studies, at the University of South Australia. She obtained her BA Hons degree in Anthropology and

African Administration at the University of the Witwatersrand (South Africa) in 1962. Between 1963-5 she carried out field work among the Kuni of Papua and obtained her Doctorate in Anthropology from the Australian National University in 1968. In 1993 she completed the Master in Environmental Studies Degree at Adelaide University.

Olga's teaching and research interests include all aspects of Australian Aboriginal cultures with particular focus on environmental land management issues. Her book on heritage, conservation and tourism at Mungo National Park "Accessing the Dreaming" was published in 1993.

Howard Groome has been involved in Aboriginal education for most of his professional life. He has been the principal of Aboriginal schools in Victoria and South Australia and has taught Aboriginal students in primary, secondary and tertiary settings. He is also interested in the teaching of Aboriginal studies and has written books for children about Aboriginal people. He has worked as a curriculum developer in this area and is currently writing a text book on this topic. He holds Bachelors Degrees in Education and Special Education and has a Master of Education. Howard lectured in and now works as a consultant on Aboriginal education.

Steve Hemming worked as a lecturer in Aboriginal Studies in the University of South Australia's Faculty of Aboriginal and Islander Studies. Prior to taking up this position he worked for ten years as a curator in the Division of Anthropology at the South Australian Museum. He has a degree in history from the University of Adelaide and is currently enrolled in a PhD in history at the University of Adelaide.

As a Museum curator he worked primarily with Aboriginal people in southern South Australia. Much of this work involved the recording of oral histories associated with historical Aboriginal sites. He has also worked with Aboriginal communities throughout Australia in his former capacity as Project Manager of the S.A. Museum's Aboriginal Family History Project.

Jenny Burden has been involved in Aboriginal affairs since the mid-1960s. She became a staff member of the Aboriginal Task Force at the South Australian Institute of Technology in 1974, teaching in the areas of psychology, communication, and developing a course in cross cultural and health psychology for task force students. Since retiring from the University of South Australia in 1994, Jenny has been engaged in various Aboriginal health related projects through the Aboriginal Research Institute, at the University of South Australia.

David Roberts is a senior lecturer in The Unaipon School at the University of South Australia and is Coordinator of the Bachelor of Arts courses in Aboriginal Studies, Aboriginal Affairs Administration and Australian Studies. He has a Diploma of Teaching from Western Teachers College, a BA (Hons) from the University of Adelaide and an MSc (cum laude) from the University of Bristol. He teaches research methods at both undergraduate and postgraduate levels, comparative Indigenous studies and Aboriginal education. His research interests include Indigenous political movements, Aboriginal education, inclusive curriculum and problem based learning.

Editors' Note

Throughout the book, some Aboriginal words are spelt in more than one way, reflecting the alternative spellings often employed by linguists and others.

Introduction

Rarely in Australia's history of contact between indigenous Australians and their non-Aboriginal counterparts has there been a favourable representation of Aboriginal and Torres Strait Islander culture and lifestyle. This book presents some positive perspectives of indigenous people on a range of issues which affect their everyday lives.

The central aim of the book is to present a realistic view of Aboriginal and Torres Strait Islander people. However, the chapters offer more than this. Their purpose is also to encourage readers to examine their own knowledge and ideas about Australia's indigenous people and provoke critical thinking.

These two objectives depend on a third objective, which is to reveal the cultural and linguistic diversity of indigenous Australians and to demonstrate to other Australians their great versatility, resilience and adaptability. This book should assist the Australian community to access the wealth of Aboriginal and Islander experience and to gain a greater appreciation of the contribution that indigenous people have made, and are making, in so many areas of Australian life.

Each chapter concentrates on a particular facet of the lives of indigenous Australians. It examines their struggle to maintain a strong identity and heritage while actively participating in Australian society. Reflected throughout the book are the ways in which indigenous Australians enrich Australian culture as a whole.

Chapter 1, "Images and Realities", takes up the issue of who defines and speaks for Aboriginal and Torres Strait Islander people. Most Australians have stereotypical images of Aboriginal people which are the result of non-Aboriginal concepts built on views of European superiority. Chapter 2, "Changing History: New Images of Aboriginal History" outlines the challenges of Aboriginal people to the history of European and Aboriginal relations since 1788 as written by the "victors". It traces the determination of Aboriginal people to be heard and to present their own versions of what has happened in the past 200 years.

Chapter 3, "Australia's First Peoples: Identity and Population", examines how, from the beginning of British settlement, the cultures and identity of Aboriginal people have been under enormous pressure from non Aboriginal actions which have fragmented and undermined that culture. Today Aboriginal people are still fighting to retain their identity as the original Australians. This identity is intimately bound to the land as examined in Chapter 4, "Two Laws One Land". The land issue highlights the clash between two incompatible systems of law. Aboriginal law is derived from the land and encompasses all aspects of spiritual, social and economic life. On the other hand, Australian law is based on the ideologies associated with capitalism. Indigenous Australians have been disadvantaged before Australian law, but the Mabo Case may herald a new phase in the Aboriginal struggle for land rights and social justice for some indigenous people.

The land and the people are bound together by traditional Aboriginal concepts of spirituality which Europeans might classify as religion. Chapter 5, "Living the Dreaming" introduces these concepts and explores the roots of contemporary Aboriginal religious experience. The impact of Christian missionary activities is outlined with a focus on Aboriginal Christianity and some other movements which have developed in response to these influences.

The Aboriginal extended kinship system and family ties have survived, albeit in many cases in a modified form, through two centuries of dispossession, discrimination, urbanisation, and traumatisation due to children being removed from their families. Aboriginal concepts of kinship, community and family and the ways in which they differ from non-Aboriginal people's concepts, particularly as they relate to cooperation, sharing and responsibility are the subjects of Chapter 6, "Family and Kin".

Chapter 7, "Australian Languages: Our Heritage", emphasises the rich linguistic heritage of indigenous Australians, which is now in danger of being lost. These languages, with their rich complexities and subtleties, have been either denigrated or ignored. Efforts are being made by Aboriginal people and linguists to redress this by implementing language programs through communities and education systems.

Chapter 8, "Living Wisdom: Aborigines and the Environment", explores indigenous Australian systems of knowledge and their wide range of application. It is a story of adaptation, change and development demonstrating the effectiveness of a lifestyle in which

Aboriginal and Torres Strait Islander people lived in harmony with their environment.

Aboriginal people, no less than non-Aboriginal Australians, appreciate the importance of education in maintaining and passing on culture and in helping to adapt to the demands of modern life. Chapter 9, "Education: The Search for Relevance", traces the history of the Aboriginal struggle to make schools and education systems meet Aboriginal needs.

Major issues for Aboriginal people are health and the delivery of health services. Chapter 10, "Health: An Holistic Approach", looks at the major factors that have contributed to the poor health status of Aboriginal people following their enforced lifestyle changes since European occupation.

Chapter 11, "Economics: Independence or Welfare", presents an outline of Aboriginal economic life in pre-contact times and the effects of colonisation and government policies. It also considers the efforts of Aboriginal people to break a cycle of economic dependency and the contributions they have made and are making to the overall Australian economy.

Traditionally, art has been integral to all facets of Aboriginal life. Chapter 12, "Art: Interpreting Reality", reveals the rich diversity of Aboriginal art forms and styles from pre-colonial times to the present. It considers the success of Aboriginal art on a world scale and shows how it has changed in the last 100 years, reflecting the political and economic realities of the day.

Chapter 13, "Self-determination and the Struggle for Aboriginal Equality", explores aspects of the contemporary struggle of Aboriginal and Torres Strait Islander peoples for control over their affairs. It also highlights the different ways in which Aboriginal people seek to achieve self-determination.

As a collection, these chapters are intended to introduce facets of indigenous Australia to a wide readership. For many, it will be their first experience of the "other" Australia. The book is not definitive; it aims to encourage readers to explore further and discover the rich heritage that exists almost undetected in contemporary Australian life.

Chapter 1

Images and Realities

Eleanor Bourke

Introduction

In Australia Aboriginal people are hostage, in the main, to images created by non-Aboriginal Australians. The power of a people to say who they are, to define their own identity and to relate their history is fundamental to their existence. To deny a people their law, languages and the use of their land is a denial of basic human rights (Skutnabb-Kangas and Phillipson, 1995). These fundamentals of civilisation were systematically stripped away from most of the indigenous people of Australia by colonisation.

This chapter examines the historical and contemporary images of Aboriginal representation.

From 1788, which Aboriginal people call the invasion and non-Aboriginal people call British settlement, most representations of Aboriginal people have been produced and controlled by others. This representation has been biased, culturally prescriptive and judged against non-Aboriginal values.

The bias came about because those new arrivals to this continent did not see any positive attributes among the Aboriginal people and believed in their own superiority. There was little, if any, communication between the Indigenous peoples and the newcomers about culture, language and beliefs. Very few people communicated directly with Indigenous Australians using Indigenous languages in the early years.

The land was declared *desert and uninhabitated* later represented as *terra nullius* and the various Aboriginal nations declared uncivilised (Castle, 1982; Cunneen and Libesman, 1995). This seemed to justify the 'extinction' of a 'Stone Age race' inevitably 'doomed' to extinction. Subsequently the 'half-caste problem' would be solved by 'breeding out the colour', a policy congruent with the idea of a White Australia" (McGregor, 1997).

Creating the images

Source materials which illustrate the European beliefs prevailing in 1770 reveal the "imperial/colonial" attitude to indigenous people. Such sources include:

- the writings of early arrivals;
- diaries;
- official documents;
- education and school textbooks; and
- paintings.

Museums house various artefacts depicting those early representations of the "noble savage" image which was used in turn to reflect a unique "Australianness" to the rest of the world. A collection of writings edited by Karp and Lavine (1991) develop this theme.

But there were some insightful perceptions such as Edward Eyre's comment in journals about his travels and meetings with Aboriginal people:

> The Continent of Australia is so vast, and the dialects, customs, and ceremonies of its inhabitants so varied in detail, though so similar in general outline and character, that it will require the lapse of years, and the labours of many individuals, to detect and exhibit the links which form the chain of connection in the habits and history of tribes so remotely separated (Eyre, 1845, vol 2:152).

The European belief that a society continues to develop towards an ideal civilisation failed to distinguish between biological evolution and cultural difference. The Social Darwinism theory invariably puts forward the view that those who are less fit, fail to survive. Indigenous Australian people were regarded as appropriate subjects for colonisation and civilising. Social Darwinism theory focussed on aspects such as cannibalism, savagery, tribal fighting to the detriment of a more positive image of Aboriginal society (McConnochie, Hollinsworth et al, 1988; McGregor, 1997).

An early image abroad was built upon the first Australian cricketers to tour England a team of "Eleven Aboriginal Black Australians". It was reported by *The Times* on the 26th May, 1868 that the team were said to represent various states (though they all came from Victoria) and having *beards and hair long and wiry* (Ward and Robertson, 1980:190). Whilst this description upheld aspects of the "noble savage" image, there were many reports of intriguing interest about this unique group, the "stalwart" First Australians touring to play competitive cricket (Mulvaney, 1988).

Issues surrounding ownership of the land are illustrations of how Aboriginal people have been misrepresented in Australian history. Land and labour exploitation were used to advance British colonisation and became the rationale for European land ownership. This led to misrepresentations of Aboriginal people and their relationships with the land. The study of anthropology in the second half of the 19th century focussed on Aborigines as remnants of a dying society.

When European missionaries from Christian denominations started to arrive in the 1820s they targeted various Aboriginal groups for conversion. They must have been viewed with some perplexity by the Aboriginal people because they were different from the other white settlers. They didn't seek to control the land or obtain Aboriginal women.

As Reynolds (1989:155) indicates they were a paradox in that while expressing goodwill and concern for Aboriginal people they were more intrusive and disruptive than other Europeans. In order to succeed in their tasks they had to break down belief systems, destroy ceremonies and wreck the very fabric of Aboriginal society. Missionaries saw, and represented, Aboriginal people as heathen children who needed to be saved (Harris, 1990; Markus, 1990; and Taplin, 1879).

In the original Australian Constitution (1900) the only reference to Aboriginal people was one of exclusion. Aboriginal people were referred to in a number of State Acts and the Commonwealth's exclusion from any responsibility towards Aboriginal people only served to confuse the status of Aboriginal people and alienate them from aspects of Australian life. Aboriginal people had no citizenship under British law and were thought to be doomed (McIntyre, 1986:79; Galligan and Chesterton, 1997).

The 1900 *Constitution Act* resulted in Aboriginal people being excluded from some Commonwealth services and programs until the seventies. This had the effect of making Aboriginal people invisible to most Australians within society.

Though the Constitution excluded Aboriginal people from being counted as citizens some Aboriginal men served as soldiers in the wars. Upon their return to Australia they were no longer prepared to be treated as less than human and started to discuss the possibility of becoming organised and asserting their citizenship rights and entitlement to land (Jackomos and Fowell, 1993; Hall, 1995; and Kartinyeri, 1996).

Most Australians have had limited personal exposure to Aboriginal people or to studies which show Aboriginal people in a favourable light. Consequently, attitudes towards Aboriginal people are based on very little knowledge, or are inaccurate because of over-generalisation. The Australian education system contributed to misconceptions by the use of ill-informed text books, the Victorian Education Department's series of readers, dating from 1927 and used until the 1960s are an example.

Many books on Australian history referred to Aborigines only in passing or briefly in the first chapter. In 1977 Professor Noel Loos wrote that "the history of frontier contact between white settlers and Aboriginals in Australia had been glossed over" (Loos, 1977:508). He noted the tendency to treat Aboriginal Australia as an episode in early Australian history. Aboriginal oral history draws attention to a universal awareness of illegal dispossession.

Loos also noted that:

> the few ethnohistorians who have researched in the area have understandably concentrated on the destruction of the pre-existing or traditional Aboriginal society … The 'doomed race' theory has thus had its effect on historians, who marched the survivors from the battlefields and the disease ridden 'blacks' camps' to the concentration camps of the reserves, out of Australian society and its history (Loos, 1977:510).

The representation of Aboriginal people in early texts on Australian history has been categorised in the following ways:

- **the colonial presumption**
  where Aboriginal people are represented as being appropriate subjects for colonisation and civilisation.

- **inadequate treatment**
  a failure to take account of Aboriginal peoples' presence in Australian history and to mention Aboriginal dimensions only in passing.
- **stereotypes and derogatory concepts**
  notions of superiority expressed in stereotypes such as childlike, simple, savage and primitive.
- **the exotic stress**
  draws attention to superficial differences but infers group's inferiority through words such as corroboree, cannibal, polygamy and bone pointing.
- **objects for study and discussion**
  references such as they, them, these people aligned with physical descriptions emphasising stereotypes such as medium stature, wiry hair, thick lips, prominent lower jaw and broad nose.
- **distortion and euphemism**
  where Australian history begins in 1788, for example, Cook discovered Australia, first settled, the Aboriginal problem, and pioneers (Spalding, 1974:11).

Such images support the argument that the new settlers were members of a superior culture and thus their acquisition of the "empty" land would lead to the creation of a superior nation. This argument was further strengthened by stereotyping Aboriginal people as "simple, primitive, dirty, ugly and degenerate" therefore in need of "progress, advancement and uplift" (McGregor, 1997).

These books impacted upon the attitudes of generations of teachers and students. Despite increased Aboriginal involvement in education systems, books written by non-Aboriginal people remain an influential educational tool. Texts making reference to Aboriginal people have often focussed on the appearance of Aboriginal people and their eating habits. This has served to further skew the image.

- They eat animals, grubs, fruit, fish anything.
- These dark skinned people need our help and care. When they smile at us, showing their lovely white teeth, they want to be friendly, and
- we must always try to make them happy in this land which once belonged to them (Bundy, 1955).

The constant reading of such stereotypes by non-Aboriginal children would obviously contribute to the development of racist attitudes in Australian society towards Aborigines.

In 1993 an exhibition of material from the Monash University Library Rare Book Collection entitled *Early Images of the Australian Aborigines,* gave a valuable insight into early representations of Aborigines in text. But it also drew attention to the availability of a valuable resource for students and researchers despite the works being primarily "written by men who had the aim of Christianising and assimilating them" (the Aborigines) (Monash University: Exhibition Catalogue).

In *The Chant of Jimmie Blacksmith,* Thomas Keneally (1973), portrays a rationalisation of white superiority and Aboriginal dispossession. Michael Cotter wrote that Jimmie Blacksmith is represented as being disenchanted with Aboriginal society as he knows it. "The destruction of his people is evident to his sensibilities and he inherits a share in white contempt for Aboriginal culture" (Cotter, 1977:583). In the novel, Jimmie is shown to aspire to equality on white terms. These are, of course, based on the institutions of western society, for example, owning his own property and marrying a white woman.

Early ethnographic films depicted aspects of Aboriginal life of those groups which were thought to be facing extinction. Early feature films included Aboriginal people occasionally as background or as primitives. After the Second World War there were a few films featuring Aboriginal characters usually made by visiting British or American directors. *Jedda* was made in 1955 by Australian director Charles Chauvel, starring Rosalie Kunoth Monks with Robert Tudawali, who was not required to speak any lines.

Impact on public opinion

Studies of race relations by Lorna Lippman (1991, 1981 and 1973), while at Monash University, and other researchers, have found that Australians hold negative attitudes toward Aborigines.

Mary Edmunds' (1987) study of public opinion, the media and attitudes towards Aboriginal people refers to the 1967 Referendum where an impressive 90.77% of electors voted to change the Constitution. She has suggested that this result has been interpreted by some commentators as support for Aboriginal people and recognition that there needed to be a change in the status of Aboriginal people's quality of life.

The Mackay Report (1988), *Being Australian,* included a chapter called "The Aborigines: a dimension to the Australian identity". This study found that the Bicentennial year, 1988 heightened the discussions about Aboriginal people and Aboriginal issues. There was an almost universal awareness that Aboriginal people believe that they are a dispossessed people and that some reparation should be made on their behalf.

The study found that Australians had become more comfortable about discussing the role, plight and future of Aboriginal Australians than a few years ago. The following comments indicate a belief that having achieved a free and open discussion about Aboriginal issues there is no need to do anything more.

> We all seem to be much more prepared to discuss it these days—I suppose that that's a good thing.

> There's so much in the media about Aborigines. They have really used the Bicentenary to push their cause. At least we have listened to them ...We are all much more aware than we used to be.

> I really wonder about the future for Australia, because I am convinced we haven't come to grips with the past. I don't think we can go on in the right way until we accept what our history really is and not glamorise it (Mackay, 1988).

This study indicated that Australians seemed to regard Aboriginal people as a curious subspecies of Australians; better educated respondents who knew Aboriginal people tended to defend the Aboriginal cause; less educated people pointed out the obvious differences with a mixture of distaste and animosity.

The 1988 Mackay Report indicated that there was an acceptance that Aboriginal people had grounds for complaint about their past treatment and about their status in Australian society. The respondents believed that there was no understanding of how Aboriginal people might change the situation for themselves. It was generally accepted that Aboriginal people would not be easily assimilated into urban Australian life.

Respondents to the Mackay study made a distinction between "good" and "bad" Aboriginal people. "Good" ones integrated totally into European culture or disappeared to take up a primitive way of life. "Bad" Aboriginal people were seen to be those who made a "nuisance of themselves" by wanting special rights while claiming all the privileges assumed to go with white civilisation. Distinctions continued to be made between "full-bloods" and "half-castes". "Full-bloods" were assumed to be much more reliable, responsible and clearer in their goals and were seen to resist assimilation into white society. "Half-castes", however, were thought to be the "real trouble-makers" because they were presumed to suffer an identity crisis.

Your half-caste doesn't know where he fits in ... (Mackay, 1988).

Though the respondents acknowledged the legitimacy in many Aboriginal issues, there was a belief that the Aboriginal way of life had nothing to offer in terms of enrichment or interest. The report concluded that in spite of a heightened awareness of Aboriginal people and Aboriginal issues, Australians generally feel superior to Aboriginal people whom they want to regard as true Australians. It was generally accepted that Aboriginal influences would be negative, that Aborigines tended to drag down the standard of living of those with whom they interacted and that Aboriginal people were committed to "taking from the system" rather than contributing to it.

The above studies indicate that as the educational diet changes so attitudes and beliefs about Indigenous Australians change. Race relations was raised as a major issue for society by Lorna Lippman. Mary Edmunds' study linked media as a source of information but found a belief that there was a need for change in dealings with Aboriginal people.

The 1988 Mackay Report indicates that the Bicentenary has changed Aboriginal participation and representation forever.

Dealing with realities

Dealing with negative imagery has been at the heart of Aboriginal educator's concerns. In 1975 the Aboriginal Consultative Group to the Schools Commission called for all teacher trainees in Australia to study courses relating to Aboriginal social organisation, and to traditional and contemporary culture. To overcome prejudice through education, Aboriginal Studies programs have been introduced into universities since 1968. The emphasis has, however, moved from traditional life and culture to contemporary situations.

In recent years there has been a distinction drawn between the needs of Aborigines for cultural education and the need for Aboriginal Studies for non-Aboriginal people. The basis for this is that Aboriginal people see Australia as comprising two distinct groups of people:

- Aboriginal and Torres Strait Islanders and their descendants, who are the indigenous people of Australia; and
- People of a number of other races, predominantly European, who have chosen to make their home in Australia.

Aboriginal Studies programs generally aim to increase understanding of Aboriginal life, activities, social organisation, beliefs and values. Such courses provide an opportunity to deal with ill informed stereotypes of Aboriginal people. Intrinsic to such studies is the attempt to present a more realistic view of Australian history and endeavour to create a more tolerant and culturally plural Australia through better understanding of contemporary Indigenous affairs.

"Who should teach Aboriginal Studies?" is a question often debated. The National Aboriginal Education Committee asked for Aboriginal involvement in the planning and teaching of Aboriginal Studies in 1977.

David Hollinsworth discussing his experience wrote:

As a non-Aboriginal person who has taught Aboriginal Studies to both Aboriginal and non-Aboriginal tertiary students for over a decade, these arguments are of intense significance, professionally, personally and politically. Arguments about the nature of Aboriginality and the means of claiming, contesting and authenticating Aboriginal identity are central to both the future of Aboriginal Studies as an academic area of study and to political and ideological struggles over Australian nationalism and the position of indigenous peoples within it (Hollinsworth, 1992:137).

Andrew Lattas commenting on Hollinsworth in the same journal noted that *paternal supervision of Aboriginal identity* was current. He added that:

> The academic desire to demystify people, to teach them that they are socially and culturally produced, strips from people the myths of their own autonomous being; it disempowers people (Lattas, 1992:160).

For this reason, Professor Colin Tatz, Macquarie University, believes that Aboriginal aspects should permeate all subjects of the curriculum. Tatz sees this as a better approach than having explicit Aboriginal Studies programs. However Aboriginal Studies is dealt with in the schools or the universities, the teaching of it usually provides another avenue for others (non-Aborigines) to represent Aboriginal beliefs, cultures and values.

In academic discussions culture, oppression and racism are simply concepts; in the context of Aboriginal Studies they are issues at the heart of relationships between Indigenous Australians and other Australians. Many of the misconceptions of the past are present today. Media coverage of the Native Title debate and reaction to the Wik decision are indicative.

Aboriginal people want to retain their languages, culture, social organisation and the management of their lands and their lives. There is a constant struggle to retain identity, practice values and maintain beliefs. Indigenous Australians desire representation which depicts them accurately as they see themselves. Indeed it is necessary to be vigilant and to avoid continuing misrepresentation as in the film *Crocodile Dundee* where Pitjantjatjara people from Central Australia, are referred to as being in Arnhem Land.

Since the 1980s there have emerged many Aboriginal writers telling their stories and, therefore, trying to balance the scales of history and representation. Aboriginal people such as Jack Davis, Ruby Langford, Sally Morgan and Eva Johnson are writing books, poems, short stories and plays. They have been followed by a plethora of Indigenous visual art expression. This is helping to redefine Australian identity. Indigenous Australians are developing the potential to influence all facets of Australian society and develop an Indigenous approach to being Australian.

Aboriginal people are moving into radio, television and print. The Central Australian Aboriginal Media Association, well known as CAAMA radio in Alice Springs and Imparja television have contributed to new images of change. Radio is widely used among Aboriginal groups to maintain social and cultural links. At Ernabella and Yuendumu Aboriginal people are developing new uses for communications in support of social and cultural links, service delivery and commercial activities. Video conferencing, computer links, telephone, radio, facsimile, local video production and broadcasting are being controlled by local groups. There is a National Indigenous Media Association of Australia in Brisbane. A perusal of the National Directory of Aboriginal and Torres Strait Islander Organisations 1996 and the Internet provides many contacts.

It is in the sports arena that Indigenous Australians probably have made their most obvious impact and contribute in a uniquely Australian way. The media plays a significant role in projecting the range of images of Indigenous Australians not only on the sports field but in the arts and elsewhere (see Tatz, 1996). This arena has provided a rich array of images in recent times in Australian Rules Football and international sports competition, providing indelible portraits of Evonne Goolagong-Cawley, Cathy Freeman and Nicky Winmar expressing their identity as Aboriginal Australians.

Nevertheless, the extent to which Aboriginal people may develop their own representations is very much controlled by the media and governments. This occurs through various policies such as the Reconciliation process or may be derived from events such as the *Mabo* and *Wik* High Court decisions. The Reconciliation Process has developed from a clear desire to do something for, with and about relations with Indigenous Australians. It grew out of the Royal Commission Report into Aboriginal Deaths in Custody (1988).

In 1994 as a response to the criticisms directed at popular misconceptions about government policy in relation to Aboriginal affairs the Commonwealth produced a publication called *Rebutting the myths*. It deals with the popular issues that form the basis of stereotypes and misinformation relating to Aboriginal Australians—such issues as:

- Aboriginal people and alcohol;
- whether Aboriginal people are really lazy;
- the availability of funds in Aboriginal affairs;
- the "special treatment" and "special privileges" of Aboriginal people;
- sacred sites, land rights and development; and
- the "free car".

The booklet intended to "banish some of the shocking and absurd prejudices which exist about Aboriginal and Torres Strait Islander people". The decision to take such a step on behalf of the Commonwealth Government through the Minister's office raises the question of public opinion about Aboriginal issues generally and about attitudinal shift.

The studies and attitudes referred to in this chapter have been used to draw attention to the fact that representations help form opinions. The seemingly funny, simple Pelaco shirt advertisement of the 1940s and 50s with an Aboriginal man from Casterton supposedly saying "Mine tink it fit fine" fulfilled a stereotype of the day. Comic strip characters such as those of Joliffe and the Aboriginal characters in Mary Grant Bruce's *Billabong* series, helped develop white myths and perpetuate misrepresentation of Aboriginal life.

It is true that these images have been replaced with other positive images such as Cathy Freeman draped in the Aboriginal flag, Nicky Winmar's raised football guernsey and the Bangarra Dancers but they are proving hard to overcome.

Aboriginal society and cultures were given a limited role in influential forums such as Australian history books, Australian movies or popular images in the past. There seems to be, however, some difficulty today in accepting the multidimensional nature of Aboriginal life and the range of Aboriginal lifestyles across a modern spectrum.

Many Aboriginal and Torres Strait Islander people today live in cities and participate in a range of cultural, political and religious activities across Australia. Diversity means that no one Aboriginal group's lifestyle and cultural activities is more or less valid than any other's. The plethora of Aboriginal media activity through radio and television is projecting fresh and unique Australian images. At the same time these representations are ensuring those images are close to the contemporary Indigenous realities.

References

Aboriginal Consultative Group (1975). *Education for Aborigines.* Report to the Commonwealth Schools Commission.

Bourke, CJ (1979). *Prejudice in School Texts: an Aboriginal Viewpoint.* Unpublished paper.

Bourke, EA (1988). *Whitefulla Ceremonies.* Paper delivered at the ACT Chapter of the Australian College of Education AGM—1988.

Brunton, R (1993). *Black Suffering, White Guilt.* Melbourne, Victoria: IPA.

Bundy, M (1955). *My Land.* A Social Study reader for Younger Children. Adelaide: Rigby.

Castles, I (1982). *An Australian Legal History.* Sydney: The Law Book Company.

Catalogue of Early Images of the Australian Aborigines, 1993 exhibition at Monash University.

Cotter, Michael (1977). "The image of the Aboriginal in three modern Australian novels". *Meanjin,* vol. 4. Aboriginal Issue.

Cunneen, C and Libesman, T (1995). *Indigenous People in Australia.* Butterworths' Legal Studies Series, Butterworth.

Edmunds, M (1987). *Opinion, Ideology and Practice or do Public Attitudes Exist Rebutting the Myths.* Canberra: AGPS.

Eyre, E (1845). *Journals of Expeditions of Discovery into Central Australia and Overland from Adelaide to King George's Sound in the years 1840-1.* London: T and W Boone.

Galligan, Brian and Chesterton, John (1997). *Citizens Without Rights: Aborigines and Australian Citizenship.* Cambridge University Press.

Hall, Robert A (1995). *Fighters from the Fringe: Aborigines and Torres Strait Islanders recall the Second World War.* Canberra: Aboriginal Studies Press.

Harris, J (1990). *One Blood: 200 Years of Aboriginal encounter with Christianity: a story of hope*. Sutherland: Albatross.

Hollinsworth, D (1992). "Discourses on Aboriginality and the politics of Aboriginal identity in urban Australia". *Oceania*, vol. 63, no. 2.

Jackomos A, and Fowell, D (1993). *The Forgotten Heroes*. South Melbourne: Victoria Press.

Karp, Ivan and Lavine, Steven D (1991). *Exhibiting Cultures: The Poetics and Politics of Museum Display*. Washington and London: Smithsonian Institute Press.

Kartinyeri, D (1996). *Ngarrindjeri ANZACs*. South Australian Museum and Raukkan Council.

Kenneally, Thomas (1973). *The Chant of Jimmie Blacksmith*. Ringwood, Victoria: Penguin.

Lattas, A (1992). "Wiping the blood off Aboriginality: the politics of Aboriginal embodiment in contemporary intellectual debate". *Oceania*, vol. 63, no. 2.

Lippman, L (1973), *Words or Blows: Racial Attitudes in Australia*. Ringwood: Penguin books.

Lippman, L (1981), *Generations of Resistance: The Aboriginal Struggle for Justice*. Melbourne: Longman Cheshire.

Lippman, L (1991). *Generations of Resistance: Mabo and Justice*. Melbourne: Longman Cheshire.

Loos, Noel (1977). "The frontier revisited". *Meanjin*, vol. 4. Aboriginal Issue.

MacIntyre, S (1986). "1901-1942 The Succeeding Age". In Bolton, G, editor. *The Oxford History of Australia*, vol. 4. Melbourne: Oxford University Press.

Mackay, H (1988). *The Mackay Report: Being Australian*.

Markus, A (1990). *Governing Savages*. Sydney: Allen and Unwin.

McGregor, R (1997). *Imagined Destinies: Aboriginal Australians and Doomed Race Theory, 1880-1939*. Melbourne: Melbourne University Press.

McConnochie, K, Hollinsworth, D, and Pettman, J (1988). *Race and Racism in Australia*. Wentworth Falls, New South Wales: Social Science Press.

Mulvaney, DJ (1988). Cricket Walkabout *The Australian Aboriginal Cricketers on Tour 1867-8,* revised edition. Melbourne University Press.

Office of Aboriginal and Torres Strait Islander Affairs (1992). *Rebutting the Myths: Some Facts About Aboriginal and Torres Strait Islander Affairs.* CanberrA: AGPS.

Reynolds, H (1989). *Dispossession: Black Australians and White Invaders.* Sydney: Allen and Unwin.

Skutnab-Kangas, T, and Phillipson, R, editors (1995). *Linguistic Human Rights: Overcoming Linguistic Discrimination.* Berlin/New York: Mouton de Greyter.

Spalding, I (1974). "Prejudice in Children's Literature", *The Aboriginal Child at School,* vol 2. no. 2, p 11.

Taplin, G (1879). *The Folklore, Manners, Customs and Languages of the South Australian Aborigines.* Adelaide: Acting Government Printer.

Tatz, Colin (1996). *Obstacle Race: Aborigines in Sport,* Kensingtion: UNSW Press.

The Victorian Readers, 1937-1940, 2nd edition. Melbourne: Government Printers.

Ward, R and Robertson, J (1980). "Such was life". In *Select Documents in Australian Social History,* vol. 2, 1831-1913.

Other Sources

Central Australian Aboriginal Media Association (CAAMA), Alice Springs, Northern Territory.

Crocodile Dundee (video recording) (1992). Rimfire Films: CBS/Fox, Artarmon, New South Wales. Director: Paul Hogan.

Indigenous Programs Unit, Australian Broadcasting Corporation.

Indigenous Cultural Affairs Magazine, Special Broadcasting Service.

Jedda (video recording) (1994). National Film and Sound Archive, Canberra. Director: Charles Chauvel.

National Indigenous Media Association of Australia, Petrie Terrace Brisbane, Queensland.

Chapter 2

Changing History: New Images of Aboriginal History

Steve Hemming

Christian Teichelmann [Lutheran Missionary, Adelaide 1842] told the story of how he cornered two recently initiated Aboriginal men and told them that they should fear Jehovah and not the "red kangaroo" (the red kangaroo being the principal Dreaming of the region). One of the Aboriginal men became very angry and replied:

> Why do you charge us with a lie, that is, reject our opinion, we do not charge you with lies; what you believe and speak of Jehovah is good, and what we believe is good.

> We [the missionaries] replied that only on one side the truth would be, and that side was ours.

> Very well, he answered, then I am a liar, and you speak the truth; I shall not speak another word, you may now speak (Teichelmann, quoted in Foster, 1990:19).

Introduction

In 1988 some Australians celebrated two hundred years of Australian history—"a celebration of a nation". But what of Australia's history before 1788 and what about the last two hundred years as seen through Aboriginal eyes? For Aboriginal people Australia's Bicentenary was a time of mourning—perhaps a celebration of the survival of Aboriginal people—but not "a celebration of a nation". The year 1788 marked the beginning of great suffering and loss for Aboriginal people—the invasion of their land. In 1939, the year after Australia celebrated its sesqui-centenary the Aboriginal political activist William Cooper, the Honorary Secretary of the Australian Aborigines League, wrote the following words:

> How much compensation have we had? How much of our land has been paid for? Not one iota! Again we state that we are the original owners of the country. In spite of force, prestige, or anything else

you like, morally the land is ours. We have been ejected and despoiled of our God-given right and our inheritance has been forcibly taken from us (Cooper, 1939, quoted in Markus, 1988:14).

In 1988 other Aboriginal people repeated Cooper's demands for justice. More recently the results of the landmark Mabo case, the High Court's Wik decision and the report on the stolen generations have prompted strong statements from contemporary Aboriginal people, echoing Aboriginal pleas for justice made since the first days of European invasion.

The images that Europeans have constructed of Australia's indigenous inhabitants have both shaped the nature of Aboriginal and non-Aboriginal relations and provided the framework within which Aboriginal history has been and is still being written. Western constructs of "race", Christian ideology and the development of Social Darwinism, with its "child" anthropology, have all been critical in the construction of images of Aboriginal people (see Dodson, 1994; McGregor, 1997). When reading histories of Australia dealing with Aboriginal people, it is important to recognise these influences and to understand the ways that the past is constructed by historians and others.

The well-known saying "history is written by the victor" should be kept in mind when understanding the representations of Aboriginal people in Australia's history. A recent and important collection of writings by Australian academics uses the theoretical framework developed by the French historian Michel Foucault to investigate the relationship between power and knowledge in the constructions of images of Aborigines (Attwood and Arnold, 1992). In the introduction to this collection Bain Attwood writes:

> Thus, in Foucault's terms, knowledge or 'truth' is not 'outside of power' but closely affiliated with it. Indeed, any 'truth' depends upon power to make it true (Attwood, 1992:II).

This understanding of the relationship between knowledge and power is clearly illustrated at the beginning of this chapter in the interchange in 1842, between the missionary Teichelmann and an angry Aboriginal man. To introduce new "truths" into Australia's history, Aboriginal and non-Aboriginal commentators and academics are in the process of challenging contemporary Australian power relations.

In recent years the boundaries between academic disciplines in the humanities have become blurred and this process can be clearly witnessed in the writing of historical works about Aboriginal people. Anthropologists, historians, sociologists and other academics are all involved in the production of what is most often termed Aboriginal history (Cowlishaw, 1992:20). However, it is perhaps the comparatively recent emergence of a large body of Aboriginal literature that has most directly challenged the old versions of Australian history and, as part of this process, non-Aboriginal constructions of Aboriginality (Morgan, 1987; Narogin, 1990; Davis et al, 1990).

Aboriginal people have started an invasion of their own over the last few decades—challenging the dominant "white" view of Australia's past. They have begun presenting their own versions of what has happened in Australia in the last two hundred years and before and introduced a new perspective, based on The Dreaming, of Australia's much longer history. Over the last few decades the increased access that Aboriginal people have had to the sources of power in Australian society has been a critical factor providing support and impetus to the rewriting of Australian history from an Aboriginal perspective.

Challenging "the great Australian silence"

In 1968 the anthropologist WEH Stanner delivered his landmark lecture, "The great Australian silence", as part of the ABC Boyer lecture series (Stanner, 1972). He highlighted Australia's longstanding habit of forgetting Aboriginal people and their views, and he argued that this habit had developed into a "cult of forgetfulness practised on a national scale" (Stanner, 1972:25). That twenty years later Stanner's "great Australian silence" made such a dramatic appearance at Australia's Bicentenary is a matter of shame for non-Aboriginal Australians. In 1988 the Australian authorities re-created the past to fit with the positive image of Australia that they wanted to project to the world. This image did not include Aboriginal versions of Australia's history. More recently, Australia's Prime Minister has advocated an approach to Australian history that appears to have much in common with the "cult of forgetfulness" described by Stanner.

In his 1968 lecture, Stanner considered the work of Australian historians from the 1930s to the 1960s and commented on the absence of Aboriginal people from the mainstream Australian histories. What these historians did was to locate Aboriginal people in what they saw as a static, primitive and "traditional" past and in so doing excluded them from the changing story of Australian history. Only so-called "full-blood" people were considered to be "real" Aborigines and they were characterised as part of a dying race, being swept aside by the march of civilisation. The majority of Aboriginal people living on reserves, on missions and in fringe-camps did not qualify, for the purposes of these histories, as "real". It was expected that they would eventually merge into the rest of the population (Langton, 1981). They were on the fringes of white Australian society, *the fringe dwellers of Australian historiography* and not considered important in Australia's past (Reynolds, 1972:ix).

The impact of genocide, invasion, institutionalisation and forced assimilation only began to be widely recognised in non-Aboriginal spheres in the 1960s.

In 1988 Aboriginal people and their supporters publicly challenged the "official" version of Australia's past and brought into focus the ways that particular constructions of the past continue the oppression of Aboriginal people in Australia. The celebration of two hundred years of "Australian" history was in direct contrast to the Aboriginal messages of mourning being presented during 1988.

Excerpts from the speeches given at the protest rally were reproduced in *Paperbark: A Collection of Black Australian Writings* (Davis et al, 1990). Aboriginal speakers questioned some of the principal, non-Aboriginal concepts at the centre of the Bicentenary and presented opposing Aboriginal perspectives in their place. The following "oppositional pairs" can be identified in the speeches and used as focal points when critiquing conventional Australian history:

history/dreaming
settlement/invasion and dispossession
pioneers/invaders

progress/subjugation
civilisation/genocide

In his opening prayer to the crowd the Reverend Charles Harris summed up the mood of the gathering:

> God of the Dreamtime, you who are with us for these 40,000 years or more before 1788, you who gave us our ceremonies, and the law, and our stories, and our sacred sites, you who gave us our Dreaming, you who gave us this land; you were with us then; you are with us now. You march with us today as we march through the streets of Sydney in the march for freedom, justice and hope.
>
> You were with us through the last 200 years of onslaught, of terrorism, and of apartheid that has been administered to our people in this land. And you have helped us and enabled us to survive through the odds that were against us.
>
> We pray that you will avenge your people, the Aboriginal and Islander people. Show to the world, today, the evil deeds of those who came and robbed us, raped our land and our people, murdered and lied to our people. Expose them to the world.
>
> Look and see the chains of oppression that keep your people, the Aboriginal and Islander people, in bondage. Hear the cry, and the call, and the plea for justice to be done in this land. Show the people that you are the God of justice and, Lord be praised, the God of the Dreamtime.
>
> Bring freedom, bring justice, and bring hope (Davis et al, 1990:332).

Harris' prayer clearly and forcefully presents an Aboriginal perspective of the meaning of the Bicentenary. His ability to incorporate Christian imagery into an Aboriginal frame, without seriously challenging the concepts associated with The Dreaming, provides a vivid example of Aboriginal resistance to domination by the ideologies brought by the European invaders. Christianity has been an important "site of resistance" and an analysis of its relationship with Aboriginal people provides examples of cultural change and adaptation that are critical to a new understanding of Aboriginal history and Aboriginality (Swain and Rose, 1988:5).

With the Aboriginal political struggle for power, and the successes that this struggle has achieved, has come the possibility for Aboriginal people to challenge the established versions of Australian history. Aboriginal perspectives have been increasingly published and have started to have an impact on the way that Australians see themselves and Australian history. Film, as a medium, has had a major role in providing a widely accessible forum for new perspectives. Good examples include the documentary *Lousy Little Sixpence*, the television series *Women of the Sun*, the film *Babakuieria* and the work of Aboriginal film-maker, Tracy Moffatt (for example, *Nice Coloured Girls and Night Cries*). In the film *Babaquaeria* the Bicentennial view of Australian history is turned on its head, and by placing non-Aboriginal people in the same powerless position that Aboriginal people continually have experienced the audience is forced to question the "official" version of Australian history.

Charles Perkins has been a prominent participant in the Aboriginal "struggle" and a vocal advocate of Aboriginal political activism, with its principal concern for changing the social, political and economic position of Aboriginal people. During the 1960s Perkins was a central figure in activities that challenged the policies of the Australian government such as the Freedom Rides (Perkins, 1975). On these "rides" young Aboriginal activists organised trips into rural New South Wales to gain support from Aboriginal and non-Aboriginal people and to expose "racist" practises. As well as stressing the centrality of the role of Aboriginal activism in forcing positive change, Perkins acknowledges the valuable role that politicians such as Gough Whitlam and Don Dunstan played in bringing about political and social change.

In response to political activism and the publication of Aboriginal viewpoints, academics in the 1960s and 1970s began taking a different approach to writing Aboriginal history and defining Aboriginal people. (See Beckett, 1958; Reay, 1964; Lippmann, 1970; Rowley, 1970 and 1971; Barwick, 1972; Reynolds, 1972). Cowlishaw writes about the interest that young anthropology students of the early 1970s took in the Aboriginal political struggle. At the University of Sydney they organised "a 'Free University' at which there were courses and discussion groups concerning contemporary Aborigines" (Cowlishaw, 1992:22). It was University of Sydney students who, in the 1960s, joined the Freedom Riders on their trips to the NSW country towns (Gilbert, 1973:31-32).

The advent of the contemporary campaign for "land rights" eventually brought anthropologists and other academics into the frontline of the struggle for Aboriginal rights. This was particularly so after the passing of the *Aboriginal Land Rights Act* (Northern Territory) in 1976. This inevitably led to a rethinking of many key concepts in the anthropological literature dealing with Aboriginal people and culture (Berndt, 1982; Langton and Peterson, 1983). New understandings of the changing nature of Aboriginal "cultures" emerged from the Aboriginal struggle for land rights. However, although anthropologists began to recognise the realities of Aboriginal Australia since 1788, the legal system, as witnessed by the 1976 Act, did not:

> In particular, there remains an immense reluctance to acknowledge the impact of colonisation and to give recognition to the creative adaptations of the pre-contact land-tenure system by which many Aborigines have ensured the continuity of relationships to the country. The failure of the Northern Territory legislation to recognise these adaptations, forced upon the people by invasion and the consequent disruptions, is its weakest point (Langton and Peterson, 1983:3).

During the 1970s and 1980s anthropology in other parts of the world was taking an interest in cultural change and adaptation and moving away from focussing on "traditional" bounded societies (Ortner, 1984). New approaches in sociology provided a serious critique of western knowledge systems and approaches to academic work (Foucault, 1974; Fabian, 1983; Lyotard, 1984; Seidman and Wagner, 1992). The development of what has been described as *postmodernist* thinking, emanating to a large extent from sociology, has revolutionised the approach that anthropology has taken to studying "other" peoples and developing authoritative accounts of their culture. The power relationship between the researcher and their object of study has been questioned by academics such as Edward Said (Said, 1978). His analysis of what he terms *Orientalism* has been applied by a number contemporary Australian academics to the ways that Aboriginal people have been studied, constructed and disempowered in the process (Attwood and Arnold, 1992; Cowlishaw, 1992).

Before the 1960s—the early struggle

Aboriginal political activism has certainly not been restricted to the period from the 1960s. It is also clear that Aboriginal men and women have played significant roles in the political movement. As the historians Jackie Huggins and Heather Goodall have pointed out:

> Aboriginal women have been involved with men in movements to regain land from the earliest struggles. For example, in NSW, a sequence can be found in the records from 1872, at Braidwood, when Kitty, Ellen and their husband, Alick, spoke for their community in demanding land: 'We want to get some land which we can call our own in reality ... We think the Blacks are entitled to live in their own country' (Brennan, 1907:213, cited in Huggins and Goodall, 1992:403).

Aboriginal people attained some successes at a local level in the earlier periods of political struggle. In the 1920s the Australian Aboriginal Progressive Association was active on the south coast of New South Wales in the defence of Aboriginal land against local farmers (Huggins and Goodall, 1992:403; Goodall, 1996). However, as Andrew Markus has documented in his history of William Cooper's political life and the Australian Aborigines' League, it was more difficult for Aboriginal people to challenge the government on wider issues involving the oppression of Aboriginal people (Markus, 1988). Such movements were relatively powerless due to the position of Aboriginal people in Australian society and the racist and ignorant views held by the majority of Australians at that time.

Similar earlier moves for political change have been documented in South Australia (Jenkin, 1976; Mattingley and Hampton, 1988). From the late 1800s Aboriginal people such as Matthew Kropinyeri were directly confronting the government on issues relating to policies and legislation affecting Aborigines (Jenkin, 1979:174). However, their pleas often fell on deaf ears, as those in authority largely believed that Aboriginal people were a primitive race and destined to die out in the face of the superior Europeans. As Markus points out in his discussion of William Cooper's role in the Australian Aborigines League (AAL):

> There was no tradition of according serious consideration to Aboriginal viewpoints and the dominant assumptions of his [Cooper's] day meant that Aborigines were dismissed as an irrelevancy, an inferior 'race' destined for extinction (Markus, 1988:20).

When Europeans first came to Australia they held views about Aboriginal people largely informed by developing forms of what has been described as "scientific racism" (McConnochie, Hollinsworth and Pettman, 1988). Captain Cook brought with him images of "native" peoples as "noble savages" largely the antithesis of Europeans. Cook was influenced by the writings of Rousseau whose followers saw "native" peoples as uncontaminated by the evils of civilisation, closer to nature and therefore God. These idealistic views were modified after 1788 and the nature of contact between invaders and Aborigines led to descriptions of Aboriginal people as "ignoble" savages and barbarous heathens (Mulvaney, 1990:10). As Social Darwinism became influential, later in the nineteenth century, the status of Aboriginal people was reduced to the level of sub-humans. It was in this intellectual climate that people such as Matthew Kropinyeri struggled for equal rights.

By the turn of the century a new Australian national identity was developing and Aboriginal people, in the literature of the time, were often depicted as the villains in the story of Australia's pioneer settlers taming a savage and unused land (Newland, 1893; Healy, 1989:55). In this growing Australian "folklore" Aboriginal people were characterised as primitive, dangerous savages leading an aimless nomadic life. Aboriginal connections with the land did not fit the European model of land ownership. In 1770 Australia had been claimed by Cook and later declared *terra nullius*—a concept only recently overturned by the High Court in the *Mabo* case (Frost,

1990; Watson, 1992; Stephenson and Ratnapala, 1993; Goot and Rowse, 1994).

Once Aboriginal people came into contact with what was considered the superior European race, it was seen as inevitable that they become extinct. Genocide was largely justified by the application of the concept of the "survival of the fittest" to humans. The Social Darwinists of the late nineteenth and twentieth centuries developed a rigid, racist view of Aboriginal people (McConnochie, Hollinsworth and Pettman, 1988). Those Aboriginal people not living in an "untouched" state were regarded as remnants of a disintegrating culture living on the fringes of white society (Cowlishaw, 1992:23-24). By the mid-twentieth century an "assimilationist" perspective dominated government policies and legislation (Broome, 1982:171). It was expected that Aboriginal people would gradually assimilate into the wider society, becoming lighter skinned as they intermarried with Europeans and adopted the "modern", dominant culture.

New approaches to Aboriginal "culture" and history

By the early 1970s historians had started to change their approach to the writing of Aboriginal history (Rowley, 1972; Reynolds, 1972). The first focus of these new histories was an attempt to provide a new perspective of the events of early contact history. The violence of relations between Aboriginal and non-Aboriginal people became a characteristic feature in what Attwood has called "revisionist" history (Attwood, 1989:135). With the publication of Reynolds' *Other Side of the Frontier* in 1981 came an attempt to discover the Aboriginal view of early contact. As Attwood writes:

> Reynolds established a model of dispossession and resistance which became the paradigm in which most scholars explored Aboriginal responses, although he also pointed to patterns of contact other than conflict (Attwood, 1989:137).

Historians became interested in Aboriginal responses to invasion, but mainly the violent ones, and usually discussed them in terms of armed resistance and massacres (Robinson and York, 1977; Loos, 1982; Elder, 1988). The dynamics of cultural change and adaptation were not investigated by these historians and a pre-occupation with the breakdown of so-called "traditional" culture left contemporary Aboriginal people in the dubious position of being labelled as having "lost" their culture.

The complexities of the interaction between Aboriginal and non-Aboriginal people have often been treated with more insight by anthropologists, who have applied a more sophisticated understanding of the cultures of the peoples that they study. A good example is Chris Anderson's study of Aborigines and the tin mining industry in Northern Queensland (Anderson, 1983). Anderson is critical of the history that was being written by historians such as Reynolds and Loos and has the following to say about this "new history":

> Much of the 'new history' of Aboriginal contact with Europeans in Australia lacks an adequate socio-cultural understanding of Aboriginal society and its diversity. Attempts to produce overall models of contact have obscured, too, the diversity of European activity and its impact. The outcome has been too hollow and passive a view of Aboriginal responses to Australian colonial situations (Anderson, 1983:473).

Anderson particularly stresses the Aboriginal "agency" in determining the outcome of interaction with non-Aboriginal people. His study is an example of "historical" anthropology, illustrating the continuing blurring of the boundaries between the disciplines involved in the study of Aboriginal history.

In his book, *The making of the Aborigines,* Attwood (1989) provides an historical background to the "making" of indigenous Australian's into "Aborigines"—an identity he argues has largely been constructed by the actions and interests of Europeans. Attwood places less emphasis than Anderson on the "agency" of Aboriginal people in the contact process.

In an earlier paper, the Aboriginal anthropologist Marcia Langton stressed the importance of recognising Aboriginal adaptations to European invasion and a commonality of "culture" among Aboriginal people across Australia in a variety of situations (Langton, 1981).

More recently other anthropologists have been producing historical accounts of Aboriginal relations with non-Aboriginal people, in particular emphasising the role of the Australian state (Cowlishaw, 1988; Morris, 1989; Trigger, 1992). Cowlishaw sees Morris' account as critical in the more recent attempts to "deconstruct the construction of Aboriginality":

> Perhaps the most important breakthrough, however, is that which insists that the study of 'Us' is part of the study of 'Them'. Morris has achieved this in his work on the Dhan-gadi Aborigines and the state, perhaps the first detailed analysis of colonialism in Australia. He views colonialism as 'the implementation of a distinctive cultural system', and reveals the Dhan-gadi's cultural responses as creative and complex (Cowlishaw, 1992:29).

Mudrooroo Nyoongah (formerly Mudrooroo Narogin and Colin Johnson), Aboriginal author and chairperson of Murdoch University's Aboriginal and Islander program, stresses the importance of Aboriginal "voices" in changing the picture of Aboriginal history (Narogin, 1990). He has recently established a new Aboriginal and Islander degree program where the emphasis is on Aboriginal people presenting Aboriginal perspectives. He sees the role of Aboriginal writers since the 1960s as being critical in challenging the "official" histories and presenting a new version of Aboriginality. (See Walker, 1966; Gilbert, 1973; Narogin, 1983.)

In the last few decades there are an increasing number of published accounts of the lives of Aboriginal people who have grown up in the rural or urban areas of Australia (eg Tucker, 1977; Ward, 1987; Huggins, 1994). Through their very telling, the images of Aboriginal identity are being extended and changed from the static, "traditional" images presented by earlier, conventional anthropology, to the diverse and dynamic images of contemporary Aboriginality. (See Walker, 1964; Gilbert, 1973; Davis and Hodge, 1985; Miller, 1985; Narogin, 1983; Morgan, 1987; Langford, 1988.) These Aboriginal authors describe the horrors of Australian history, but also call into question the recent past and the present. They make white Australia aware that for Aboriginal people the invasion of their country and the violence of the early contact period have continued to the present day.

Nyoongah also attacks the treatment that the Aboriginal oral history tradition has received at the hands of non-Aboriginal historians and anthropologists (eg Shaw, 1983; Muecke, 1983; Rose, 1995). He sees oral histories which have been transcribed to the published page, as "captured", "calcified" and transformed from living, dynamic, tradition, to nothing more than "artefacts". He writes:

> Increasingly, traditional discourse is becoming fossilised, and the young people are turning away from the remains. The languages of their communities are becoming objects of shame, ridiculous moments of stone-age culture. This is only too evident in a work such as My country of the pelican dreaming. If an Aborigine needs help it is to them he applies, and if he does something wrong it is by them that he is punished—and if his story is to be written, it is to be written by the coloniser and in the coloniser's own discourse (Johnson, 1987:28).

However, in the collection of Black Australian writings, *Paperbark* (Davis et al, 1990), Muecke's technique for transcribing and presenting oral texts is used. The value of this approach is recognised, along with a warning that it still contains some restrictions.

> ... this can only be a partial representation of the complex gestures, inscriptions, melodies and intonations which characterise Aboriginal storytelling and singing (Davis et al, 1990:1).

New images of Australia's history

New images of Australia's history are emerging and a growing understanding of the history of Aboriginal people and their relationship to the Australian state is being developed. This process is occurring both through the efforts of Aboriginal people and through contributions by non-Aboriginal people. A different interpretation of Australia's history, from Aboriginal perspectives, is becoming available due to the growing body of Aboriginal literature. The following images of Australia's history graphically depict why Aboriginal people saw 1988 as both a year of mourning and as an opportunity to say that as a people "we have survived".

Aboriginal people believe that they have always lived in Australia, since the beginning—The Dreaming. Archaeologists have a different view of history and through excavation they have pushed the dates for the Aboriginal occupation of Australia back past 40,000 years (Flood, 1983). The western "scientific" approach to constructing the past has caused considerable conflict between archaeologists and Aboriginal people—the case of the reburial of the Lake Mungo human remains is a recent example (Pardoe, 1992:138). However, it appears that on both sides of this debate accommodations are being made and archaeologists who recognise Aboriginal ownership of the pre-European, Australian past are finding support for their research from Aboriginal communities. Many Aboriginal people see value in archaeological research and they don't believe that it necessarily challenges their world view (Pardoe, 1992:139). Western constructs of time, adapted to fit with Aboriginal concepts, can be clearly seen in the prayer of the Reverend Harris quoted at an earlier point in this paper. The popularity of Aboriginal art, in particular the dot paintings of the Western Desert, has led to the widespread exposure of concepts such as The Dreaming (Sutton et al, 1989). New images of Australia as an "ancient land", created in The Dreaming, are competing with scientific images of Australia's past. This has, however, led to problems for Aboriginal people, with the reinforcement of "traditional" stereotypes of Aboriginal culture often the result.

The violence of early contact between Aboriginal people and Europeans has been a major focus for new interpretations of Australian histories, produced by both Aboriginal and non-Aboriginal people. A recognition that the Europeans were invaders and that they forcibly stole Aboriginal lands has emerged from this literature. Many writers have sought to show that Aboriginal people violently resisted this invasion and that a state of warfare existed in many areas (eg Miller, 1985). This didn't all occur 200 years ago. In the Western Desert first contact was still taking place in recent decades and there is comparatively recent evidence of massacres of Aboriginal people in Central Australia, for example, the Coniston massacre in 1928 (Elder, 1988:141-153). A focus in many recent studies has been the continued, violent repression of Aboriginal people by the Australian state through institutionalisation, policing and oppressive policies. Many Aboriginal authors have argued that their resistance to invasion has not ended and, that sovereignty was never ceded.

Along with the violence of the frontier came another invasion—the introduction of Christianity through missionaries. This was both a physical invasion and an "invasion of the mind" (Attwood, 1989:1). Reynolds has this to say about the arrival of the missionaries:

> Religion moved from the background to the foreground in Aboriginal experience of European culture with the arrival of missionaries in the 1820s when the tribes targeted for conversion were directly challenged by the doctrines and practices of the newcomers. Of all Europeans the missionaries must have seemed the most enigmatic. They didn't seek land; they were often, though not always, disinterested in black women. They were so unlike the majority of frontier settlers; and, while they expressed goodwill and concern for the Aborigines, they were far more intrusive and interfering than other Europeans, often seeking to disrupt ceremonies and beliefs that were at the heart of Aboriginal society (Reynolds, 1989:155).

For many Aboriginal people life on a mission was the only alternative as their lands were taken over by the Europeans. Many Aboriginal people were forcibly moved onto missions. However, the reactions of Aboriginal people to Christianity and to the establishment of missions have been diverse. There are examples of Aboriginal people rejecting Christianity (Tonkinson, 1974), examples of the destructiveness of missionaries (Attwood, 1989) and numerous examples of Aboriginal people adapting Christianity to fit their particular situations (Calley, 1964; Bos, 1988).

Until recently the significant role that Aboriginal people have played in the Australian economy has been largely ignored. However, in many situations, such as on missions, their labour was often forcibly obtained and wages were very low or non-existent. Through studies by anthropologists, historians and the reminiscences of Aboriginal people, the story has emerged of how Aboriginal people became essential to the survival of one of the most important non-Aboriginal "industries"—pastoralism (Berndt and Berndt, 1987; McGrath, 1987; May, 1994). However, Aboriginal people have not benefited financially from their involvement with industries such as pastoralism, as can be seen from Sally Morgan's family history in her novel *My Place* (Morgan, 1987).

In 1788 the Australian state began its control of Aboriginal people's lives. The police and the prison system have always been instrumental in this control. The recent Royal Commission into Black Deaths in Custody has clearly mapped out the role of non-Aboriginal institutions in the oppression of Aboriginal people. Policies of protection, segregation and assimilation have been applied to Aboriginal people by Australian governments and resulted in inhuman practices such as the removal of children from parents (Matthews, 1977; Howard, 1982; Read, 1984; Mattingley and Hampton, 1988; Edwards and Read, 1989).

It was not until the 1960s that Aboriginal people began to gain some access to "power" in Australian society. Only in 1967, through an Australia wide Referendum, were Aboriginal people recognised as "equal" citizens and included in the Census. In 1972 a symbolically significant event for the Aboriginal cause took place with the setting up of a Tent Embassy on the lawns of Parliament House in Canberra. This embassy was set up in protest over statements made by the McMahon government over land rights. The earlier "walk off" by the Gurindji people at Wattie Creek, over wages decisions by the Arbitration Commission, was also crucial in the struggle for land rights (Broome, 1982; Coombs, 1994).

Since 1988 there has been ample opportunity for more reflection by non-Aboriginal Australians on Australian history from an Aboriginal perspective. In these few years Australians have witnessed the Royal Commission into Black Deaths in Custody, the establishment of the Government's new attempt to provide Aboriginal people with more control over their lives—the Aboriginal and Torres Strait Islander Commission, the introduction of the concept of "reconciliation" rather than the immediate development of a "treaty", as proposed in 1988, the establishment of the "Provisional Government"; the landmark case concerning Aboriginal land rights, the *Mabo* case and the Stolen Generations Report (Rowse, 1992; Watson, 1993; Attwood, 1996). Out of the Royal Commission into Aboriginal Deaths in Custody and the High Court decision over the *Mabo* case has come a serious questioning of the past images of Australian history. What Australia has to do to develop as a nation, and as a new republic, is to move towards a shared understanding of Australian history. Aboriginal perspectives have to be respected and recognised for their value in developing a mature nation, willing to face its past.

References

Anderson, C (1983). "Aborigines and tin mining in north Queensland: a case study in the anthropology of contact history". *Mankind,* vol. 13, no. 6, pp 473-498.

Attwood, B (1989). *The Making of the Aborigines.* Sydney: Allen and Unwin.

Attwood, B (1992). "Introduction". In *Power, Knowledge and Aborigines,* edited by B Attwood and J Arnold. [A special edition of the *Journal of Australian Studies.*] Bundoora: La Trobe University Press in association with the National Centre for Australian Studies, Monash University, pp i-xvi.

Attwood, B and Arnold, J, editors (1992). *Power, Knowledge and Aborigines.* [A special edition of the *Journal of Australian Studies.*] Bundoora: La Trobe University Press in association with the National Centre for Australian Studies, Monash University.

Barwick, D (1972). "Coranderrek and Cumeroogunga: pioneers and policy". In *Opportunity and Responses: Case Studies in Economic Development,* edited by T Epstein and D Penny. London: [publisher unknown].

Beckett, J (1958). "Marginal men: a study of two half-caste Aborigines". *Oceania,* vol. 29, pp 91-108.

Benterrak, K; Muecke, S and Roe, P (1984). *Reading the Country : An Introduction to Nomadology.* Freemantle: Freemantle Arts Centre Press.

Berndt, RM, editor (1982). *Aboriginal Sites, Rights and Resource Development.* Nedlands: University of WA Press.

Berndt, RM and Berndt, C (1987). *End of an Era: Aboriginal Labour in the Northern Territory.* Canberra: Australian Institute of Aboriginal Studies.

Bos, R (1988). 'The Dreaming and social change in Arnhem Land'. In *Aboriginal Australians and Christian Missions,* edited by T

Swain and D Rose. Adelaide: Australian Association for Religious Studies.

Broome, R (1982). *Aboriginal Australians: Black Response to White Dominance. 1788-1980.* Sydney: Allen and Unwin.

Calley, R (1964). "Pentecostalism among the Bandjalang". *Aborigines Now: New Perspectives in the Study of Aboriginal Communities,* edited by M Reay. Sydney: Angus and Robertson.

Coombs, HC (1994). *Aboriginal Autonomy.* Cambridge: University of Cambridge Press.

Cowlishaw, G (1988). *Black, White or Brindle: Race in Rural Australia.* Melbourne: Cambridge University Press.

Cowlishaw, G (1992). "Studying Aborigines: changing canons in anthropology and history". In *Power, Knowledge and Aborigines,* edited by B Attwood and J Arnold. [A special edition of the *Journal of Australasian studies.*] Bundoora: La Trobe University Press in association with the National Centre for Australian Studies, Monash University, pp 20-31.

Davis, J; Muecke, S; Narogin, M and Shoemaker, A (1990). *Paperbark: a Collection of Black Australian Writings.* St Lucia: University of Queensland Press.

Davis, J and Hodge (1985). *Aboriginal Writing Today: Papers from the 1st National Conference of Aboriginal Writers—Perth, WA.* Canberra: Australian Institute of Aboriginal Studies.

Dodson, M (1994). "The end is the beginning: re(de)fining Aboriginality", Wentworth Lecture. *Australian Aboriginal Studies,* no. 1, pp 2-13.

Edwards, C and Read, P, editors (1989). *The Lost Children.* Moorebank, NSW: Doubleday.

Elder, J (1988). *Blood on the Wattle: Massacres and Maltreatment of Australian Aborigines Since 1788.* Frenchs Forest: Childs and Associates.

Fabian, J (1983). *Time and the Other: Now Anthropology Makes its Object.* New York.

Flood, J (1983). *Archaeology of the Dreamtime: the Story of Prehistoric Australia and its People.* Sydney: Collins.

Foley, G (1990). "The year of mourning". In *Paperbark: a Collection of Black Australian Writing*, edited by Davis et al. St Lucia: University of Queensland Press, pp 330-332.

Foster, R. (1990). "The Aborigines Location in Adelaide: South Australia's First 'Mission' to the Aborigines". *Journal of the Anthropological Society of South Australia*, vol. 28, no. 1, pp 38-63.

Foucault, M (1974). *The Order of Things: an Archaeology of the Human Sciences*. London: Tavistock.

Frost, A (1990). "New South Wales as terra nullius". In *Through White Eyes,* edited by S Janson and S MacIntyre. Sydney: Allen and Unwin.

Gilbert, K (1973). *Because a White Man'll Never do it*. Sydney: Angus and Robertson.

Goodall, H (1996). *Invasion of Tent Embassy*. St Leonards: Allen and Unwin.

Goot, M and Rowse, T (1994). *Make a Better Offer: the Politics of Mabo*. Leichardt: Pluto Press.

Healey, JJ (1989). *Literature and the Aborigine*. St Lucia: University of Queensland Press.

Howard, M (1982). "Australian Aboriginal politics and perpetuation of inequality". In *Oceania*, vol. 53, no. 1, pp 82-101.

Huggins, J (1994). *Auntie Rita*. Canberra: Aboriginal Studies Press.

Huggins, J and Goodall, H (1992). "Aboriginal women are everywhere. Contemporary struggles". In *Gender Relations in Australia: Domination and Negotiation,* edited by K Saunders and Evans. Sydney: Harcourt, Brace and Jovanovich, pp 398-424.

Jenkin, G (1979). *Conquest of the Ngarrindjeri*. Adelaide: Rigby.

Johnson, C (1987). "Captured discourse, captured lives". *Aboriginal History,* vol. 11, nos. 1-2, pp 27-32.

Langford, R (1983). 'Our heritage, your playground'. *Australian Archaeology,* vol. 16, pp 2-6.

Langton, M and Peterson, N, editors (1983). *Aborigines, Land and Land Rights*. Canberra: Australian Institute of Aboriginal Studies.

Langton, M (1981). "Urbanising Aborigines, the social scientists great deception". *Social Alternatives,* vol. 2, no. 2, pp 16-22.

Lippmann, L (1970). *To Achieve our Country. Australia and the Aborigines.* Melbourne: Cheshire.

Loos, N (1982). *Invasion and Resistance.* Canberra: Australian National University Press.

Lyotard, J (1984). *The Postmodern Condition: a Report on Knowledge.* Manchester: University Press.

Markus, A (1988). *Blood from a Stone: William Cooper and the Australian Aborigines' League.* Sydney: Allen and Unwin.

Matthews, J (1977). *The two lives of Jimmie Barker.* Canberra: Australian Institute of Aboriginal Affairs.

Mattingley, C and Hampton, K, editors (1988). *Survival in our Own Land.* Adelaide: Wakefield Press.

May, D (1994). *Aboriginal Labour and the Cattle Industry.* Cambridge: Cambridge University Press.

McBryde, I, editor (1985). *Who owns the Past?.* Melbourne: Oxford University Press.

McConnochie, K; Hollinsworth, D and Pettman, J (1989). *Race and Racism in Australia.* Wentworth Falls: Social and Science Press.

McGrath, A (1987). *Born in the Cattle: Aborigines in Cattle Country.* Sydney: Allen and Unwin.

McGregor, R (1997). *Imagined Destinies: Aboriginal Australians and the Doomed Race Theory, 1880-1930.* Melbourne: Melbourne University Press.

Miller, J (1985). *Koori—a Will to Win: the Heroic Resistance, Survival and Triumph of Black Australia.* London: Angus and Robertson.

Morgan, S (1987). *My Place.* Fremantle: Fremantle Arts Centre Press.

Morris, B (1989). *Domesticating Resistance: the Dhan-Gadi Aborigines and the Australian State.* Oxford: Berg.

Mulvaney, DJ (1990). "The Australian Aborigines 1606-1929: opinion and fieldwork". In *Through White Eyes*, edited by S Janson and S MacIntyre. Sydney: Allen and Unwin.

Narogin, M (1983). *Doctor Wooreddy's Prescription for Enduring the End of the World.* Melbourne: Hyland House.

Narogin, M (1990). *Writing from the Fringe: a Study of Modern Aboriginal Literature*. Melbourne: Hyland House.

Newland, S (1893). *Paving the Way. a Romance of the Australian Bush*. London: Gay and Bird.

Ortner, S (1984). "Theory and anthropology since the sixties". In *Comparative Studies in Society and History,* pp 126-166.

Pardoe, C (1992). "Arches of radii, corridors of power: reflections on current archaeological practice". In *Power, Knowledge and Aborigines,* edited by B Attwood and J Arnold. [A special edition of the *Journal of Australasian studies.*] Bundoora: La Trobe University Press in association with the National Centre for Australian Studies, Monash University, pp 132-141.

Perkins, C (1975). *A Bastard Like Me*. Sydney: Ure Smith.

Read, P, editor (1984). *Down there with me on the Cowra Mission: an Oral History of Erambie Aboriginal Reserve, Cowra, New South Wales*. Sydney: Pergamon Press.

Reay, M, editor (1964). *Aborigines Now: New Perspectives in the Study of Aboriginal Communities*. Sydney: Angus and Robertson.

Reynolds, H (1989). *Dispossession: Black Australians and White Invaders*. Sydney: Allen and Unwin.

Reynolds, H (1972). *Aborigines and Settlers: the Australian Experience 1788-1939*. Melbourne: Cassell Australia.

Reynolds, H (1981). *The Other Side of the Frontier: Aboriginal Resistance to the European Invasion of Australia*. Ringwood, Vic: Penguin.

Robinson, F and York, B (1977). *The Black Resistance*. Camberwell, Vic: Widescope International.

Rose, DB (1995). *Hidden Histories*. Canberra: Aboriginal Studies Press.

Rowley, C (1972). *The Destruction of Aboriginal Society*. Harmondsworth: Penguin.

Rowley, C (1970). *The Destruction of Aboriginal Society*. Canberra: Australian Institute of Aboriginal Studies.

Rowley, C (1971). *Outcasts in White Australia*. Canberra: Australian Institute of Aboriginal Studies.

Rowse, T (1992). *Remote Possibilities: the Aboriginal Domain and the Administrative Imagination*. Darwin: Northern Australian Research Unit.

Said, E (1978). *Orientalism*. London: Routledge, Keegan Paul.

Seidman, S and Waggner, DG (1992). *Postmodernism and Social Theory: the Debate over General Theory*. Cambridge: Blackwell.

Shaw, B (1983). *Banggaiyerri: the story of Jack Sullivan*. Canberra: Australian Institute of Aboriginal Studies.

Stanner, WEH (1972). *After The Dreaming*. The Boyer Lecture, Sydney: ABC.

Stephenson, MA and Ratnalapa, S (1993). *Mabo: a Judicial Revolution*. St Lucia: University of Queensland Press.

Sutton, P, editor (1989). *Dreamings: the Art of Aboriginal Australia*, New York: Viking.

Swain, T and Rose, DB, editors (1988). *Aboriginal Australians and Christian Missions*. Adelaide: Australian Association for Religious Studies.

Tonkinson, R (1974). *The Jigalong Mob: Aboriginal Victors of a Desert Crusade*. California: Cummins.

Trigger, D (1992). *Whitefella Comin': Aboriginal Responses to Colonialism in Northern Australia*. Cambridge: Cambridge University Press.

Tucker, M (1977). *If Everyone Cared*. Sydney: Ure Smith.

Walker, K (1964). *We are Going*. Brisbane: Jacaranda Press.

Walker, K (1966). *The Dawn is at Hand*. Brisbane: Jacaranda Press.

Ward, G (1987). *Wandering Girl*. Broome: Magabala Books.

Watson, I (1993). "Has *Mabo* turned the tide for justice?" *Social Alternatives*, vol. 12, no. 1, pp 5-9.

Chapter 3

Australia's First Peoples: Identity and Population

Eleanor Bourke

Introduction

> Benelong's children survived as did a lot of other Aboriginal
> peoples' children ... But they were told they were no longer
> Aboriginal because they didn't live in a certain way and because
> they didn't look a certain way ... they no longer came from where
> the new boundaries said they came from, they were then told they
> were no longer Aboriginal (Peters, 1994).

There is speculation about the actual numbers of Aboriginal people
in Australia at the time of European settlement in 1788—who they
were, whether they originated in this continent, how long they had
been here and the numbers of languages spoken. Despite this,
traditional Aboriginal historical accounts generally indicated
Aboriginal people have always been here, that they developed in
Australia and did not come from elsewhere. Estimates of the number
of Aboriginal people inhabiting the continent when the British
arrived vary from around 300,000 to over 1 million. In 1928
Radcliffe-Brown developed the lower estimation, while Professor
Noel Butlin, geographer and demographer, in 1983 estimated the
population at about a million (Butlin, 1993:92). In addition it has
been estimated that from 250 languages with up to 600 dialect
groups were viable when the British arrived (Butlin, 1993).

In 1911 it was speculated that the Aboriginal and Islander
population had fallen to about 31,000, a fall primarily due to
excessive deaths through violent confrontations with the settlers,
disease, poor health and malnutrition. Relatively low fertility and
the definition of who was counted as an Aborigine may also have
contributed. In the 1930s, however, the population began to grow.
Between the 1947 and 1976 censuses, persons identified as
Aboriginal or as Torres Strait Islander increased from about 51,000
to 160,916, an average annual growth rate of about 4% (Horton,
1994:2.889).

When the First Australians identified themselves to the Europeans they did it in a way that made it possible to discern associations with specific places by name. An example of this is given by Myers (1991:28) writing about the "Pintupi" who never used this name to refer to themselves until they came into contact with white people. Rather they talked about people coming "from the west", giving a nominal social identity. Myers believes that "social identities hold little meaning" and that "identity, is situational" (1991:28).

The word Aboriginal was introduced later, definitions were created and distinctions made between people on the basis of geography, lifestyle and ancestry. But the people who became the "Aboriginal", were also called "natives" or were described as the Murray River tribes or the Goulburn blacks. The use of Aboriginal, became dominant long after the knowledge of their own names for "the people" had been lost.

The association of Aboriginal people with the land was disrupted as colonisation took effect. Aboriginal groups had to struggle to adapt to new situations under extremely adverse circumstances. For example, traditional hunting grounds and sacred sites were selected for sheep and cattle grazing and waterholes were contaminated. Alienation of Aboriginal people from the land disrupted ceremonial life and changed Aboriginal lifestyles and family ties. It changed Aboriginal identity for ever. There is also speculation that there were two severe smallpox outbreaks between 1788 and 1850 (Butlin, 1983; Critchett, 1990) to which Aboriginal people would have had little or no resistance, resulting in great loss of life.

The official records of the first settlement show that it was the intention of the British Government to deal fairly with the original Australians. This is highlighted by an extract from the Select Committee on Aborigines (British Settlements) from the House of Commons on 26 June 1837 in London:

> These people, unoffending as they were towards us, have, as might have been expected, suffered in an aggravated degree from the planting among them of our penal settlements. In the formation of these settlements it does not appear that the territorial rights of the natives were considered, and very little care has since been taken to

protect them from the violence or the contamination of the dregs of our countrymen.

The consequences have been dreadful beyond example, both in the diminution of their numbers and in their demoralization.

Many deeds of murder and violence have undoubtedly been committed by the stockkeepers (convicts in the employ of farmers in the outskirts of the colony), by the cedar cutters, and by the remote free settlers, and many natives have perished by the various military parties sent against them ... (Cannon, 1992 vol. 2A:62).

As well as ravaging the population at the time of contact, the impact of the new settlement has been persistent and remains an issue. The right of most Indigenous Australians to identify themselves as the First Australians is often questioned.

Protection and Aboriginal identity

Colonisation decimated the Aboriginal population, fragmented the Indigenous people and their cultures and challenged their identity and survival. Aboriginal people had to adapt. Changes occurred to ensure their survival as a people

The first *Aborigines Protection Act* was legislated in 1869 in Victoria. This Act, and subsequent protection acts, was premised on the racial superiority of the British and the belief that Aboriginal people were uncivilised. The Acts were designed to exclude designated or prescribed Aboriginal people from many aspects of modern Australian life as it was evolving. Specific Acts even deemed that Aboriginal people were not able to be employees, work with food or carry the mail (McCorquodale, 1987). Legislation generally prescribed an identity based on race and pedigree.

The impact of such acts has been far reaching for Aboriginal people and have underpinned official attitudes and legitimated policies which have discriminated against Aboriginal people. They have been used to validate the idea of "real" Aboriginal people meaning "full-bloods", thereby challenging the identity of Aboriginal people in the more densely European occupied parts of Australia.

In Victoria the *Aborigines Protection Act 1886* narrowed the definition of "Aborigine" to:

> full-bloods, half-castes over 34, female half-castes married to Aborigines, the infants of Aborigines and half-castes who were licensed by the Board of Protection for Aborigines to reside on a station.

The Protection Acts through reference to blood quantum were used to sanction divisions between Aboriginal people and to legitimate the idea that some Aboriginal people were more Aboriginal than others. They justified discrimination against Aborigines and division among them. John Murray, in the Victorian Parliamentary Debates in 1911, summed up an attitude to "half-caste" identity:

> A good many people make a mistake about the character of the half-caste. He is really more of a blackfellow than the full blooded Aboriginals. The infusion of blood does not make him more capable than the full blooded Aboriginal to compete with the white man in the battle of life (VPD Assembly, 1910:1386).

In South Australia the *South Australian Aborigines Act 1911* emphasised control and expanded segregation. The *South Australian Aborigines Amendment Act 1939* broadened the definition of Aboriginal to include all people of Aboriginal descent. However, it introduced the exemption certificate, referred to by Aboriginal people as the "dog tag". The law made possible "exemptions from Act, for any person, who, in the opinion of the Board, by reason of his character, standard of intelligence, and development should be exempted" (McCorquodale, 1987:71). Exemption was also used as punishment to expel Aboriginal people from institutions and reserves in South Australia.

Many Aboriginal people deeply resented having to carry the exemption paper which declared them to be "honorary whites". Exemption classified some Aboriginal people as white people and this caused divisions in many families with lasting effects. Val Power, a Ngarrindjeri of Raukkan in South Australia whose mother was exempted, said:

> My mother was fair-skinned with blue eyes. A lot of people with fair skins hid their Aboriginality. But my mother didn't want to do

that. She didn't want to lose her identity as an Aboriginal person. It was no use saying she was a Maori or something because she still had brothers at Point McLeay who had dark skins (Mattingley and Hampton, 1988:50).

The *Queensland Aboriginals Protection and Restriction of the Sale of Opium Act 1897* had the following notation to the clause defining half-castes:

Note: Offspring of a white woman and Aboriginal father not half-caste.

The subsequent 1939 *Queensland Act* in its definition indicated that:

Any Aboriginal may be removed to and detained in a reserve ... [This even included] a child on a reserve with a mother who is an Aboriginal ... (McCorquodale, 1987:58-59).

Protection meant that many Aboriginal people were sent to designated areas away from their own country and away from their families further eroding their sense of identity.

John McCorquodale in his analysis of Aborigines and European law identified that there were some 800 pieces of legislation dealing with Aboriginal people and within it some 67 definitions of Aboriginality (McCorquodale, 1987). The legislation codified and institutionalised the notion of superior and inferior peoples and cultures.

The White Australia Policy which was designed to control the movement and employment of "coloured" aliens such as Asians and South Sea Islanders presented another complication for Aboriginal people. As non-whites who were indigenous to Australia they, too, were excluded from employment on the basis of race under acts intended to control the employment of aliens. William Cooper, as Honorary Secretary of the Australian Aborigines' League, in 1936 argued for Aborigines to be treated fairly.

... the full-bloods are the descendants of the original owners of Australia. They are the lineal descendants of their fathers. The change in ownership by conquest should not invalidate their title to reasonable part of those lands and these rights should be admitted without cavil ...

The half-caste is the descendant of the Aboriginal and therefore joint heirs with the full blood. They are also descendants of the white man and thus heirs with the white race for all rights of British nationhood ... (Cooper in Markus, 1988:48).

In a document called *Aborigines Demand Citizenship Rights* (1938) also known as the Aboriginal Manifesto, the Aborigines Progressive Association wrote about the identity of Aboriginal Australians:

You are the New Australians, but we are the Old Australians. We have in our arteries the blood of the Original Australians, who have lived in this land for many thousands of years (Argus, 13 January 1938).

Population and identity

William Cooper tried to form the first national Aboriginal movement and to petition King George V regarding the plight of Aboriginal Australians. In hindsight it is obvious that William Cooper and his peers (in New South Wales the Aborigines Progressive Association was active leading up to the Sesquicentenary) had a great impact on the Aboriginal consciousness and identity.

Cooper won support from the National Missionary Council for the first National Aboriginal Day to celebrate Aboriginal survival in 1940. It was to be celebrated annually on the Sunday preceding the Australia Day weekend. It became known as Aboriginal Sunday in the eastern states. National celebrations now occur in the second week of July each year and are regarded by many Aboriginal people as a national celebration of their existence and survival in Australian society. These celebrations strengthen Aboriginal identity by focussing on Aboriginal people, their culture and their contribution to society. Today NAIDOC (National Aboriginal and Islander Observance Day Committee) is synonymous with National Aboriginal week celebrations.

NAIDOC has become a national celebration of Aboriginal identity drawing in many other Australians.

The post-war drift to urban centres found Aboriginal people seeking each other out in the cities. Some left their families, taking with them the name of an Aboriginal contact in the city. This resulted in Aborigines congregating in pockets within cities. Urban Aboriginal identity, apart from skin colour, meant belonging to an Aboriginal community, identifying as Aboriginal, seeking out new values to blend with a common heritage and a proud tradition. This meant acknowledging loss but celebrating survival as well. Some fair- skinned Aboriginal people faced a dilemma. They could deny their identity, compete for jobs and escape racism or they could identify as Aborigines and be excluded like their darker brothers and sisters.

Colin Bourke of the Gamilaroi wrote in 1978 about the yearning of Aboriginal people for a place in modern Australian life:

> Few Aborigines are completely comfortable with their Aboriginality. There is a large vacuum of unfulfilled Aboriginal needs. It is these unsatisfied desires—to be able to see oneself as a person of value, to be proud to be an Aborigine, to be able to work at one's own identity and heritage in a positive light which negate all the programs derived for Aboriginal advancement (Bourke, 1978:3).

Such a feeling of uncertainty came from the exclusion of Aboriginal people from many aspects of Australian society. The *Commonwealth Constitution Act of 1901* specifically excluded Aborigines as citizens and from some entitlements. As a result they were not eligible for Commonwealth Social Services such as the Age Pension and Unemployment Benefits. Until 1966 Aboriginal people who lived away from towns were not included in the census. However, estimates were made by the various government agencies responsible for Aboriginal welfare after Federation. These estimates were included in every national census. The following table is an attempt to track the Aboriginal population from 1788.

Population: Structure and Future Growth

Estimates of the past and present distribution of the Aboriginal population of Australia, 1788 to 1966

Year†	State or Territory						Australia *
	New South Wales	Victoria	Queensland	South Australia	Western Australia	Northern Territory	
1788	40,000	11,500	100,000	10,000	52,000	35,000	251,000
1901	8,065	521	26,670	3,070	5,261	23,363	66,950
1921	6,067	573	15,454	2,741	17,671	17,973	60,479
1947	11,560	1,277	16,311	4,296	24,912	15,147	73,817
1954	12,214	1,395	18,460	4,972	16,215	17,157	70,678
1961	14,716	1,796	10,696	4,884	18,276	19,704	79,253
1966a	14,219	1,790	19,003	5,505	18,439	21,119	80,207
1966b	20,601	2,707	23,040	6,584	21,146	22,306	96,632
1966c	23,130	3,500	41,700	7,760	21,890	24,120	122,100

* This column includes Tasmania and the Australian Capital Territory, separate figures for which are not shown.

† The 1966a figures are for persons of half or more Aboriginal descent. The 1996b figures include additionally persons who described themselves as less than 50 percent Aboriginal. The 1996c figures are estimates made by the State and Territories. See Australia, Department of Territories, The Australian Aborigines, Sydney, 1967:62 (Broom and Lancaster, 1973:43).

The repeal in 1967 of section 127 of the *Commonwealth Constitution Act* by amending S 51 (xxvi) of the Constitution, enabled Aboriginal population figures to be included officially from 1971. Since then census procedures have been improved to try to ensure that Aboriginal people are counted accurately. At the 1986 census approximately 230,000 people identified themselves as Aboriginal or Torres Strait Islander. Over half of the Aboriginal population were under 20 years of age. Aboriginal people were to be found in all parts of Australia, with the largest populations in New South Wales and Queensland. Aboriginal percentages of the whole population were greatest in the northern part of Australia—north western Australia, the Northern Territory and northern Queensland. New South Wales was the State with the largest Aboriginal population while Queensland had the largest indigenous population.

State and Territory Indigenous Population 1996
Census Usual Residence Counts

State and Territory	1991	1996	% change
New South Wales	69,993	101,636	45.2
Victoria	16,701	21,503	28.8
Queensland	70.072	95,374	36.1
South Australia	16,227	20,421	25.8
Western Australia	41,844	50,699	21.2
Tasmania	8,912	13,929	56.3
Northern Territory	39,857	46,362	16.3
Australian Capital Territory	1,583	2,844	79.7
Jervis Bay Territory	192	181	0.5
Australia (a)	265,371	352,970	33.0

(a) 1996 figures include Cocos (Keeling) and Christmas Islands in the Australia total (ABS Census, 1996).

The 1996 Census count indicates a dramatic Aboriginal and Torres Strait Islander population increase of 33% from 1991. This compares with an increase of 5% in the corresponding usual residence census count for non-Indigenous Australians.

Increases in the counts of Indigenous people between 1991 and 1996 were greatest in metropolitan and large urban centres, where they averaged more than 50%. Increases were less marked in small rural centres (13% on average). In all areas average increases were much larger for counts of the Indigenous than total Australian population.

Over half of the Aboriginal population were still under 20 years of age. Aboriginal percentages of the whole population are greatest in the northern part of Australia—north western Australia, the Northern Territory (25%) and northern Queensland. New South Wales became the State with the largest Aboriginal population (over 100,000) while Queensland has an Indigenous population over 95,000 (ABS Statsite http://www.abs.gov.com.au).

The rapid increase in the Indigenous population has caused some difficulties for statisticians endeavouring to explain unprecedented growth. Increased identification rate, higher birthrates, a higher percentage of females of child bearing age and marriages between Aboriginal and non-Aboriginals have been advanced as some of the causal factors.

Contemporary Aboriginal identity

Aboriginal organisations, in addition to being formed in response to government policies, are expressions of Aboriginal identity. While they have been established with a view to meeting Aboriginal needs they also serve to bring to the fore a distinctive Aboriginal cultural heritage and an Aboriginal presence. In this way Aboriginal cultural heritage has been modified and changed in response to new experiences and knowledge.

McGrath (1987:171) writes *of* traditional owners who taught their children:

> Watch out you don't forget this; hold on to this dreaming which you inherit from your father; You in turn must use this at initiations; we must not lose this. Our ancestors never lost it, and now we must hand over the Dreamings to our sons, otherwise they might get mixed up and say: I don't know what design to put on at the initiation, I don't know which is my father's dreaming.

She also recorded that the:

> lighter skinned Aborigines taken away from their station-dwelling parents who literally lost information about their origins, and learnt to feel ashamed of their Aboriginality ... (McGrath, 1987:168).

Garnet Wilson, Chairman of the South Australian Aboriginal Lands Trust, speaking at a United Nations International Day for the Elimination of Racial Discrimination in 1983 said:

> If you are an Aboriginal Australian—an Aboriginal Australian— you are robbed of your identity and heritage! Instead of being a proud guardian of a spiritually and physically beautiful country you are captured in poverty and hopelessness! (Mattingley and Hampton, 1988:265).

Ronald and Catherine Berndt (1988:528) affirm that there is:

> A wave of feeling, of Aboriginal identity, pointing toward pan-Aboriginality, seeks to establish a common socio-cultural heritage.

They added that:

> ... the significance of Aboriginal identity is of considerable importance, because it defines persons of Aboriginal descent in contrast to non-Aborigines.

There have been some recent challenges to Aboriginal expressions of identity developed by Aboriginal people using their own experiences. The Aboriginal novelist, Colin Johnson, writing as Mudrooroo Nyoongah has written "that the search for Aboriginal identity must come from within and that Aboriginal people must determine for themselves an identity within parameters established by them" (Oceania, 1992:156).

A World Indigenous Movement with good networking through indigenous pathways around the world has also developed. Dr Thom Alcoze, Northern Arizona University has written:

> There is a rebirth experienced by Native Americans today. Expressions of historic understandings and identity as nations, cultures, and societies of great value and sophistication have emerged.

Lois O'Donoghue, CBE, AM, founding Chairperson of the Aboriginal and Torres Strait Islander Commission said in 1992 when presenting the Barunga statement to the United Nations Working Group on Indigenous People:

Australia is a big country. We come from the north, south, east and west of Australia, the Torres Straits and Tasmania ... Point 6 from the Barunga statement seeks respect for and promotion of our Aboriginal (indigenous) identity, including the cultural, linguistic, religious and historical aspects, including the right to educate in our own languages and in our own culture and history (United Nations Working Group on Indigenous Populations, 10th session, 1992:22).

The National Report of the Royal Commission for Aboriginal Deaths in Custody reported that Aboriginal people resent non-Aboriginal attempts to define and categorise them.

Brunton (1993) discussed the *tensions between public constructions of Aboriginality*. He located this discussion within the Aboriginal movement based on the understandings and experiences of individual Aboriginal people. He identified the following issues which appear as contradictions in discussions about Aboriginality:

- possible pressure to conform to certain ideas of Aboriginality; and
- conflict between local regionalised identity as against a concept of pan-Aboriginality based on a common cultural framework.

Brunton raises these points in a discussion about the consequences of Aboriginality and the idea that Aboriginal identity attracts preferential treatment and benefits. He repeats Dierdre Jordan's observation that:

... it is a commentary on the perceptions of white society that contemporary theorists, even the most enlightened, assume that Aborigines of mixed ancestry should identify with the race of their black parent, rather than their white parent, and that the identity offered by mainstream society is one of exclusion from claims to European ancestry (Brunton, 1993:15).

The "new" Aborigines to use the Berndts' term are all those who are of Aboriginal descent or who identify themselves as Aboriginal people and who have carved out for themselves a particular niche in Australian society. The Berndts (1988:526) write of *Aborigines being rediscovered* by other Australians and that a romantic image of traditional Aboriginal life was portrayed by novelists, poets, artists, musicians and dancers in the 1970s.

This image includes the emergence of national and state spokespersons; it includes a range of opinions designated as "moderate" to "extremist" in political terms. This has been expressed in the espousing of a distinctive Aboriginal contribution to Australian society and Aboriginal ways of doing things.

Aboriginal people, as First Nations people, do feel compelled to seek acknowledgment of their prior ownership, their sovereignty and the recognition of a continuous identity. David Suzuki writing generally about indigenous nations said:

> Indigenous people are the descendants of a given geographic territory that may have been taken over militarily, politically or by settlement of outsiders ... as historically, politically, and culturally dominated--though not conquered—world wide they know who they are. The sense of self-identification is the single most crucial element of any working definition of indigenous Aboriginal or first peoples (UN Working Group, 1992:7).

Schwab commented on the nature of Aboriginal identity in Adelaide:

> Identity among most Aborigines in Adelaide is clear and explicit because it is based in large part, as it was in the past, on a local ground of kinship, sense of self, as well as relation to and identification with other Aborigines in Adelaide ... (Schwab, 1988:79).

Unlike non-Aboriginal constructions of Aboriginality, Aboriginal people believe that their identity is based on their own cultural heritage and is not merely a reaction to non-Aboriginal actions. While it cannot be denied that the policies in relation to Aboriginal people in the main are articulated by non-Aboriginal people, there needs to be acknowledgment of many traditional Aboriginal values, as well as an ancient heritage of adaptation and change. Those who say that Aboriginality is new or that "part-Aboriginals" have not had enough time to develop a sense of identity or continuity, do not see Australian history through Aboriginal eyes or they choose to misinterpret it.

Europeans have based Aboriginal identity mainly on race whereas Aboriginal people speak of "my people", representing the notion of peoplehood. This is derived from knowledge of genealogies, and belonging to specific extended family groups. Aboriginal identity and culture is based on a distinctive cultural heritage which incorporates special meanings given to the land and people and is centred on core values.

Aboriginal people see opportunities for their cultures to be further developed, extended and refined through education. This will be achieved through participation, not separation and degradation, in Australian life for Aboriginal people. This requires Aboriginal identity to be affirmed and recognised by all Australians. How then do Aboriginal people see themselves?

> Aboriginal culture cannot be separated from the land. On the land are stories—Aboriginal stories that explain why people, rockholes, the hills and the trees came to be there. The land is full of stories. Every square mile is just like a book, a book with a lot of pages, and it's all a story for the children to learn (Yami Lester in Mattingley and Hampton, 1983:73).

An Aboriginal social identity is no longer simply an aspiration. It is now a reality, relevant to virtually all persons of Aboriginal descent. Even though the content varies, there are a sufficient number of elements held in common by Aboriginal people to distinguish it.

> To me as a black theologian, God is black as much as white. Why? Because God speaks our language, knows our culture and made this land we now live in and enjoy. If I am to have my true identity before God, you cannot lock me into white ways. You must give me freedom to be me. God has the same concern for the Aboriginal as for the white (Gondarra, 1986:13)

Some academics are claiming that Aboriginal identity is largely a response to European invasion and domination of the land. von Sturmer, for example, argues that Aboriginality simply does not exist: "Aboriginality is a fiction which takes on a meaning only in terms of white ethnocentrism ..." (von Sturmer in Tonkinson, 1990:199). To some Aboriginal people this would parallel a claim that European Jewish identity is a result of its reaction to Nazi Germany.

This is not to deny that Aboriginal people and their culture today are affected by all factors prevailing in Australian society. Legal, health, education, technological and economic factors all affect the Aboriginal population. They place pressure on Aboriginal cultures, identity and spirituality and it is hard for some to retain their Aboriginality today.

Aboriginal people have formed organisational structures to meet their needs and serve as cultural symbols and, in at least one instance, to serve as proof of Aboriginal cultural continuity in the modern sense. In 1976, Justice Lush in a Victorian Supreme Court case had to rule whether or not Aboriginal people still existed in Victoria, said that "Aborigine" was a word probably used much more widely in Australia than in other English speaking countries. He said that "the Aborigines" was used to describe "persons in groups or societies irrespective of mixture of blood". In the case of *Bryning Re* Justice Lush found that Aboriginal people and their descendants continued to exist in Victoria and cited the existence of the Australian Aborigines' League from the 1920s as evidence (McCorquodale, 1987:251).

However, Aboriginal culture and identity continue to be under increasing pressure. Aborigines are flooded with mass media and are themselves using and participating in Western media forms. The dominance of English and the loss of Aboriginal languages provide just one indicator of how Aboriginal culture can be diminished. Aboriginal arts and crafts are popular commercially but this commercialism may pose a threat to traditional purposes and meanings. The way in which Aboriginal Australians will choose to deal with these and other aspects of Aboriginal culture will serve to further shape modern Aboriginal identity.

Gaynor MacDonald has written about the "traditions of the Wiradjuri" and the "acceptance of Aboriginality" within Aboriginal groups. She notes the deeply "engrained ... ongoing traditions" such as the Wiradjuri kinship system which continues to provide important channels for personal identity for Wiradjuri today (MacDonald, 1998).

It is Cathy Freeman who has given the strongest depiction and expression of Aboriginal identity when she created a controversy in 1994 by carrying the Aboriginal flag after a Commonwealth games victory.

In 1997 she said after winning the World 400m Championship in Athens "I could have no energy and still be able to carry those two flags. How could I stand by and not? I am such a proud Indigenous Australian" (*Sydney Morning Herald*, August 1997).

References

Argus Newspaper (Melbourne), January 13, 1938.

Australian Bureau of Statistics, 1996 Census, Canberra.

ABS Statsite http://www.abs.gov.com.au.

Berndt, RM and Berndt, CH (1988). *The World of the First Australians: Aboriginal Traditional Life, Past and Present*. Canberra: Aboriginal Studies Press.

Bourke, C (1978). "Aboriginal culture and schools". *Polycom*, vol. 14, p 3.

Broom and Lancaster Jones (1973). *A Blanket a Year*. Canberra: ANU Press.

Brunton, R (1993). *Black Suffering, White Guilt?* Victoria, Australia: Institute of Public Affairs Ltd.

Bryning Re (1976). Victorian Supreme Court.

Burger, A (1979). *Neville Bonner*. Melbourne: Macmillan.

Butlin, N (1983). *Original Aggression Aboriginal Population of South Australia 1788-1850*. North Sydney: Allen and Unwin.

Butlin, N (1993). *Economics and the Dreamtime*. Melbourne: Cambridge University Press.

Cannon, M (1982). "The Aborigines of Port Phillip 1835-1839". *Historical Records of Victoria* vol, 2A. Melbourne: Victorian Government Printer.

Critchett, J (1990). *A Distant Field of Murder: Western District Frontiers 1834-1848*. Melbourne: Melbourne University Press.

Eyre, Edward John (1845). *Journals of Expeditions into Central Australia*, vol. 2 (Facsimile). London: T and W Boone.

Gondarra, Djiniyini (1986). *Series of Reflections of Aboriginal Theology*. Darwin: Bethel Presbytery, Northern Synod of the Uniting Church.

Hollinsworth, David (1992). "Discourses on Aboriginality and the politics of identity in urban Australia". *Oceania,* vol. 63, no. 2, pp 137-155.

Horner, J (1974). *Vote Ferguson for Aboriginal Freedom.* Sydney: ANZ Book Co.

Horton, D, editor (1994). *Encyclopaedia of Aboriginal Australia,* vol. 2. Canberra: Aboriginal Studies Press.

Jordan, D (1985). *Census Categories: Enumeration of Aboriginal People or Construction of Identity.* Adelaide: University of Adelaide Paper.

Keen, I, editor (1988). *Being Black.* Canberra: Australian Studies Press.

MacDonald, G (1998). "Continuities of Wiradjuri Tradition". In Edwards, WH, editor (1998). *Traditional Aboriginal Society.* Second edition. South Yarra: Macmillan.

Markus, A, editor (1988). *Blood From a Stone.* Australia: Allen and Unwin.

Mattingley, C and Hampton, K (1988). *Survival in Our Own Land.* Adelaide: Wakefield Press.

McCorquodale, J (1987). *Aborigines and the Law: a Digest.* Canberra: Australian Studies Press.

McGrath, A (1987). *Born in the Cattle.* Sydney: Allen and Unwin.

Murray, John (1910). *VPD Assembly,* vol. 125, 27 September 1910.

Myers, FR (1991). *Pintupi Country, Pintupi Self: Sentiment, Place, and Politics among Western Desert Aborigines.* Berkeley: UCLA.

Peters, F (1994). "What happened to the Original People". In *Other Boundaries.* Sydney: UTS.

Royal Commission for Aboriginal Deaths in Custody (1991). *National Report.* Canberra: AGPS.

Schwab, J (1988). "Urban Aboriginal Identity in Adelaide". In Keen, I, editor (1988). *Being Black.* Canberra: Australian Studies Press.

Tonkinson, Myrna (1990). "Is it in the blood? Australian Aboriginal identity". In *Cultural Identity and Ethnicity in the Pacific.* Edited by J Linnekin and L Poyer. Honolulu: University of Hawaii.

UN Working Group on Indigenous Populations 10th Session—
1992. Switzerland: The Australian Contribution.

Chapter 4

Two Laws: One Land

Colin Bourke and Helen Cox

Introduction

The Aboriginal peoples of this country had well-developed systems of law long before the arrival of the First Fleet from England in 1788. Underpinning these systems was the relationship of the people to the land. This relationship remains an important source of spirituality for many people today.

This paper describes the main features of traditional Aboriginal legal systems. The impact of European "settlement" and the imposition of English law is described and analysed from a legal viewpoint. The imposed criminal justice system has incarcerated Aborigines at a disproportionate rate.

The relationship between Aboriginal and European law is examined with reference to the denial of human rights and failure to recognise native title to land. This leads to the contemporary situation with a discussion of the decision of the High Court in *Mabo*. A focus on the traditional relationship between Aboriginal people and the land cannot be avoided in any discussion of the law.

Traditional Aboriginal law

The Aboriginal ancestors travelled the country during The Dreaming, the creative period from the time immemorial. They established the code of life which today is called The Dreaming or The Law. The Law has been passed on for countless generations of people through the remembrance and celebration of the sites which were the scenes of the ancestral exploits. Song, dance, body, rock and sand painting, special languages and the oral explanations of the myths encoded in these essentially religious art forms have been the media of The Law to the present day. (Statement of Marcia Langton, World Council of Churches, 1981:13).

Traditional Aboriginal Law is often referred to as *customary law*. It is difficult to define in non-Aboriginal terms because it covers the rules for living and is backed by religious sanctions and it also prescribes daily behaviour. Through The Dreaming the law is prescribed for the land and its inhabitants.

Aborigines had occupied all of Australia before 1788, but they had no *lingua franca*. No shared language spanned the continent. There were also variations in the laws from one group to another and one region to another. However, in all regions, law and spirituality were intermingled and common features can be identified. The broad roles and responsibilities of men and women in sacred ritual, economic affairs, marriage and other aspects of daily life had been laid down in The Dreaming. The ancestors were the source of Aboriginal life and law and there were religious sanctions for the traditional dictates of right and wrong.

Aboriginal government was very decentralised and it was largely informal and loosely organised. This had a direct bearing on the maintenance of law and order. Within each group there were recognised forms of behaviour with which its members were in fundamental agreement. Children were enculturated into the correct forms of behaviour by their own family (Edwards, 1988:107; Berndt and Berndt, 1967:102).

The people most conversant with all the features of their own culture are those who are fully initiated and no longer young— usually the elders. They have the most wisdom and knowledge and their opinions carry the most weight when it comes to a debatable point or upholding The Law (Berndt and Berndt, 1967:102).

In Aboriginal Australia there were no formal courts of law with specially designated persons vested with authority and power to deal with cases, to judge and to punish. Instead most problems were handled informally within the group by a council of elders. Intra-group difficulties would be settled when the opportunity arose such as when groups came together for ceremonies or when particular food supplies, such as yabbies, Bunya pine nuts, Bogong moths, were in abundance (Berndt and Berndt, 1967:103-104).

Traditional law can be compared to the Ten Commandments. It covered homicide, sacrilege, sorcery, incest, abduction of women, adultery, physical assault, theft, insult, including swearing, and the usurpation of ritual privileges and duties—a reasonable comparison. However, Aboriginal traditional laws also included offences of omission towards other people, such as failure to share food, to avoid particular relations, perform rituals or ceremonies or to educate nominated group members (Edwards, 1988:61; Meggitt, 1962).

In 1962 Meggitt published his study of Walbiri society which had had minimal European contact. He produced a summary of the rules of customary law which categorised a number of offences which the Walbiri recognised as unlawful. The Law covered ritual, economic, residential and kinship rules and conventions. It also covered the care of sacred objects, the division of labour by gender, the avoidance of mother-in-laws and even the rising of the sun. Meggitt believed that in pre-contact times rules of law and norms of politically appropriate behaviour were probably not distinguished (Meggitt, 1962).

Most social behaviour was public. It was nearly impossible to offend without others knowing. It was rare for any discussion to occur in the group as to the question of guilt. There was almost no privacy in any camp, so everyone knew what had occurred. Punishment was meted out in public. This would certainly have been a deterrent to breaking the more important rules.

The range of penalties included death, wounding, fear of sorcery, corporal punishment and abuse or ridicule to shame people into compliance (Berndt and Berndt, 1967:103; Edwards, 1988:62-64). There were no gaols or fines. Close relatives could plead for leniency but they could also seek the heaviest penalty.

European impact—post 1788

Much of Aboriginal law did not openly conflict with British law, but those aspects which required secrecy or inflicted punishment directly by the group raised considerable difficulties as whites spread across Australia. Most problems were, however, caused by colonists breaking Aboriginal law, especially land seizure and the treatment of Aboriginal women by Europeans.

Many of the Aboriginal groups tried to incorporate the newcomers into their system of law by extending kinship rules and networks and sharing resources. However, many of the intruders failed to conform to the traditional laws. In particular they were ignorant about the principle of *reciprocity*. Sharing was expected. The European settlers appeared greedy and selfish as they rarely shared their resources even when they were granted favours by Aboriginal people (Reynolds, 1981:68-70; Edwards, 1988:61).

Many Aboriginal people strongly resisted the invading Europeans. Pemulwuy led the Eora resistance to the establishment of Sydney, while the Kalkadoons in north Queensland struggled for many years to protect their physical and spiritual life against the invading colonists.

British response: application of terra nullius

The British sought to extend their laws to the land now called Australia and its Aboriginal inhabitants. The laws of England were imported to the new colony of New South Wales to the extent that they were applicable to those times and conditions. (Australian Law Reform Commission [ALRC], 1986:34).

Despite Aboriginal resistance England declared itself the sovereign or ruler of Australia. The established legal doctrine that enabled it to do this is known as *terra nullius*. The European legal view at the time was that the Crown had absolute title to all land. Under the doctrine colonising powers such as England could apply their own law to land which they peacefully occupied, if the land was uninhabited, or was occupied by a people without settled laws or customs. In conquered or ceded (surrendered) countries the pre-existing laws of that country were applied until they were displaced or altered by the new sovereign (Hanks, 1991:1).

Australia was declared to be a land that was not occupied by a people with settled laws. In legal effect, it was *terra nullius*. This was upheld in the case of *Cooper v Stuart* (1889) 14 Appeal Case 286. The legal order of the Aboriginal peoples was not seen as sufficiently organised to be recognised. This view was not supported by Justice Blackburn in *Milirrpum v Nabalco* (1971), however his judgement followed the precedent set in the previous cases.

> They [previous cases] all affirm on the principle, fundamental to the English law of real property, that the Crown is the source of all title to land.

Generally Aboriginal people were expected to abide by these imported laws, even though they were largely ignorant of them and had never agreed to be bound by them. Some attempts were made to educate Aborigines about the new system of law. For example, in Tasmania in 1828 Governor Arthur ordered picture boards to be nailed to trees in the bush depicting a black man spearing a white man and then being hanged as well as a white man shooting a black man and meeting the same fate. (Although this may have been done in an attempt to encourage peaceful relations rather than to educate per se [Ryan, 1981:96-97]). Aboriginal people were officially regarded as British subjects and, in theory, were entitled to the protection of the British system (ALRC, 1986:19).

Although the existence of the many Aboriginal groups was recognised by the early European explorers and settlers, their laws, customs and rights under British laws were not acknowledged. Resistance, massacres and genocide were also ignored in the application of the doctrine of *terra nullius* which justified the acquisition of land. Aboriginal resistance was far from insignificant and there are many documented examples.

Some non-Aborigines were horrified by what was happening and wrote to England deploring the situation. This was largely to no avail. In 1828 the Governor of Tasmania (Arthur) proclaimed martial law, which was tantamount to a declaration of war against Aborigines. During the three years in which martial law remained in force the military were entitled to shoot on sight any Aboriginal person in the settled districts (Ryan, 1981:99; Plomley, 1966:29; ALRC, 1986).

Yet the legal fiction that the islands and the mainland were settled peacefully was maintained. By ignoring Aboriginal customs and law and the resistance to white settlement English law was applied to Aboriginal Australians. To do otherwise would have meant that not only would Aboriginal law have to be acknowledged but so too would Aboriginal sovereignty and rights to the land. So long as Australia was seen to be settled under the doctrine of *terra nullius* there need be no common law recognition of Aboriginal land rights or, indeed, any Aboriginal law.

Relationship between Aborigines and European law

Not only were Aboriginal people denied recognition of their own laws, in reality they were also deprived of the protection of the new system. Edward John Eyre made the following report when he was resident Magistrate at Moorunde on the river Murray:

> In declaring the natives British subjects and making them responsible to British laws, indigenous people were placed in an anomalous position of being made amenable to laws of which they are quite ignorant, and which, at the same time did not afford them the slightest redress from any injuries they may receive at the hands of Europeans. This arose from their being unable legally to give evidence in a Court of Justice, and from its rarely happening that any aggressions upon them take place in the presence of other Europeans who might appear as witnesses for them ...
>
> It is impossible to explain to the natives the reason of their being unable to give evidence; they only see that their own people are always punished for offences, that the Europeans almost always escape (EJ Eyre, Resident Magistrate at Moorunde, Report SAGG, 9 February 1843:44).

Aboriginal people could not give evidence in court because they were not Christians. Thus it was very difficult for them to defend serious charges or to have European offenders brought to justice (Ryan, 1981:88). In practice Aborigines were not accorded the same rights as British subjects in judicial proceedings (Ryan, 1981:39).

The legal system of Australia was used to deny Aboriginal people fundamental human rights and it continued to do so. Under the rhetoric of protection children were removed from parents, the right to marry was limited, freedom of movement was restricted and special laws regulated Aboriginal employment. Aborigines were forced to live on reserves, settlements and missions (ALRC, 1986:21). Those Aborigines who demanded their rights were oppressed. As late as 1962 the Council for Aboriginal Rights found that the Director of Native Affairs in Queensland may cause any Aborigine "to be removed from any district to a reserve and kept there. He may also cause any Aboriginal on a reserve to be removed to another reserve and kept there" (Murray, 1962:17).

The law also provided that the Director of Native Affairs and not the parents "shall be the legal guardian of every Aboriginal child in the State while such a child is under the age of twenty one years". The government controlled marriage, property and employment.

Even wages were not paid in full. All or most were put into a bank account controlled by the Director.

In Western Australia the Commissioner of Native Welfare had control over all Aboriginal children and the property of Aboriginal people and could restrict the movements of Aboriginal people and censor the mail of those in institutions. Regulation 28 of the *Native Welfare Act* included the undefined offence of "insubordination" (Murray, 1962:41). Particular offences were created to control Aborigines.

The 1957-58 Annual Report of the Northern Territory disclosed 8,000 or about 48 per cent of the Aboriginal population were residents in institutions. They were controlled, submissive and isolated. Their legal rights were compromised. Aboriginal people were forcibly removed from their lands and families were separated (Murray, 1962:31).

The Melbourne Herald on March 19, 1958 carried a report from Douglas Lockwood:

> Aboriginal prisoners are chained by the ankle to a verandah post at Halls Creek police station while awaiting trial and serving their sentences. ... It is done here because the 80 year old building has only one cell. A few months ago 12 prisoners were on the chain at the same time. When one wanted to move, the other 11 had to move with him.

Aboriginal people were subject to the law but unable to have a legitimate input into the content of the laws or choice of parliamentary representative. Aboriginal people did not have the right to vote in federal elections until 1962. The movement for full citizenship rights gathered momentum and in 1967 90% of Australians voted "yes" to a referendum removing the constitutional provision excluding "Aboriginal natives" from being counted in the national census (S127) and giving the Commonwealth Government (S51 [XXVI]) power to legislate in relation to Aboriginal Affairs (ALRC, 1986:22). The injustices, however, continued.

The lack of justice for Aboriginal people led to the establishment of Aboriginal legal services in all states during the 1970s. The legal services have endeavoured to have the legal system give justice to Aborigines. Despite this Walker found in 1987 that "overall, in Australia, an Aboriginal is over sixteen times more likely to be in prison than a non-Aboriginal" (Hazelhurst, 1987:107). Walker raised the distinct possibility that Australia, in a more subtle way, is as racist as South Africa in its treatment of the indigenous people.

In October 1987 the Royal Commission into Aboriginal Deaths in Custody was established. If non-Aborigines had died at the same rate, it has been estimated there would have been up to 9,000 deaths during the period 1980-1989 investigated by the Royal Commission (RCADC *Final Report. Summary SA State Aboriginal Affairs 1991*:3). However, the primary reason for the high number of deaths (99) was found to relate to "the disproportionate rate at which Aboriginal people are detained in this country" (RCADC, vol. 4, p. 1).

In 1991 the *National Report: Overview and Recommendations* was delivered by Commissioner Elliot Johnson, QC. This report documented the institutionalised racism rampant in Australian society. The socio-economic problems faced by many Aboriginal and Torres Strait Islander people were linked to the limited access to land and failure to protect sacred sites. The Commissioner recommended:

> That in all jurisdictions legislation should be introduced, where this has not already occurred, to provide a comprehensive means to address land needs of Aboriginal people. Such legislation should encompass a process for restoring unalienated Crown land to those Aboriginal people who claim such land on the basis of cultural, historical and/or traditional association (RCADC, vol. 5, p. 37, recommendation 334).

Legal responses to native title

Although the British common law failed to recognise Aboriginal rights to land, many Aboriginal and Torres Strait Islander people have maintained their claim to and connection with their land.

Over time it has also become clear to more and more non-Indigenous Australians that many Aboriginal and Torres Strait Islander peoples refer to sophisticated sets of traditional rules. ALRC Report 31 acknowledged that "... there are many indications that Aboriginal customary laws and traditions continue as a real controlling force in the lives of many Aborigines" (1986:33).

Some of these rules are intertwined with mechanisms for "ownership" of land. Legal cases were mounted but lost on the basis that Australia was *terra nullius—land belonging to no one*. (Although these issues were raised in *Coe v Commonwealth* (1979) at 403, the case did not proceed to a full hearing).

In the case of *Milirrpum v Nabalco Pty Ltd* (1971) 17 FLR 141 the Yolgnu (Aboriginal) people from Yirrkala on the Gove Peninsula tried to protect their native title by asserting their rights in the Supreme Court of the Northern Territory. After the discovery of bauxite in 1953 a mining lease was granted by the federal government and mining activity commenced. Sacred sites were threatened and destroyed. In 1963 the Yolgnu people presented a bark petition to the House of Representatives. A Committee of Inquiry was held and a report produced but no action was taken. In 1968 the federal government granted a 42 year lease to the mining company Nabalco which included an agreement for the establishment of a town. No consultation occurred. The Yolgnu brought proceedings in the Northern Territory Supreme Court. This attempt failed as Justice Blackburn felt bound by the established precedent that Australia was *terra nullius*, even though he found that:

> The evidence shows a subtle and elaborate system highly adapted to the country in which the people led their lives, which provided a stable order of society and was remarkably free from the vagaries of personal whim or influence. If ever a system could be called 'a government of laws, and not of men', it is that shown in the evidence before me (Milirrpum v Nabalco Pty Ltd (1971) at 267).

Williams (1987) provides an analysis of the coexistence of two legal systems on the Yolgnu people and makes reference to the impact this case had on the Yolgnu's understanding of Australian legal systems.

Land rights

As the common law refused to recognise native title, Aborigines, Torres Strait Islanders and other Australians fought for land rights through legislative reform. In 1972 an Aboriginal Tent Embassy was set up on the lawns of Parliament House, Canberra.

In the 70s and 80s numerous land rights marches were held. In many ways they were successful. Although Australia has lagged behind other comparable countries in the recognition of common law native title it has been at the forefront of land rights legislation.

In 1966 South Australia passed the first Australian land rights legislation. The *Aboriginal Lands Trust Act* (South Australia) set up an Aboriginal body to which the Governor might transfer Crown lands or Aboriginal reserves. In 1970 Victoria was the first state to pass an act granting land. It gave full title of the Lake Tyers and Framlingham reserves to their residents in trust. Since then all state parliaments except Tasmania have adopted some form of land rights legislation. However, most of this legislation is limited in its application. It is land granted by an act of parliament rather than land gained as of right.

For Aboriginal people holding the view that "the land is our mother" land rights legislation is an important aspect of self determination.

Native title and mabo

In the past Australian courts were not sympathetic to the notion of a common law native title but Australian indigenous people refused to acquiesce. The term *native title* refers to the interests in land held by indigenous inhabitants by virtue of their prior occupation. It is necessary to go to customary law to establish what these rights and interests are and they will vary on a case by case basis. In Australia acknowledgment of native title was precluded by the application of the doctrine of *terra nullius*.

In May 1982 Eddie Mabo and four other Meriam people from the Murray Islands in the Torres Strait began an action seeking legal recognition of their family's common law title in the land. This action apparently commenced because Mr Mabo was refused permission by the Department of Aboriginal and Islander Affairs to visit his family on Murray Island. The Meriam people were actually asking the courts to review the doctrine of *terra nullius*. The Queensland Government tried to head off this claim by developing legislation extinguishing any native title that may have existed.

This was found to be contravening the *Racial Discrimination Act 1975* so the claim proceeded.

In what is now known as the *Mabo* case the Australian High Court reviewed the law in the light of established facts: that Torres Strait Islander people had settled laws, that these laws covered relationships with land and that some people continue to maintain a connection with their land in accordance with their native laws and customs. The case had been in the courts for 10 years before the High Court gave its decision in June 1992 (Reynolds, 1991).

The High Court stated that at the time of occupation Australia was **not** *terra nullius* and rejected the application of this doctrine and its consequences for native title.

In their joint judgment Justices Deane and Gaudron went so far as to say:

> The acts and events by which that dispossession in legal theory was carried into practical effect constitute the darkest aspect of the history of this nation. The nation as a whole must remain diminished unless and until there is an acknowledgment of, and retreat from, those past injustices ... The lands of this continent were not terra nullius or 'practically unoccupied in 1788' (Mabo and Orr, 1992:100).

Justice Brennan also dismissed the legal fiction that Australia was terra nullius. Brennan stated (Mabo and Orr, 1992:47):

> The common law of this country would perpetuate injustice if it were to continue to embrace the enlarged notion of terra nullius and to persist in characterising the indigenous inhabitants of the Australian colonies as people too low in the scale of social organisation to be acknowledged as possessing rights and interests in land.

Justice Brennan (Mabo and Orr, 1992:46) said:

> If native title survives the Crown's acquisition of sovereignty as in my view, it does, it is unnecessary to examine the alternative arguments advanced and... the common law of Australia rejects the notion that, when the Crown acquired sovereignty over territory which is now part of Australia it thereby acquired the absolute beneficial ownership of the land therein and accepts that the antecedent rights and interests in land by the indigenous

inhabitants of the territory survived the change in sovereignty. Those antecedent rights and interests thus constitute a binder on the radical title of the Crown.

Under native title the Crown is the ultimate owner of the land (as is the case with all land in Australia) but this ownership is subject to the rights of the indigenous people using the land. Native title supports rights to use and occupy the land but may not be full ownership. The extent and content of the rights are determined by the traditional laws.

Justice Brennan (at page 47 of *Mabo*) went on to describe native title in the following way:

Native title has its origin in and is given its content by the traditional laws acknowledged by and the traditional customs observed by the indigenous inhabitants of a territory. The nature and incidents of native title must be ascertained as a matter of fact by reference to those laws and customs.

Thus, for many non-Indigenous Australians native title is a very unclear and imprecise concept as it requires an understanding and knowledge of traditional Aboriginal culture.

Limitations to mabo

Mabo was a seminal High Court decision but it may not produce many successful claims or compensation as the Court laid down several limiting factors. Native title can be extinguished and many groups and individuals may have lost the right to assert such rights over the last 209 years. If the people have left the land either voluntarily or forcibly and lost connection with the land as defined by their laws and customs then the title is lost. If the government has dealt with the land in a way that is inconsistent with traditional native title then that title may be either extinguished or suppressed. Once the title has been extinguished in any way, it seems that it cannot be revived. The legal implications of suppression are yet to be fully explored. It is generally agreed, however, that any land that is held freehold cannot be subject to a Mabo style claim. This effectively rules out any claims over cities, towns or developed areas.

Indigenous claimants asserting recognition of native title need to establish a continuous connection with the land. Native title is defined by the rights and interests possessed under the traditional laws acknowledged and customs observed by Aboriginal and Torres Strait Islander peoples. Native title is not freehold title. It arises out of the relationship that a particular individual or group of people has with identified land or perhaps, water.

Native title to land may be extinguished by native title holders dealing with the land in a manner which is inconsistent with evolving traditional laws and customs. The land cannot be sold or transferred except perhaps within Indigenous groups. in accordance with traditional customs. This restriction arises because native title is not a proprietary right but a personal and usufructuary right. The preservation of native title however, does not demand that traditional practices remain static.

Evidentiary problems can also arise in establishing native title. How does one prove native title? What if it involves revealing information that may be secret or protected? Native title is based on traditional laws and involves evidence based on oral histories. Justice RS French, President of the Native Title Tribunal writes: "The proof of native title at common law potentially requires detailed and time consuming inquiry of traditional laws and customs, their content and application to the subject land and the history of communal association with that land" (Paper *The Role of the Native Title Tribunal*, 16 June 1997 at 9/10 delivered in Perth on 16 June 1994 and circulated by the Native Title Tribunal). The issues relating to establishing the proof of Aboriginal customary laws and the taking of Aboriginal evidence in Australian Courts are discussed in Australian Law Reform Commission Report 31, chapters 24-35).

The majority of the High Court in *Mabo* decided that compensation for past acts of dispossession is unlikely and in most cases impossible. However, this was not a final determination by the Court. There are many bars to compensation, although the *Racial Discrimination Act 1975* may ensure that native title destroyed since the introduction of this Act will require compensation. Issues also arise by virtue of section 51 (XXXI) of the Commonwealth Constitution which speaks of *just acquisition*. If the Commonwealth compulsorily acquires property it is required to do so on *just terms*. However, this provision only binds the Commonwealth and not the State governments. Native titles extinguished by the states will not be caught by this provision, but state destruction of titles post 1975 may run foul of the *Racial Discrimination Act 1975*.

The *Mabo* decision left a range of issues inadequately explored and created uncertainty. What relevance did *Mabo* have for Indigenous people who had resided in urban areas for several generations? How substantial must the connections to the land be and must a spiritual connection be evidenced by physical contact?

Mabo did not settle questions relating to the impact of native title on exploration or mining leases, pastoral leases, reservations of lands for parks or off-shore areas. Many of these matters are yet to be decided in pending cases. The uncertainty has resulted in great concern being expressed by powerful interest groups (Howard, 1993:8-9).

Uncertainties also exist for Indigenous communities whose elders and leaders must make decisions about taking legal action. Questions arise as to who pays the cost of asserting a claim and who potentially is entitled to benefit (how are members of a group to be defined and by whom?).

For many, while the decision sets the record straight, it does not change what happened. This sentiment is echoed by Frank Brennan: "The court did not undo the injustices of the past: it has set the foundations for just land dealings in the future" (*The Australian*, November 4, 1992:11).

Recognition of native title has broader implications as it amounts to a recognition and protection of some customary law by the wider Australian legal system. The Australian Law Reform Commission in the *1986 Report on Aboriginal Customary Law* observed that although there had been some recognition of customary law and traditions by some courts and some legislation, generally, such recognition has been exceptional, uncoordinated and incomplete (page 82). To what extent does the recognition of native title herald the recognition of other customary laws?

Native Title Act

The *Mabo* decision was handed down by the High Court in June 1992. In response, the Commonwealth Parliament introduced the *Native Title Act 1993* which commenced operation on 1 January 1994. the purpose of the legislation was to recognise and protect Native title. The Act established the Native Title Tribunal and provided and alternative process for claiming title. The *Native Title Act* adopts the definition of native title based on the common law interpretation established in Mabo.

As at August 1997, 612 applications for determination of native title claims had been lodged with the Native Title Tribunal. These claims apparently cover 45% of Australia (Media Release Senator Nick Minchin, Parliamentary Secretary to the Prime Minister with responsibility for Native Title).

Wik

The first case to reach the High Court since *Mabo* is that of *The Wik Peoples v The State of Queensland & Ors; The Thayorre People v The State of Queensland & Ors*. The decision was delivered on 23 December 1996. The Wik people from far north Queensland commenced proceedings in the Federal Court of Australia in June 1993 against the State of Queensland, the Commonwealth of Australia, Comalco Aluminium Limited, Aluminium Pechiney Holdings Pty Ltd claiming native title and other possessory rights over an area of land and sea. The Thayorre peoples were later joined in the proceedings as they made claim to part of the land claimed by the Wik Peoples. Justice Drummond of the Federal Court decided that pastoral leases over the land claimed granted exclusive possession to the lessees and therefore extinguished native title. The Wik and Thayorre people appealed to the Full Federal Court and their appeals were subsequently moved to the High Court (The Wik Peoples v The State of Queensland & Ors; The Thayorre People v The State of Queensland & Ors).

The substance of the appeal was based on whether the grant of a pastoral lease necessarily extinguished native title rights. The answer is based on the question whether the pastoral leases granted exclusive possession of the land to the pastoralists.

The argument advanced by the respondents was that the leases conferred exclusive possession which was inconsistent with native title and therefore the existence of the leases extinguishes native title rights.

The Court was also asked to consider whether native title rights revived on expiry, surrender or forfeiture of the pastoral lease.

Toohey outlined his approach (page 126)

> Inconsistency can only be determined, in the represent context, by identifying what native title rights in the system of rights and interests upon which the appellants rely are asserted in relation to land contained in the pastoral leases. This cannot be done by some general statement; it must "focus specifically on the traditions, customs and practices of the particular aboriginal group claiming the right". Those rights are then measured against the rights conferred on the grantees of the pastoral leases; to the extent of any inconsistency the latter prevail.

As the pastoral leases were created by statutes interpretation of the relevant legislation was pivotal to determining the nature of the rights and obligations flowing from the grant of each lease. It is also necessary to identify native title rights by reference to Indigenous "traditions, customs and practices". Where there is any inconsistency the rights of the pastoralist prevail over native title rights. The effect of inconsistency, that is whether the native title rights are extinguished or suppressed, was not determined by the Court.

The Parliamentary Joint Committee on Native Title and the Aboriginal and Torres Strait Islander Land Fund Third Minority Report states that:

> The main implication of the High Court's decision in Wik is that native title may have survived on the estimated 42 percent of the Australian land mass covered by pastoral leases (Third Minority Report Extracts, 27 October 1997:13).

The approach of the Cape York Land Council, following the *Wik* decision was commended in this report. The Cape York Land Council has demonstrated leadership by convening a summit within one month of the decision being handed down which major stakeholders such as representatives of pastoral, mining, Aboriginal interests, state and federal governments attended. The Minority summary report states:

> It is a matter of shame on those detractors [referring to Queensland Premier Rob Borbridge and Deputy Prime Minister Tim Fisher] and on the Government that in the weeks following the High Court's decision the only leadership shown, the only attempts to resolve issues, was by an Aboriginal Land Council (page 14).

Sovereignty / self determination

Throughout the cases the courts have clearly agreed on one thing— the issue of sovereignty.[1] The courts have consistently refused to entertain any concept of Aboriginal sovereignty as the courts do not have the power to question the legitimacy of Australian sovereignty which provides the source of their jurisdiction.

Although the recent cases create many uncertainties one thing is certain: the issue of Aboriginal and Islander self-determination is back on the political agenda. It is not only native title or land rights that are being discussed but the nature of the future relationship between indigenous and other Australians. Dodson (1993:6) says: "The Mabo decision, which is a win, gives impetus to Aboriginal and Torres Strait Islander calls for a new deal". Reconciliation is high on the agenda.

The changes have brought uncertainties. As a result there has been a mass of anti-native title propaganda by groups seeking to protect their current position.

The federal government has responded by introducing a ten point plan contained in amendments to the *Native Title Act*. The Government's stated objectives in developing the amendment Bill are to reduce uncertainty, improve and streamline claim processes, balance the interests of all the parties while maintaining respect for native title (Media Release Senator Nick Minchin, Parliamentary Secretary to the Prime Minister with responsibility for Native Title).

However, a range of groups have seen the amendments as creating further injustice. The Minority Report of the Parliamentary Joint Committee on Native Title and the Aboriginal and Torres

Strait Islander Land Fund is damning of many of the proposed amendments.

There are issues as to whether the proposed amendments are constitutional. It is argued that section 51 (xxvi) of the Australian Constitution can only be used for making laws of benefit to a particular race. See for example Frank Brennan's article (1997) *Grading John Howard's 10 Point Plan*. Further, extinguishment of native title may amount to acquisition of property on unjust terms which is contrary to section 51 (xxii) of the Constitution (Executive Summary Third Minority Report, page 3).

In addition the Bill may be in breach of the *Racial Discrimination Act 1975*.

The cost of uncertainty, but the gain is the promise of justice. Frank Brennan writes:

> The law of the land is now more complex because it reflects more justly the history of land use and extends the rule of law to all citizens whose country it is (*The Australian*, 4 November 1992:4).

Conclusion

As Australian cases followed English precedents, it is obvious that Aboriginal rights would receive inadequate recognition. They were not part of English law and had not been developed in English law. Legislation was very much enacted to support the foundation of a colony, not to protect indigenous people.

European settlement produced a conflict between two systems of law and two cultures. This was not officially acknowledged for nearly two hundred years. The introduced British legal system has assumed that Aborigines and Torres Strait Islanders are subject to its rule. The existence of traditional laws has been ignored.

The British invasion was the beginning of the modern Aboriginal movement in Australia. The issues of land ownership, culture, development, progress and law were at the centre of Aboriginal and non-Aboriginal relations from the first days of the colony. They are still the habit of relations between Indigenous peoples and other Australians today.

Non-Indigenous Australians are prone to argue that they should not have to be guilty for the sins of their forefathers. They wish to forget what happened to Aborigines but, as Henry Reynolds (1981:201) says:

> Forgetfulness is a strange perception coming from a community which has revered the fallen warrior and emblazoned the phase 'Lest we Forget' in monuments throughout the land.

Aborigines cannot forget. Too many warriors have fallen. Black memories are scarred. Aboriginal people have fought long and hard for justice, for their land, preservation of culture and development on their own terms. Perhaps the High Court decisions on *Mabo* and *Wik* will enable the indigenous Australians to at last be given justice through the Australian legal system and a true process of reconciliation can be commenced.

References

Australian Law Reform Commission (ALRC) (1986). *The Recognition of Aboriginal Customary Law, Report No. 31.* Canberra: AGPS.

Berndt and Berndt (1967). *The First Australians.* 2nd edition. Sydney: Ure Smith.

Bird, Greta (1988). *The Process of Law in Australia: Intercultural Perspectives.* Sydney: Butterworths.

Brennan, Frank (1997). "Grading John Howard's Ten Point Plan". *Land Rights Queensland*, Issue 2, 1997.

Dodson, Patrick (1993). "Reconciliation and the High Court's decision on native title". *Aboriginal Law Bulletin*, vol. 3, no. 61.

Edwards WH (1988). *An Introduction to Aboriginal Societies.* Wentworth Falls: Social Science Press.

Executive Summary and Selected Extracts, Third Minority Report of the Parliamentary Joint Committee on Native Title and Torres Strait Islander Land Fund, 27 October 1997.

Hanks, J (1991). *Constitutional Law in Australia.* Sydney: Butterworths.

Hazelhurst, KM (1987). *Ivory Scales.* Kensington: NSW University Press.

Howard, Colin (1993, February). "The *Mabo* case". *Adelaide Review*, pp. 8-9.

Justice RS French (1994). *The Role of the Native Title Tribunal*, 16 June.

Land Rights Queensland, issue 2, 1997.

Mattingley, C and Hampton, K (1988). *Survival in Our Own Land*. Adelaide: Wakefield Press.

McRae, H; Nellheim, G and Beacroft, L (1991). *Aboriginal Legal Issues*. Sydney: Law Book Co.

Meggitt, MJ (1962). *Desert People: a Study of the Walbiri Aborigines of Central Australia*. Chicago: The University of Chicago Press.

Murray, William M, editor (1962). *The Struggle for Dignity*. Melbourne: Council for Aboriginal Rights.

Plomley, NJB, editor (1966). *Friendly Mission*. Tasmania: Tasmanian Historical Research Association.

Reynolds, Henry (1981). *The Other Side of the Frontier*. Penguin.

Reynolds, Henry (1991). "For seven judges two hundred years of questions". *Australian Society,* vol. 10, Janaury/Februuary, 1991, pp. 12-13.

Royal Commission into Aboriginal Deaths in Custody (1991). *National Report*. Canberra: AGPS.

Ryan, Lyndall (1981). *The Aboriginal Tasmanians*. St. Lucia, Qld: University of Queensland Press.

The Native Title Act 1993

Williams, Nancy. (1987). *Two Laws Managing Disputes in a Contemporary Aboriginal Community*. Canberra: Australian Institute of Aboriginal Studies.

Cases

Coe v Commonwealth (1979) 53 ALJR 403.

Cooper v Stuart (1889) 14 App Cas 286.

Mabo and Orr v Queensland (1992) High Court of Australia CLR

Milirrpum v Nabalco (1971) 17 FLR 141

State Government Insurance Commission v Trigwell (1979) 142 CLR 617 at 625634

The Wik Peoples v The State of Queensland & Ors (1996) 187 CLR

Endnotes

[1] The sovereign is the supreme power over the land and the people.

Chapter 5

Living the Dreaming

Bill Edwards

Introduction

The roots of contemporary Aboriginal religion lie in a variety of traditions and experiences. First and foremost, are the various stories, ceremonies, values and structures which sustained Aboriginal peoples throughout their long period of relatively unchallenged occupation of the continent. Colonisation was accompanied by the introduction of Christianity and many Aboriginal people have been influenced by Christian teaching and values and other introduced religions. The responses of Aboriginal people to two centuries of invasion, dispossession, suffering and racism have shaped further their understandings about life and purpose, fusing with the other traditions to shape their contemporary religious ideas and feelings.

In recent decades Aboriginal land rights, and now the High Court decision in Mabo, have focussed attention on Aboriginal understandings about the world and their place and purpose in it. Earlier misconceptions and prejudices have been exposed as researchers have sought to discover Aboriginal viewpoints and Aboriginal people themselves have revealed more about their relationships to the world in order to substantiate their claims to land. Appearing before the Ranger Uranium Inquiry in 1975, the late Silas Roberts, as Chairman of the Northern Land Council, stated that "Our connection to all things natural is spiritual" (Cole, 1979:162). This assertion of the centrality of spiritual beliefs to Aboriginal life contrasts with some of the statements made by early colonial observers in which the existence of any kind of spiritual understandings was denied.

The Nineteenth Century Presbyterian leader in New South Wales, the Rev. John Dunmore Lang, allowed Aborigines "nothing whatever of the character of religion, or of religious observance, to distinguish them from the beasts of the field" (Harris, 1990:542). Writing in Victoria in 1978, A. Le Souef asserted that "I never could discover among them anything amounting to religion ... My opinion is that they have no religious notions or ideas whatever" (Stanner, 1984:139).

Recent archaeological discoveries suggest that in fact Aboriginal people are inheritors of the longest surviving tradition of religious beliefs and practices in the world. Radio-carbon dating of skeletal remains has provided evidence of human occupation of sites 40,000 years ago, and that cultural practices, including belief and ritual systems, have been maintained over this long span of time, for example, the use of red ochre, and the arrangement and adornment of bodies in ancient burial sites (Edwards, 1988:7).

The early European observers of Aboriginal life came with preconceived ideas about what constituted religion and the sphere of spiritual existence, based on their experience in Western Europe of Christianity, church buildings, forms of worship, the roles of priests and ministers, belief in one God, and the importance of scriptures. When they observed similar phenomena of rites, holy men, shrines or temples and sacred books in Africa and Asia they acknowledged the presence of religious systems. However, as the forms of religious expression in Australia were so different and subtle, their very existence was denied.

In contrast to those early views, recent observers have emphasised the centrality of beliefs in spiritual powers in Aboriginal cosmology. Tonkinson, who studied the Mardudjara people of Western Australia wrote of the "profoundly religious view of life that characterises the Aborigines" (Tonkinson, 1978:15). Rose, who researched in the Victoria River region of the Northern Territory wrote that "We are talking about a profoundly moving representation of humanity's search for religious meaning" (Rose, 1987:266). Since the earlier pejorative comments were made, the definitions of religion have broadened and more detailed study of Aboriginal societies has revealed the variety, complexity and depth of the belief and ritual systems. Morphy (1988) provides a summary of developments in the anthropological study of Aboriginal religion from 1961 to 1986. These and more recent studies have shown that Aboriginal systems of beliefs provided answers to the great universal religious questions of humankind, the questions about origins, meaning, purpose and destiny.

The Dreaming

The term, The Dreaming, is used commonly to describe the Aboriginal creative epoch. Each language group had its own term to refer to this epoch and all associated with it. Ngarinyin people in the north-west of Western Australia refer to it as *Ungud,* the Aranda of Central Australia as *Aldjerinya,* the Pitjantjatjara of north-west South Australia as *Tjukurpa,* the Yolngu of north-east Arnhem Land as *Wongar,* while in the Broome region it is referred to as *Bugari.* While the term used in some of the languages is related to the word for Dreaming this does not apply to all of them. The use of the English word Dreaming should not suggest that it refers to some vague reflection of the real world. Rather, Aboriginal people see the world of The Dreaming as the fundamental reality. The indigenous terms have a meaning of story and they refer to each group's stories which enshrine their understandings about their origins.

Previously referred to as the Dreamtime, the term was changed to The Dreaming by Professor Stanner in a paper first published in 1956, (Stanner. 1987) in acknowledgment of the fact that the Aboriginal creative epoch cannot be understood within a Western framework of linear time. Western concepts of linear time with the separation of past and present make it difficult to describe The Dreaming as it is conceived in Aboriginal thought. While there is a sense in which The Dreaming activities occurred at the beginning of the world, and are past, there is a sense also, in which they are still present. Through ritual, humans are able to enter into a direct relationship with The Dreaming. The Aboriginal concept of time is therefore cyclic, rather than linear, but in the sense that each generation is able to experience the present reality of The Dreaming. Rose refers to it as the *heroic time which existed in the past and still exists today* (Rose, 1988:260). Stanner coined the term "everywhen" in an attempt to convey this idea. "One cannot 'fix' The Dreaming in time: it was, and is everywhen" (Stanner, 1987:225).

In a recent study of Australian Aboriginal being, Swain suggests that the attention given to time in relation to The Dream events has diverted attention from the significance of place. "Were we to cling to the dream-root, this would be best rendered as

'Dreaming-event' (a qualitative rather than temporal distinction) or Dream-place" (Swain, 1993:24).

The concept of The Dreaming does not assume the creation of the world from nothing, a creatio ex nihilo. It assumes a pre-existent substance, often described as a watery expanse or a featureless plain. Spirit beings lay dormant under the surface of this substance. According to The Dreaming stories the Spirit beings emerged from the formless earth and assumed forms and identities which combined, in many instances, features of humans and the various animal and plant species which now inhabit the cosmos. They appeared as kangaroo-men, shark-men, serpent-women, brolga-women, mulga seed-women and bush fig-men. The stories of each area reflected the faunal and floral species of the various environments. Some of the Dreaming beings were humans, for example, the Two Youths, while other stories ranged over objects and incidents of the Aboriginal environment, for example, grind stones, wind, coughing and diarrhoea.

The Spirit Beings on emerging from the formless substance moved over the surface of the earth, performing the everyday activities of the humans and other species they represented. They hunted, ate, fought, cheated, made tools, sang, danced, gathered foods, dug for water and died. At times they are said to have performed human type activities such as hunting, making tools, or dancing. At other times they performed the activities of the other species they represented, such as munching grass or hopping over a sandhill. As they travelled they and their tracks, artefacts and activities were transformed into the rocks, mountains, waterholes, caves, sandhills, trees, watercourses, stars, and the other phenomena of the environment. For example, a kangaroo-man sitting up to view the country became a rocky ridge, the winding track of a serpent became a watercourse, bush tomatoes gathered by some women became small stones, a bush shelter built by a group of sisters became a cave and these sisters eventually went into the sky to become the star constellation known as the Pleiades. For more examples see Edwards, 1988: 16-18 and Isaacs, 1980.

The land

This brief outline of The Dreaming illustrates the significance of land in Aboriginal thought. The whole of the landscape is conceived as having been formed through the activities of the Spirit Beings. The whole environment is viewed as the arena in which the dramatic events of The Dreaming were and are enacted. The continent is dotted with significant sites associated with the stories, for example, places where the Spirit Beings first emerged, where they performed a ceremony or where they died and re-entered the earth. It is criss-crossed with the tracks of the Spirit Beings as they travelled from site to site. Aboriginal people today do not invent sacred sites as is sometimes suggested by opponents of land rights. In one sense, all the land is a sacred site. The Spirit Beings are said to be present continually in the forms of the landscape which were created through their activities.

The Ancestral Spirit Beings of The Dreaming are believed to be the ancestors of both the Aboriginal groups which live in the areas of the various stories and of the species associated with them. For example, one group of people are said to be descended from the Kangaroo-man who is also progenitor of the kangaroos. People derive their spiritual essence from the Ancestral Spirit Beings and share the same spiritual essence which inhabits the land and other species.

In contrast, Western ideas about reality and religion are based largely on the general acceptance of dichotomies between natural and cultural, material and spiritual, past and present, secular and sacred, subject and object. Reference has been made earlier to the different concept of time in Aboriginal thought. Just as the clear demarcation between past and present is lacking in Aboriginal conceptualisation, the other dichotomies are not present. In Western thought, culture as human achievement, is distinguished from the natural world. Aborigines envisage other species taking part in cultural activities (Rose, 1987:264). Sutton comments that "In traditional Aboriginal thought, there is no nature without culture" (Sutton, 1988:18). The distinction between subject and object breaks down as people identify rocks, trees or birds as representations of their own beings, and not as things solely objective and external to them. Rose sees a difference between Aboriginal and other forms of mysticism which tend to focus on the transcendent and supernatural. "Aboriginal religion leads people into this world and towards an immanent experience of unity in the here and now" (Rose, 1987:268).

The realm of spiritual existence is not divorced from the material world but is embedded in it. The various languages have terms which are similar to the English concept of spirit. For example, the Pitjantjatjara people refer to *kurunpa. Kurunpa* is present in all aspects of the world. The Ancestral Beings left their spiritual essence in the rocks, the trees, the animal and other species. People walk with care over the earth in an awareness that spiritual forces surround them and that they must heed the laws and taboos which dictate relationships to them. For example, a person nearing a waterhole may throw a stone into the water to alert the water serpent spirit of his or her approach to avoid the danger of being bitten.

Animism and totemism

These beliefs led to the application of two terms in early studies of Aboriginal religion. An anthropologist at Oxford University, Edward Tylor, introduced the term "animism" from the Latin, *anima,* for soul or spirit, to describe these Aboriginal beliefs because of this attribution of possession of spirit to a wide range of inanimate objects as well as to animate beings. The term "totemism" has been applied to describe the association existing between a local descent group of people and the animal or plant species with which they are thought to share descent. This shared descent bestows on the local groups the rights to utilise the resources in the area and the obligations to care for sites and carry out the associated rituals designed to ensure the continued existence of the related species. (For a detailed description of totemism, see Berndt, 1981:231-40).

While the terms animism and totemism point to important aspects of Aboriginal understandings about the presence of spiritual essence in the world and the relationship of people to other parts of the world, they were reductionist terms introduced by theorists who viewed Aboriginal religion as a primitive expression of the human search for meaning. Neither terms adequately convey the complexity, and varieties, of Aboriginal religious systems.

Another of the dichotomies underlying Western thought is that between the secular and the sacred. Aboriginal thought had contained no such distinction. Because all life was conceived as originating from the activities of the Ancestral Spirit Beings, all parts of the cosmos partook of their spiritual essence and were sacred. There are, however, places, objects and ceremonies which are believed to have associated with them a special quality of power, sacredness and danger. Access to, use of and participation in them is restricted to those who are thought to have the prerequisite knowledge and experience. Differences in age and sex are basic factors related to the knowledge and experience.

The passing on of the Dreaming stories from one generation to the next was a most important aspect of education. Knowledge of the story was the most prized possession of senior Aboriginal people. Males and females knew differing and complementary parts of stories. Bell (1998) emphasises the importance of the role of women in ritual and in the preservation and transmission of religious knowledge. This knowledge was not passed on indiscriminately but only as recipients were seen to be ready to accept the obligations which accompanied the knowledge. Keen (1994:45), in his study of the religion of the Yolngu of north-east Arnhem Land, recognises the difficulty of attempting to categorise clearly, aspects of Aboriginal religions. He notes that "religious mystery was created through ambiguity" (1994:42).

The stories record that the Ancestral Spirit Beings gave their first descendants the various languages in which the stories have been related. For example, the kangaroo-men left the dialects of the Western Desert groups and the first Mother, Waramurungundji, emerged from the sea and as she gave birth to the first children of Arnhem Land, she gave them the languages they were to speak.

The Ancestral Spirit Beings left as a legacy the other forms of symbolism—songs cycles, paintings and rituals—through which their exploits were recorded and passed on. The correct narration of the stories, painting of the symbols, singing of the songs and performance of the rituals is designed to ensure the maintenance of the cosmos and society. The well-known Wandjina paintings in the caves of the Kimberley region of north-west Western Australia are thought to have been first painted by the Wandjina Spirit Beings.

As the paintings are touched up, the spirit powers are renewed and released for appropriation by the descendants of the Ancestral Beings. Keen (1994:135-6), writing of ceremonies, asserts that "Yolngu did not see them primarily as modes of communication with ancestral spirits but as modes of identification with the *wangarr* and access to ancestral power".

A *pattern for life*

The Dreaming ancestors provided the model for life. They established a pattern for the daily round of economic, social, political, cultural and ritual activities. People hunt and share food, make tools, punish offenders, draw designs and relate to each in certain ways because the ancestors are believed to have acted in these ways, and to have left examples to be followed. The stories reflect the daily events in the lives of the people of the particular region. Just as Aboriginal people depended on hunting, fishing and gathering for daily sustenance, the ancestors are portrayed as engaging in these pursuits in The Dreaming. Strehlow commented that in the stories we see the Aborigine "at his daily task of hunting, fishing, gathering vegetable food, cooking and fashioning his implements. All occupations originated with the totemic ancestors" (Strehlow, 1947:35). The particular roles of males and females in hunting and gathering, the ways in which foods were prepared, cooked and shared, and the use of implements were all pre-ordained by the ancestors. Morphy (1988:249) quotes a Yolngu man's expression about the purpose of life as "we are always running to catch up with what has been done before". Even in the most mundane tasks people re-live the events of The Dreaming. All living is in a sense sanctified.

For an attempt to illustrate the unity of all aspects of Aboriginal life, as centred on the principle of The Dreaming, see the design in Edwards (1988:13).

Yami Lester, a Yankunytjatjara man from the north-west of South Australia, recalls learning about the land, people and culture as a child, when his parents:

> ... just talked about the country. And I believed what they said. You couldn't doubt, it was just something real. The country wasn't just hills or creeks or trees. And I didn't feel like it was fairy tales they

told me. It was real, our kuuti, the force that gives us life. Somebody created it, and whoever created it did it for us, so we could live and hunt and have a good time. That's how we come to be here because that malu and ngintaka created this image for us to live and breathe: the plants, the language, the people (Lester, 1993:10).

Malu is the kangaroo, and *ngintaka* is the perentie.

The relatively limited technological development in Aboriginal societies was counter-balanced by the sophisticated elaboration of social relationships. The Pitjantjatjara word for relation, *walytja,* is a basic concept. This aspect of Aboriginal life is described in Chapter 6.

Relationships are of vital importance in Aboriginal societies. Members of the various groups can identify their relationships to all other members of the group. These relationships dictate much of the day-to-day behaviour of individuals. The same kinds of relationships and obligations which flow from them are accorded to the Ancestral Spirit Beings. The reciprocal obligations between individuals and groups dictated ways in which offenders against the rules and structures should be punished. The rules, taboos and punishments are enshrined also in The Dreaming stories. Thus Aboriginal people today commonly gloss their own terms for The Dreaming with the English word *Law.*

Rituals

Religion and spirituality are concerned with access to spiritual powers. The Aboriginal belief that they share the same spiritual essence with all parts of the cosmos encourages them to seek contact with the Spirit Beings and access to spiritual powers through rituals. The Ancestral Spirit Beings had themselves performed ceremonies on their travels and left songs, dances and other rites to be followed to ensure the continual existence of the world and all its life forms. Rose wrote of "all those ceremonies through which cosmic life is regenerated" (Rose, 1987:264). Some rituals were designed to ensure the continued supply of the species whose Dreaming exploits they re-enacted. Others marked the passage of individuals through significant stages of life, such as puberty, marriage and death. Some rituals belong to the domain of males, others to that of females. In some, both sexes have complementary roles. Each group is responsible for preserving the stories, maintaining the sites and ensuring the performance of the rituals related to its totemic species. As all groups undertake their responsibilities, all species and the whole world is nurtured and regenerated. In his classic study of the religion of the Murinbata of the Northern Territory, Stanner (1963:4) wrote that "The facts of the ceremony are dense with meanings".

Ritual linked the performers with The Dreaming. They were not just re-enacting the creative deeds of the Ancestor Spirit Beings but as they were painted with the symbols of the stories, sang the songs and danced the steps, they entered into the very being of those ancestors. Eliade wrote that for Aboriginal people: "The communication with the Dream Time, regenerates life, and assures its continuation. In short, the ritual 're-creates' the world" (Eliade, 1973:61). He quotes Strehlow's comment that the performer as the reincarnation of one of the ancestors "himself has played a part in that first glorious adventure" (Eliade, 1973:57). Stanner (1963:139) perceived Murinbata rites as, "at the most fundamental level, attempts to make social life correlative with the plan and rhythm of the cosmos".

In inland regions, the most significant rituals relating to the passage of individuals through stages of life were the male initiation ceremonies. Less attention was given to mortuary rituals. As people were scattered in arid regions, there were few people on hand on most occasions when a person died, and burial took place as soon as possible. It was believed that the spirit of the person left the body after death, wandered around the area for a short while and returned to the realm of spiritual existence, adding to the store of spirit essence from which spirits entered women to cause conception and generate further births.

In northern tropical areas, mortuary ceremonies are more significant. More fertile ecological conditions allow for larger population clusters which enables more people to be involved. The mortuary ceremonies of some groups in Arnhem Land have three stages, concluding with the placing of the bones in a hollow log coffin. Clan symbols painted on the coffin are designed to be recognised by the ancestors who receive the spirit of the dead person (Morphy, 1987:22).

Reference has been made to the idea that The Dreaming provides a pattern for the way life is to be lived now. There are problems associated with this interpretation of The Dreaming. It is not a pattern of an idealised perfect state. All the affairs of human life, good and evil, are included in the stories. Sutton writes that the Ancestral Beings "exhibit all the faces of human virtue, vice, pleasure and suffering" (Sutton, 1988:15). The stories enable people to reflect on all the vicissitudes of life.

> The key characters of the more important myths are hardly models of approved behaviour. Liberal misdemeanours by mythic ancestors are frequently unjustified and go unpunished, or if punished, then to an extent that often goes beyond any conceivable justice. Explicit moral comment is rarely a feature of traditional Aboriginal narratives, or even of historical reminiscences. Listeners must make their own judgments, if any (Sutton, 1988:18).

Another problem associated with the above description of The Dreaming is that it gives an impression of a fixed, static and unchanging pattern of culture whereas change is inevitable in any society as groups adapt to changing environmental conditions, external contacts and internal pressures for change. While in Aboriginal societies there is a rhetoric of the unchangeableness and immutability of The Dreaming and of the social life lived in its image, referred to by Stanner as "a metaphysical emphasis on abidingness" (Stanner, 1987:234), change and innovation were present, even though very gradual, and the changes in the material and social conditions of life were reflected in changes to The Dreaming stories.

The impact of colonisation

Aboriginal societies which had known only gradual and minimal change over their long histories suffered sudden and momentous changes with the advent of English colonial settlement, or invasion, from 1788. Many of the groups subject to the initial impact of settlement were wiped from the face of the land by killings, the introduction of new diseases and the loss of will as they were driven from lands which had been central to their way of life (Broome, 1982:62). The dispossession of the land was justified by emerging

Western theories culminating in Social Darwinism, which assumed that earlier forms of social organisation would be replaced inevitably by more progressive and more highly developed forms.

Other groups in remote regions had more time to adjust to this impact and did not face the same pressure of invasion. They were able to survive despite a severe decline in population. Colonial authorities revised their policies for administering the surviving groups according to changing ideologies, the demands of the dominant population and the resistance of the groups to the policies. Broome refers to the twin objectives in early policies of civilising and Christianising the Aborigines (Broome, 1982:31). As adherence to traditional beliefs and practices were seen as inimical to the process of civilising there was pressure to discard them.

The objective of Christianising was instituted by the establishment of missions. Mission work in Australia among Aboriginal and Torres Strait Islander people was part of a world-wide movement. Influenced by Evangelical revivals and concerns for indigenous peoples, who were suffering as a result of slavery and colonial expansion, churches in Europe and America in the late 18th and 19th centuries sought to obey the command of Jesus to "make disciples of all nations" (Gospel of St Matthew 28:19). While missions in Australia provided a refuge which in many regions enabled Aboriginal groups to survive, the failure on the part of many missionaries to recognise and appreciate the values of Aboriginal societies and the tendency to regard all aspects of these societies as pagan and immoral led to suspicion, antipathy and despair. The first missionary in New South Wales, Walker, expressed a common theme that no good could be done with the adults of the "scattered, uncivilised, unsocial and cannibal tribes" (Quoted in Harris, 1990:47) but that the work must be commenced with the young men and children. Some early missionaries did however draw attention to the frontier brutality and the atrocities inflicted on Aboriginal groups by settlers. Threlkeld saw the cruelty associated with the convict system as degrading "the white to a lower degree than that of the despised aborigine of New South Wales" (Gunson, 1974:48).

An itinerant Presbyterian missionary in New South Wales, William Ridley, recognised the worth of Aboriginal culture and inconsistency between the white peoples' profession of religion and their stealing of Aboriginal women and dispossessing Aborigines of their land. He wrote in 1861:

> One poor fellow on the Mooni addressed me in a long and pathetic harangue on the wrongs which his people have suffered at the hands of the white men (Harris, 1990:234).

Since the commencement of missionary activity in 1824 the Christian mission enterprise amongst Aborigines has been persistent and widespread. The work has been sponsored by a variety of denominational and interdenominational mission societies and basic philosophies and approaches have varied. In many early, and some recent missions, no value was seen in traditional Aboriginal cultures and attempts were made to eradicate languages, rituals and other practices. In others, missionaries such as the Rev. JRB Love, who worked at Kunmunya in the north-west of Western Australia in 1915 and from 1927 to 1940, respected the structures and values of the societies in which they worked and sought to graft the Christian message on to existing cultures. Love wrote of his experience of a Worora ceremony:

> As I looked at these rites the amazing realisation flashed upon me that here, among one of the most primitive tribes...I had been witnessing rites akin to the most sacred observances of the Christian faith. I had been witnessing, in all their primitiveness and crudeness of administration, the rites of the Laying-on of hands, of Baptism, and of a sacred meal that could without irreverence be call a Communion (Love, 1936:219).

It is not the purpose of this chapter to attempt to provide a history of the Aboriginal-Mission encounter and to evaluate the effectiveness of the missionary endeavour. Rather, an outline is given of some of the contemporary Aboriginal movements which have their roots in this missionary enterprise. Aboriginal responses to missions have been varied. Some groups have reacted to the challenge presented by new stories and ceremonies by incorporating elements of them into the former systems but seeking to retain the traditional systems as paramount. Others have responded positively to Christian evangelism and themselves have become active in, and expressed their spirituality through, the life and mission of Christian churches. Still others have rejected the Christian message because of the paternalism and severity of much of the missionary practice, and the involvement of missions in the break-up of families and the loss of traditions.

In the Torres Strait Islands, the annual celebration of the Coming of the Light, suggests that the mission enterprise gained wider acceptance. According to Beckett, the available sources enable us to form only a vague impression of island life in pre-colonial times (Beckett, 1987:30). The traditions suggest that the fear of violent death was ever-present, warfare was common, and sorcery was feared as men sought supernatural power. The London Missionary Society established work in the Islands in 1871 and teachers from the South Pacific played important roles in the building of local churches. They encouraged the cessation of many traditional practices. The protection afforded by the warfare and sorcery, encouraged the Islanders to accept their authority and influence (Beckett, 1987:40). As local church leaders were trained they became mediators between Europeans and Islanders. The London Missionary Society withdrew from the islands in 1914, having passed on its role to the Anglican Diocese of Carpentaria.

Syncretic movements

Syncretism, or the merging of elements from different, even seemingly irreconcilable world views, is a feature of all religious systems as they seek to adapt to their environments. Some syncretic movements have been referred to as revitalisation or nativistic movements as through them leaders have sought to revive elements of traditional authority and practice in the face of the challenge of introduced ideas, influences and authorities. Syncretic movements range from those in which reaction is strong and they resist the external pressures strongly, to those where syncretic elements may be present in movements which are more accepting of the introduced systems. The former tend to be secretive and closed, with knowledge of them by outsiders limited. Cultic movements present in Western Australia from the 1930s to the 1970s appear to have characteristics of such movements.

The *Woagaia* movement emerged from traditional complexes in Central Australia and took on nativistic features at Lagrange on the north-west coast in the 1960s. Another movement in that region during the 1960s focussed on a black Jesus, known as *Jinimin,* with a mixture of traditional and Christian forms in the ceremonies. For example, in some ceremonies the distribution of food appears to have copied Christian eucharistic practices. A syncretic movement observed by Ronald Berndt at Elcho Island, off the north coast of Arnhem Land in the late 1950s was linked more openly to both church and traditional systems, with traditional sacred objects, *rannga,* and the Christian cross featured in public displays. Kolig, (1988) provides a brief description of some syncretic movements.

Aboriginal Christian movements

The control of Christian missions by white missionaries and mission boards tended to inhibit the emergence of Aboriginal leadership and Aboriginal forms of worship. Even when Aboriginal Christians were encouraged to incorporate indigenous elements of music or ritual they were diffident in their response. Because of the close association of form and meaning in Aboriginal rituals it was difficult for them to take the forms and give them new meaning. There was a tendency to accept the ways in which the Christian message was introduced to them as the correct way, the given Christian Dreaming way. Changes in the Aboriginal policy and political arenas over the past two decades have been accompanied by the emergence of new Christian movements. Former missions have come under the control of local community councils. Because the missions had provided education and some opportunities for leadership, Aboriginal Christians emerged as leaders in their communities and organisations as policies of self-management were implemented. They were encouraged in turn to seek more responsibilities in their churches. Increasing mobility has brought together Aboriginal Christians from widespread groups.

An early movement in the modern era was a Pentecostal movement amongst the Bandjalang people of north-east New South Wales in the 1950s. Some traditional elements were incorporated with characteristic features of Pentecostalism. The movement, which had anti-white overtones, brought purpose and pride to a group which had suffered severe breakdown and anomie. The Bandjalang had been evangelised by the interdenominational United Aborigines Mission. This mission society and another fundamentalist society, the Aborigines Inland Mission established several mission stations, childrens' homes and other institutions throughout Australia. These included Warburton Ranges Mission and Mount Margaret Mission in Western Australia, Nepabunna and Colebrook Home, in South Australia, and the Retta Dixon Homes in Darwin. Aboriginal people influenced by these societies were encouraged to forsake any association with traditional belief and ceremonial systems, with even the use of Aboriginal languages being discouraged, as they were viewed as pagan. It should be acknowledged that these views were modified by some later missionaries in these organisations and some engaged in language study and translation. Also the popularity of hymns, such as The Old Rugged Cross, at many funeral services of Aboriginal people indicates the continuing influence of this tradition on contemporary Aboriginal spirituality.

Aboriginal leaders who were trained within these and similar contexts established the Aboriginal Evangelical Fellowship in 1971. A fellowship had been formed in Western Australia in 1967 and a meeting with leaders from eastern states in 1968 led to a conference of 70 leaders at Port Augusta over the Christmas/New Year period of 1970-71. Conventions held at Port Augusta annually have attracted Aboriginal people from all over Australia and attendances reached 2000 in the late 1970s. A leader in this movement, Pastor Jack Braeside, commented that:

> The value of the convention is that people come into a deeper experience of God and go back to their own places contributing to their churches and fellowships. Others are being inspired to start churches of their own and become an asset to their community churches. People are being educated as Christians in organising things in the convention, contributing choir items, preaching and attending council meetings. Doing this ourselves has been an educational exercise (Hart, 1988:8).

The Aboriginal Evangelical Fellowship was formed by Aboriginal people and remained under their control. A significant movement in its early years, when it provided leaders for other Aboriginal movements, (for an example see Gilbert, 1978:60) its influence has declined in recent years, partly because of the narrowness of the tradition which gave it birth. Differing attitudes to traditional culture, disputes over doctrine and varying responses to the charismatic movement have caused divisions and a decline in membership. Harris (1990) provides a brief history of the movement.

From mission traditions where Aboriginal cultures and values were accorded more respect, such as at Ernabella in South Australia and Elcho Island and Yirrkala in Arnhem Land, have emerged Aboriginal Christian leaders who are at the same time upholders of many aspects of their traditional cultures and active participants in Church life. A significant movement which originated on a denominational mission and spread to many Aboriginal communities in widespread regions of Australia was the Elcho Island revival which commenced in 1979. Elcho Island had been a Methodist Mission until control passed to a local council in the early 1970s. As with the Bandjalang movement this revival brought a new spirit to a community suffering from severe social problems. Leaders in the movement were sons of men who had been involved in the movement referred to early which Berndt had observed at Elcho Island in the 1950s. Keen (1994:276-88) provides an outline and analysis of these movements.

Most members of the community were caught up in this charismatic movement which featured well attended nightly services with singing, prayer and healing. The movement spread throughout Arnhem Land and to communities as far distant as Wiluna in Western Australia and Yalata in South Australia. While the initial enthusiasm waned, the movement has left a lasting impact on many Aboriginal people and on styles of Aboriginal Christian worship in many regions. The leaders of the movement saw it as offering a model for other churches and Christians in Australia. The Rev. Djiniyini Gondarra, a past Moderator of the Northern Synod of The Uniting Church has written:

> The Christian churches in Australia need to be more open to recovering joyfully the blessings and insights offered through Aboriginal culture and spirituality (Gondarra, 1988:6)

Djiniyini Gondarra is a leader of the Uniting Aboriginal and Islander Christian Congress, formed under the inspiration of a former Assemblies of God pastor, Charles Harris, who had called Aboriginal Christian leaders from several traditions to meet at a conference in 1982. Constituted in 1983, the Congress had its charter adopted by the National Assembly of The Uniting Church in Australia in 1985 (Edwards and Clarke, 1988:198). The Congress has challenged Australian churches through a Manifesto which includes the following:

> Aboriginal culture has never understood life in this divided way. All parts of life belong together as they do in the Bible. Our people have always lived their spiritual lives in the political processes of our community life (UACC, 1988:6).

The Congress played an important role during the 1988 Australian Bicentennial year by organising an Aboriginal march in Sydney through its Justice, Freedom and Hope Committee.

Aboriginal Christians in churches where traditional belief systems are still strong have tended to compartmentalise these systems with the Christian stories. They have been willing to accept the validity of Dreaming stories at the same time as acknowledging God as creator. Dreaming stories do not assume the logic of western thought and they have seen no incongruity in affirming both belief systems. An attempt by a small group of Aboriginal Christians in North Queensland, to explore the dialogue between Aboriginal traditions and Christianity, is found in the book *Rainbow Spirit Theology* (Rainbow Spirit Elders, 1997). Through the Congress and other movements, Aboriginal Christians are seeking to express their Christian faith through forms which are congruent with their own traditions. At the ordination of the first Aboriginal woman minister in The Uniting Church, Liyapidiny Marika, in 1991, her clan brought her forward in a traditional ceremony accompanied by clap sticks. She wore both the white ordination alb and a traditional feather headdress.

An Aboriginal Roman Catholic woman in the Northern Territory, Miriam-Rose Ungunmerr is another who sees this combination of traditional Aboriginal and Aboriginal Christian forms and values offering hope to others in Australia. In 1984 she produced a series of paintings of the Stations of the Cross based on Aboriginal symbols (Ungunmerr, 1984).

Aboriginal Catholics have been encouraged to explore Aboriginal spirituality through the address to them by Pope John Paul II in Alice Springs in 1986:

> For thousands of years you have lived in this land and fashioned a culture that endures to this day. And during all this time, the Spirit of God has been with you. Your 'Dreaming' which influences your lives so strongly that, no matter what happens, you remain for ever people of your culture, is your own way of touching the mystery of God's Spirit in you and in creation (Hendricks and Hetteran, 1993:90).

Around Australia, Aboriginal Catholic movements are revising liturgies to introduce elements from their own traditions. From this tradition, an Aboriginal deacon, Boniface Perdjert, has written:

> their traditional religion did give my people deep awareness of the spirit and things of the spirit. Their religion contained some elements that are on a wave-length rather close to the Christian wave-length. It is up to the Christian apostle, with delicacy and skill, to tune these two wave-lengths together, so that the resultant harmony may be recognised by the Aborigines as truth, the truth that sets him free (Hendriks and Hefferan, 1993:39).

Contemporary Aboriginal spirituality

While many Aboriginal people have accepted the Christian message, either following it exclusively, or attempting to graft it on to their traditional beliefs, other Aborigines in contemporary Australia have rejected formal Christian structures and seek to express their spirituality by reaffirming Aboriginal beliefs and values. For some it has involved a process of relearning stories which had almost been lost to their parents' generation. Some have sought enlightenment from other religious systems, such as Islam, the Baha'i faith and the Rastafarian movement. Reacting to the dominant materialism of Australian society many are turning again to the centrality of spiritual existence and values in their lives. Some see this emphasis on spirituality as central to their identity as Aborigines.

Aboriginal people are encouraged in the recovery, reaffirmation and sharing of their story about the world and life, through growing links with other indigenous peoples throughout the world. Early in 1993 Aboriginal delegates who met with other indigenous people in New Zealand at a World Conference on Spiritual Healing experienced this encouragement. Non-Aboriginal Australians are giving Aboriginal beliefs about land, relationships and spiritual existence greater respect as the world faces threats to the ecology of the land, to social and family life and to economic systems. Some sense that Aboriginal concepts of spirit and of peoples' relationship to land offer insights to all who are concerned about these problems.

Aboriginal writer, the late Kevin Gilbert, expressed an Aboriginal attitude which accords with the views of many environmentalists.

> The Aboriginal way is that everything created is equal and sacred; that the soil, the clay, the rocks are all sacred within, say, creation, and that all have a personality, a distinct personality. I had the strength of knowing my creator is not above me somewhere, but is always with me (Jones, 1990:56).

Gilbert saw no need for church or systems of religion.

> There's no need to meditate distinctly; there's no need to go to any church; there's no need to think spiritual or religious thoughts. There's a constant flowing of life and we are very much a part of that life (Jones, 1990:57).

The contemporary Aboriginal songwriter/singer, Kevin Carmody, although referring in his songs to Jesus and religious symbols has no time for the formal structures of religious systems. Aboriginal people now, as they have always done, are expressing their fundamental ideas about reality through story, song and art.

As many people in the modern world are turning both from traditional religious systems and materialist interpretations of the world, there is renewed interest in a variety of spiritualities—eastern, new-age, celtic, feminist and others. As part of this movement Aboriginal beliefs and values, which sustained them for many thousands of years in environments which others have found alien and threatening, are attracting new interest and respect. In the

Introduction to her book, *The Search for Meaning*, the broadcaster Caroline Jones, has written as follows:

> Aboriginal people gave meaning to my life by showing through their suffering, their courage, their unselfishness, their sense of family, their forgiveness, their survival and their sense of the sacred what it is truly like to be human. For me they are the steady beating heart at the centre of our Australian spirituality (Jones, 1989:17).

Her words reflect the comment of Miriam-Rose Ungunmerr, that Aboriginal spirituality is the gift for which *Australia is thirsting* (Ungunmerr, 1988:9).

References

Beckett, Jeremy (1987). *Torres Strait Islanders: Custom and Colonialism.* Cambridge: Cambridge University Press.

Bell, Diane (1998). "Aboriginal Women's Religion: A shifting law of the land". In *Traditional Aboriginal Society*. Second edition. Edited by WH Edwards. South Yarra: Macmillan.

Berndt, RM and CH (1981). *The World of the First Australians*. Sydney: Lansdowne Press.

Broome, Richard (1982). *Aboriginal Australians: Black Responses to White Dominance, 1788-1980*. Sydney: Allen and Unwin.

Cole, Keith (1979). *The Aborigines of Arnhem Land*. Adelaide: Rigby.

Edwards, WH (1988). *An Introduction to Aboriginal Societies*. Wentworth Falls, NSW: Social Science Press.

Edwards, WH and Clarke, BA (1988). "From missions to Aboriginal churches: The Uniting Church in Australia and Aboriginal missions". In *Aboriginal Australians and Christian Missions,* edited by Tony Swain and Deborah Bird Rose. Bedford Park SA: Australian Association for the Study of Religions.

Eliade, Mercia (1973). *Australian Religions*. Ithaca: Cornell University Press.

Gilbert, Kevin (1978). *Living Black: Blacks Talk to Kevin Gilbert*. Ringwood, Victoria: Penguin Books.

Gondarra, Djiniyini (1988). *Father you Gave us The Dreaming*. Darwin: Bethel Presbytery.

Gunson, Neil, editor (1974). *Australian Reminiscences and Papers of L. E. Threlkeld, Missionary to the Aborigines 1824-1859*. Canberra: Australian Institute of Aboriginal Studies.

Harris, John (1990). *One blood: 200 Years of Aboriginal Encounters with Christianity: a Story of Hope*. Sutherland, NSW: Albatross Books.

Hart, Max (1988). *A Story of Fire: Aboriginal Christianity*. Blackwood, SA: New Creation Publications.

Hendriks, Joan and Hefferan, Gerry, editors (1993). *A Spirituality of Catholic Aborigines and the Struggle for Justice*. Brisbane: Aboriginal and Torres Strait Islander Apostolate.

Isaacs, Jennifer (1980). *Australian Dreaming*. Sydney: Lansdowne.

Jones, Caroline (1989). *The Search for Meaning*. Crows Nest. NSW Australian Broadcasting Corporation.

Jones, Caroline (1990). *The Search for Meaning*: Book Two. Crows Nest. NSW: Australian Broadcasting Corporation.

Keen, Ian (1994). *Knowledge and Secrecy in an Aboriginal Religion: Yolngu of North-east Arnhem Land*. Oxford: Clarendon Press.

Kolig, E (1988). *Religious Movements, in the Australian People: an Encyclopedia of the Nation, its People and Their Origins*, edited by James Jupp. Wentworth Falls, NSW: Angus and Robertson.

Lester, Yami (1993). *Yami: the Autobiography of Yami Lester*. Alice Springs: Institute for Aboriginal Development Publications.

Love, JRB (1936). *Stone-age Bushmen of To-day*. London: Blackie and Son Limited.

Morphy, Howard (1987). "The art of Northern Australia". In *Traditional Aboriginal society: a reader*. Edited by WH Edwards. South Melbourne: Macmillan.

Morphy, Howard (1988). "Religion". In *Social Anthropology and Australian Aboriginal Studies: a Contemporary Overview*, edited by RM Berndt and R Tonkinson. Canberra: Aboriginal Studies Press.

Rainbow Spirit Elders (1997). *Rainbow Spirit Theology*. Blackburn: Harper Collins.

Rose, Deborah B (1987). "Consciousness and responsibility in an Aboriginal religion". In *Traditional Aboriginal Religion: a Reader*, edited by WH Edwards. South Melbourne: Macmillan.

Stanner, WH (1963). On Aboriginal religion. *Oceania Monograph 11*. Sydney: University of Sydney.

Stanner, WH (1984). "Religion, totemism and symbolism". In *Religion in Aboriginal Australia: an Anthology*, edited by Max Charlesworth et al. Brisbane: University of Queensland Press.

Stanner, WH (1987). "The Dreaming". In *Traditional Aboriginal Religion: a Reader*, edited by WH Edwards. South Melbourne: Macmillan.

Strehlow, TGH (1947). *Aranda Traditions*. Melbourne: Melbourne University Press.

Swain, Tony (1993). *A Place for Strangers: Towards a History of Australian Aboriginal Being*. Cambridge: Cambridge University Press.

Sutton, Peter, editor (1988). *Dreamings: the Art of Aboriginal Australia*. Ringwood: Viking—Penguin Books.

Tonkinson, R (1978). *The Mardudjara Aborigines*. New York: Holt, Rinehart and Winston.

UAICC (1988). *Manifesto of The Uniting Aboriginal and Islander Christian Congress*. Sydney.

Ungunmerr, MR (1984). *Australian Stations of the Cross*. North Blackburn: Collins Dove.

Ungunmerr, MR (1988). "Dadirri". *Compass,* vol. 22.

Chapter 6

Family and Kinship

Colin Bourke and Bill Edwards

Background

All aspects of Aboriginal society have been directly affected by the arrival of British colonists. Land use, law, spiritual beliefs and ways of life have been traumatised. All parts of Aboriginal society have felt the full force of the invasion, but it is arguable that traditional Aboriginal family life and the supporting kinship structures have taken the maximum disruptive impact especially in areas of highest non-Aboriginal population density.

Aboriginal family life has been irreversibly changed in most of Australia. Many of the changes have come about merely by the presence of Europeans in this country, many others are attributable to the direct actions of the colonisers, actions which were deliberately aimed at destroying family life as it existed in Aboriginal society.

Despite this, Aboriginal societies have strong continuities with their forebears, and they "are as much a part of their own tradition as they are of European domination" (Macdonald, 1998:297). Macdonald in her study of the Wiradjuri of New South Wales illustrates ways in which colonialism has interacted with traditional lifeways to produce the present day Aboriginal societies.

Aboriginal kinship and family structures are still cohesive forces which bind Aboriginal people together in all parts of Australia. They provide psychological and emotional support to Aboriginal people even though they create concern among non-Aboriginal people who would prefer Aborigines to follow European social preferences for nuclear families with few kinship responsibilities. Aboriginal family obligations, often seen as nepotism by other Australians, may be reflecting cultural values, involving kinship responsibilities.

Removal of children

Nearly all Aboriginal families know of relatives who were removed as children and put into European custody. Aboriginal people refer to them as "taken" or "stolen". The effects of such policies and practices are still reverberating in the Aboriginal community. Aboriginal adults who were taken away from their families as children experience difficulties adjusting without having an Aboriginal family supported childhood. Though wanting to join their own people, some have a crisis of identity. They have been raised to think "white" and "be like white people". To gain acceptance in Aboriginal society they have to learn new values and new rules and in many cases overcome negative views of their Aboriginal heritage.

The removal of Aboriginal children from their parents has been official policy in all states of Australia since the so-called "protection era". Missionaries established the practise in the early 1800s to instil Christian virtues of obedience, punctuality and religious observance. They wished to create an Aboriginal working class by developing marketable skills which would make Aborigines employable (Edwards and Read, 1989:x). The missionaries tried hard, but they failed and the Aboriginal people living near these early missions simply moved away.

The separation of Aboriginal children from their families began in earnest in 1883 when the NSW Aborigines Protection Board was established to control what non-Aborigines perceived to be a growing problem of Aboriginal populations congregating around towns (Edwards and Read, 1989:xii). It was argued that the children of these people could be turned into useful citizens if they were taken from their parents and socialised as Europeans. A policy of child removal began based on the "idleness" of the parents from which the child should be "protected". It is ironic that the so-called protection policies era actually devastated Aboriginal life.

In New South Wales alone, official records show some 5,625 children, at least, had been removed from their parents between 1883 and 1969 (Read, nd:9) and placed in Aboriginal Children's Homes. There are no records of Aboriginal children sent into other state or religious homes. Unofficial removals would also significantly inflate the figure. Similar situations prevailed in the rest of

Australia. The passing of the *Child Welfare Act* in NSW in 1939 did not stop the practice. It was not until the 1950s that a reduction in the stream of enforced separations occurred. It was still believed, however, that non-Aboriginal parents could more quickly assimilate an Aboriginal child, so great pressure was placed on young Aboriginal mothers to have their children adopted by non-Aboriginal people. The number of Aboriginal children who were fostered increased in the 1950s. In 1957 the NSW Protection Board placed advertisements in newspapers seeking foster parents to look after Aboriginal children. Peter Read in *The stolen generations* noted that the response was extraordinary and within two years there were more Aboriginal children fostered out than were in the homes.

Aboriginal families were often regarded as either homeless or as living in squalor by government officials so Aboriginal children were never placed with black families. After being removed from their family and community support most were subjected to racism, ignorance and prejudice. They grew up confused and unsure about their own identity. Peter Read believes that in Australia today there may be 100,000 people of Aboriginal descent who do not know their families or the communities from whence they come.

These people have been institutionalised, fostered or adopted, loved, hated or ignored. They all share the mental torment of not belonging in the society into which European Australia had decided to put them. Australian society accepted the young Aboriginal children into its institutions but rejected them when they became adults.

Many of these adults have sought, and some are still seeking, to find their families. They know of their Aboriginal ancestry but they need to know more about what it really means. They wish to be re-united with their families. They seek their Aboriginal identity. They need to know who they are and where their families are from. The psychological scars and damage to self-concepts are immeasurable for those removed from their families. The effects of being deprived of parental care are still being felt in Aboriginal society.

The National Inquiry into the separation of Aboriginal and Torres Strait Islander children from their families (1997) was conducted by the Human Rights and Equal Opportunity

Commission. It concluded that between one in three and one in ten Indigenous children were forcibly removed from their families and communities between 1910 and 1970.

The Inquiry found that the children and their families were actively discouraged from contacting each other. Many children were taught to feel contempt for Aborigines while institutional regimes were strict with severe punishment common. While the conditions and resources of missions, institutions and children's homes were poor (Human Rights and Equal Opportunity Commission, 1997:14-15).

The education offered the children was inadequate and the 1994 Australian Bureau of Statistics (ABS) survey found that the children who were forcibly removed were no better educated than their peers raised in their communities (Human Rights and Equal Opportunity Commission, 1997:16).

Many of the children were sexually abused because the welfare system failed to protect the children. Some children found happiness, but their mothers left behind suffered great personal loss and often felt helpless and useless with extremely low self-esteem. Indigenous parenting skills have been lost as the children in many cases have suffered depression, insecurity and feelings of worthlessness with a subsequent lack of trust and intimacy (Human Rights and Equal Opportunity Commission, 1997:17-19).

The Inquiry found there has been a great loss of heritage, language and culture and many people have been left with nowhere to belong and no sense of identity. Contrary to some publicly expressed views the Inquiry found that the experiences of forcibly removed children overwhelmingly contradicted the view that it was in their "best interests at the time". In 1994 the ABS survey found people who were forcibly removed in childhood were twice as likely to assess their health as poor or fair (29%) compared with people who were not removed (15%) (Human Rights and Equal Opportunity Commission, 1997:19).

Societies can place emphases on either the individual or the social identity of a person. Western society places an emphasis on the individual. It values the rights and freedom of choice of the individual. Being strongly individualistic, there is less emphasis placed on group development.

Aboriginal society places greater emphasis on social identity, membership of a group and the obligations and responsibilities of individuals to conform to the expectations of others. It is a communal society where even though the autonomy of each individual is respected (Myers, 1986:18), the individuality of each member receives less emphasis than their cooperative contribution. Being removed from such a society leaves the individual adrift without a point of reference and uncertain as to how to try to re-enter a society whose mores they do not know and whose kinship structure is not understood.

Kinship

In Western societies the structures of social interaction and roles and obligations change as individuals move out from the immediate family circle to the wider society. In contrast to this, in Aboriginal societies the family structures and the sets of rights and obligations underlying them are extended to the whole society. As an individual moves out from the immediate family to the local group and to the total linguistic group, he or she is able to identify all other members of the groups by the same relationship terms which apply in the family. Terms usually applied to lineal relatives are used to refer also to collateral relatives. This is made possibly by the application in Aboriginal societies of what is called the Classificatory System of Kinship.

A basic principle of this system in traditional societies is the *equivalence of same-sex siblings*. According to this principle, people who are of the same sex and belong to the same sibling line are viewed as essentially the same. Thus two brothers are considered to be equivalent. If one has a child, that child views not only his biological father as father but applies the same term to the father's brother. The same principle applies to two sisters with both being mothers to any child either one bears. As a father's brother is also identified as father, the latter's children will be brothers and sisters, rather than cousins. This system is known as the classificatory system of kinship because all members of the larger group are classified under the relationship terms. There is no need to expand the range of classifications or relationship terms. Several people are identified by an individual within each classification. Thus a person has several fathers, several mothers, and many brothers and sisters. A mother's brother, being on the same sibling line but of the other sex, is identified as an uncle. A father's sister is an aunt (See Edwards, 1988:48-49, for diagrams illustrating kinship terms).

When speaking to, or about, another person in Aboriginal societies, the person's personal name is rarely used. A person is addressed by the appropriate relationship term, eg. father, aunt, or older brother. Another person is referred to as so-and-so's son or mother. The personal names are seen as essentially part of the person and are used with discretion.

Because an individual is always interacting with others who are clearly identified by specific relationship terms much of the behaviour in traditional societies is governed by the rights and obligations associated with the various relationships. According to the anthropologist, Robert Tonkinson, "All over Australia, kinship is undeniably the most important single factor in restructuring Aboriginal social relationships" (Tonkinson, 1987:210). This applied in all spheres of life, in economic activities, social relationships, marriage, social control, ritual, education and politics. A person who brought in large game from the hunt, such as a kangaroo, was obliged to share a portion of it with specific relatives. Mothers, aunts and grandmothers had special roles in educating young children. In societies which did not have chiefs or designated leaders with wide powers, kinship was important in resolving conflict and restoring harmony. If a member of a group did something wrong certain members of the group, according to the relationships, were responsible for punishing the offender.

Individuals are limited in the choice of marriage partners, by their relationships. In most Aboriginal societies a person married a person classified as a cross-cousin. Thus a man married either a mother's father's daughter or a father's sister's daughter, this varying according to the accepted rules in the group. This did not mean that marriage was between first cousins but was between members of these categories. People identified as uncles (mother's brothers) had special obligations related to the training, discipline and initiation of youths. In turn, in some groups, they promised one of their daughters to the young man as a prospective wife. In Aboriginal societies, marriages are significant, not only for the relationship between the two partners, but as forging alliances between groups.

Some relationships allow for great freedom in interaction, eg between grandparents and grandchildren. In others, deference or restraint has to be shown at all times. One prominent type of relationship in Aboriginal societies is known as avoidance relationships. These provide control over relationships which could give rise to extreme tensions in small groups. For example, a man may have to avoid all face to face contact with his mother-in-law. Brothers-in-law are also kept at a distance from one another. Brothers and sisters are expected to show some reserve in their relationship as they mature.

An important principle underlying all interaction is that of reciprocity. Pitjantjatjara people refer to this as *ngapartji-ngapartji*, or "in return". Between individuals, local groups and larger groups there are systems of rights, obligations and responsibilities based on this principle. If an individual or group gives food or a marriage partner to another individual or group they expect to receive something or somebody in return. If a person or a group offends another person or group they can expect retribution in return. These systems of checks and balances are designed to maintain equilibrium between individuals and groups. The kinship systems with their sets of rights and obligations provide individuals with a guide to their own behaviour and some security and confidence in predicting likely behaviours when meeting other people. Teaching about the relationships and associated behaviours is a major element in the traditional education of Aboriginal children.

The kinds of structures outlined above are identified as *egocentric*. From each individual's position, he or she can specify their relationship, and the concomitant rights and obligations, to all other members of the group. The systems vary across the continent and other sources should be consulted for details of specific systems. All groups have complementary systems of social organisation which are identified as *sociocentric*. In these systems all members of the group are viewed as members of social groups or categories.

Social categories

Whereas an individual is identified by various relationship terms according to the person who is applying them, eg, a son calling him father, or another man calling him brother, people are placed into specific social categories according to their descent. In some societies this was determined by descent from the mother (matrilineal), in others by descent from the father (patrilineal). Membership of the categories is therefore ascribed by birth.

A basic division in Aboriginal societies is that between the moieties. Moiety means half and each group was divided into two groups or moieties (see Figure 1a). Membership of a moiety is significant in ritual, social interaction and marriage. In ceremonies people sit in two circles according to moiety membership to sing the song cycles. Marriage in Aboriginal societies was normally exogamous in relationship to moieties, that is, a person married someone from the other moiety group. In north-east Arnhem Land, where children belong to the same moiety as their fathers, both their physical and their social environments are divided into two moieties, *Dhuwa* and *Yirritja* (See Figure 1b). A *Dhuwa* person must marry a *Yirritja* person, and visa versa. Some areas of land are *Dhuwa*, and other areas are *Yirritja*. Animal, bird and plant species and implements are classified as either *Dhuwa* or *Yirritja* (Williams, 1981:106). In Victoria the Gunditjmara were divided into the *Krokitch* moiety symbolised by the white cockatoo, and the *Kaputch* moiety symbolised by the black cockatoo.

Some Aboriginal societies in the Western Desert and Broome regions placed emphasis on social category based on generation levels. These systems also divided the total society into two groups but in a way which cross-cuts the moiety divisions. A person belongs to a generation level group which includes his or her own siblings, and people from the levels two above and two below their own level, that is, the levels of their grandparents and grandchildren. The other category is made up of people from the levels of one's parents and one's children (see Figure 2a). This type of system is illustrated from Pitjantjatjara society (see Figure 2b),

Many Aboriginal societies were further divided into systems in which there were four or eight categories. All members of the societies belong to one of these categories, according to descent and generation. The systems with four categories are known as section systems. Those with eight categories are known as subsection systems. Each section or subsection group is identified by a specific name. The use of these names enables strangers when meeting to work out their relationship and responsibilities without having to trace the precise relationship link. The systems are therefore interpreted by some as a shorthand way of identifying one's place in society. While the systems are often used to illustrate marriage arrangements they served a much wider purpose in ordering social interaction. Maddock suggests that Aboriginal people viewed these systems as part of a cosmic order, "The classifications made by Aborigines appear rather to manifest a passion for order that has driven them to try to apply to the whole world a single system" (Maddock, 1974:95).

In section systems all members of the society belong to one of four categories. For the purpose of illustration these can be called A, B, C and D (see Figure 3a). Moiety membership and generation level are important constituents in these systems. A and B belong to the same generation level, C and D to the alternate generation level. A and C belong to the same moiety, B and D to the other moiety. Under this system a person must marry someone who is the same generation level but in the other moiety. Therefore a man who is a member of section A must marry a woman who is a member of section B. A man who is a member of section C must marry a woman who is a member of section D. Children of A and B belong to either C or D, depending on whether descent is viewed as patrilineal or matrilineal.

Tonkinson observed amongst the Mardudjara of the desert areas of Western Australia that when strangers met they identified themselves by their section names as this reduced the range of possible kin relationships. Once a person had decided on the basis of this information which kin term to give to one of the strangers, the relationship to all members of both groups could be worked out (Tonkinson, 1987:214). See Figure 3b for the application of section names from one Aboriginal society in Western Australia. In some areas of Western Australia two of the sections in the four section system were divided into two subsections, to provide a variant of the section system.

Some groups, such as the Warlpiri of Central Australia and the Yolngu of north-east Arnhem Land, made a further division into eight categories, known as subsections. This can be illustrated by dividing each of the categories A, B, C and D into two, and symbolising them as A1, A2, B1, B2, C1, C2, D1 and D2 (see Figure 4a). In the naming of these subsections a further division is made by distinguishing the sex in each category. This refinement of the section system enables distinctions to be made between sets of relatives which are not made under the section system. For example, second cross-cousins, who are preferred as marriage partners, are distinguished from cross-cousins. See Figure 4b for the application of subsection names from Warlpiri society.

Williams (1981) is a detailed, well illustrated guide to the study of kinship in Aboriginal societies. Keen (1988) provides an overview of the development of anthropological studies of Aboriginal kinship.

Aboriginal kinship and social systems are complex and varied. They were incorporated in the mythology of The Dreaming and viewed as a legacy of the Ancestral Spirit Beings. They provide a sense of personal identity and social cohesion and are the coordinating force for all social interaction. They provide a code to enable people to live in relative harmony with one another.

However, as outlined earlier in this chapter, these systems of traditional Aboriginal societies were disrupted severely by colonial settlement and the domination of European political, social, education and religious systems. There has been debate as to the extent to which these traditional systems, which are still strong in some remote regions, are present in contemporary rural and urban Aboriginal societies.

According to Macdonald (1998:301) kinship has remained the foundation of social life, including political and economic relations in Aboriginal societies throughout colonial history. Based on her study of Wiradjuri society in New South Wales she sees kinship as a dynamic and responsive system which is used to maintain a continuity of traditions, and a system of shared meanings based on mutual experience (1998:299). Kinship locates a person within the social structure so that they belong and have a social place. The use of such terms as "my people", "my relations" (rellies) or "my mob" by Aboriginal people in towns and cities reflects the traditional usage and contributes to an expression of Aboriginal identity.

Moieties

Figure 1a

All members of a society belong to one of these two categories. In patrilineal societies members belong to a group because of descent from the mother determines membership. A person marries someone from the other moiety. Thus moieties are exogamous. X indicates marriage.

Figure 1b

The names given to the moiety groups in Yolngu societies of north-east Arnhem Land. As well as people, animal and plant species, artefacts and places belong to one of these moieties. X indicates marriage.

Generation Levels

Generation Level 1 Includes one's own, one's grandparents, and one's grand-children's generation levels.	**Nganantarka (our bone)** Includes one's brothers, sisters, cousins, grand-parents, grandchil-dren.
Generation Level 2 Includes one's parent's, and one's children's generation levels.	**Tjanamilytja (their flesh)** Includes one's parents, uncles, aunts, sons, daughters, nephews, neices.

Figure 2a   Figure 2b

Alternate generation levels. Generation levels are enogamous in that one marries a person who belongs to the same level.

The names given to the generation levels in Pitjantjatjara society in the north-west of South Australia.

Sections

Figure 3a

If the divisions based on moieties and generation are combined there are four categories, shown in the above figure as A, B, C and D. These are called sections. Aboriginal societies which have this section system have names for each section. As the moieties are exogamous and people marry within their own generation level, A marries B and C marries D. Childern of A and B will be either C or D and children of C and D will be either A or B, depending on whether descent in the society is patrilineal or matrilineal. X indicates marriage.

Figure 3b

Section names as used in some inland regions of Western Australia. X indicates marriage. The arrowed lines indicate descent.

Subsections

MOIETY 1		MOIETY 2	
A1	✕	B1	
A2	✕	B2	Generation level
C1	✕	D1	
C2	✕	D2	

Figure 4a

In some societies each section is further divided into two subsections, thus providing a system with eight categories. Names are given to each of the subsections, with the males and females in each subsection being distinguished by differences in the names. X indicates preferred marriage.

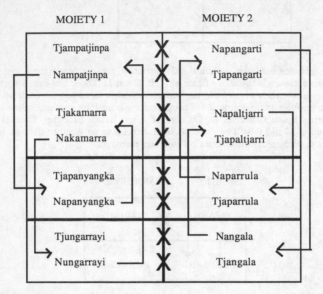

Figure 4b

Warlpiri subsection names (Northern Territory). Names commencing with Tj indicate the males of the subsection. Those commencing with N indicate the females. X indicates preferred marriage, eg a Tjampatjinpa man should marry a Napangarti woman, although marriage to a Napaltjarri woman is acceptable. The arrowed lines indicate descent, that is, the arrow points to the subsection to which the children of the couple at the other end of the line would belong.

Urban kinship and families

In the towns and cities of Australia today Aboriginal families retain to varying degrees the kinship system of their ancestors. Some Aboriginal people have non-Aboriginal spouses and live in situations where they appear to be absorbed into non-Aboriginal society. Therefore, the family structures of rural and urban Aborigines is different from those of the more traditionally oriented groups. However, in the cities where most Aborigines are of mixed descent and have had long exposure to Europeans they are still an identifiable, separate cultural group. Aboriginal people, wherever they are, distinguish themselves from other Australians and are linked together by a sense of belonging to a locality and to an extended family.

Aboriginal families in urban and rural areas have developed a culture of their own through family, community and organisational structures. These structures give them psychological and physical support and provide security. Much of this security lies in the knowledge that urban Aborigines can continue to rely on group support and don't have to depend on non-Aborigines. Aboriginal people identify as a cultural group and have a growing pride in their Aboriginality. Today, depending on their location, they are known as Kooris, Murris, Nungas, Nyoongahs, Yolngu and Anangu, among other local names.

The battles for land rights, education and better living conditions, together with a growing interest in Aboriginal traditions, has led to the development of other social and political groupings not based wholly on kin. A heightened sense of cultural and political identity has developed a feeling of pan-Aboriginality. Aboriginal people from all parts of Australia are acknowledging a common cultural background of Aboriginality while maintaining a diverse range of lifestyles throughout Australia.

The focus by earlier anthropologists on remote, so-called traditional Aboriginal societies tended to divert attention from the importance attached to kin and country by mixed race Aboriginal people. Thus a sociologist wrote in the 1960s that generally speaking, "the part-aborigines of New South Wales have no culture of their own to preserve" (Bell, 1964:64). Models of cultural survival and a subculture of poverty were used to explain the survival of kinship or country allegiances. Research studies such as those by Beckett (1964) in rural New South Wales and Gale (1972) in Adelaide were uncommon. More recently, Macdonald (1998) has given attention to the extent to which kinship and attachment to land are important for Aboriginal people in rural New South Wales.

Urban tertiary educated Aboriginal professionals are still absorbed by genealogical ramifications, and, kinship terms and courtesy titles are frequently used. Many people are referred to as aunty, uncle, sister, brother, cousin when there may be no blood relationship. This practice is often abhorred by some people, usually non-Aborigines, who believe that only traditionally oriented Aborigines should use such terms. At Aboriginal social gatherings placing people in kinship terms in relation to those present is a most important part of the gathering.

The Aboriginal family is central to the survival of Aboriginal culture. The structure, values and practices can be based on the traditional complex kinship systems or the extended family, kinship ties and locality allegiances of rural and urban people. The values, beliefs and identity of Aboriginal culture can be best developed from within the family.

Fay Gale's study of urban Aborigines in 1972 described the phenomenon of urban Aboriginal people moving house within Adelaide to be near their kin. Aboriginal families are subjected to enormous acculturation pressures, as well as psychological, social and economic stresses. Non-Aboriginal programs and institutions continue to be destructive of Aboriginal urban, rural and traditionally oriented families as they were in the past. Aboriginal families will survive and thrive when Aboriginal people gain control of their own lives.

Gaynor Macdonald argues that "all aspects of daily life (today) are informed by traditions which stem from classical Wiradjuri culture, from the practice and beliefs of Wiradjuri ancestors" (1998:297).

Children

Many Aboriginal people fear that their children may lose their cultural values and beliefs and, therefore, not identify strongly with Aboriginal society. Traditionally oriented people are concerned their children are losing their language and increasing their use of English. At the same time they are also adopting new values and traditional skills are being lost.

The Aboriginal Women's Taskforce Report 1986 *Women's Business* noted:

> Children are the responsibility of the entire family rather than to the biological parents alone. Many Aboriginal people have been 'grown up' by members of the family other than their biological

mother and father and this practice of growing up children is still very widespread today. Often it is the children's grandparents who carry out the growing up. They also are very important members of the family unit and are heavily relied upon to play a large part in child rearing. As a result of the children being encouraged to think and have responsibility at a very early age, they have a large degree of personal autonomy (Aboriginal Women's Taskforce, 1986:27).

This report also noted that if a mother leaves the family, for whatever reason, the children continue to grow up within the extended family. "Fostering", therefore, has a different meaning for Aboriginal people. Often there is no attempt to legalise the arrangements through the courts because it is the family which is involved. There is a reluctance to use the "white man's law" to give legal guardianship to members of a family to whom the children already belong. People are also reluctant to admit that the mother has left the child in someone else's care because of the long history of children being removed and placed into institutions by welfare officers. Another factor is that Aboriginal people have a different cultural view of child care. Such a mother would be seen by non-Aboriginal people as "no good" or "unworthy". In fact, she may be acting in a culturally acceptable way, given the rights and obligations that Aboriginal families share.

The raising, care and discipline of children by the family is often extended to the wider Aboriginal community. Generally, there is the feeling that children belong to everybody and in a large gathering children are the responsibility of all, be they female or male, young or old. The movement of children between their relatives is a convenient and accepted practice that provides the children with the opportunity to learn many aspects of the traditional way of life.

Where Aboriginal people may not have members of their extended family living in close proximity, the traditional child raising and care practices (in which grandparents and other extended family members play an important role) is not available. In a fragmented society where Aboriginal people—through necessity, by persuasion or by force—have had to adopt a way of life which does not reflect their values, aspirations or expectations, the care of children becomes difficult (Aboriginal Women's Taskforce, 1986).

More recently this has resulted in the establishment of Aboriginal child care and pre-school centres in the cities.

Aboriginal families are still trying to cope with the effects of the removal of children. As the National Inquiry found, people brought up in institutions or passed around different foster homes didn't learn about good parenting. As parents, many of the stolen generation children have problem children who are at risk of being institutionalised because they are at risk or are offenders (Human Rights and Equal Opportunity Commission, 1997:19-20).

Women play many roles in the Aboriginal family. They are expected to be, for example, wife, mother, grandmother, aunt, niece, daughter, each day of their adult lives. With Aboriginal family life under increasing pressure the role of Aboriginal women has increased. In many urban situations Aboriginal women are not only the base foundation of the family, they are also the strength of the Aboriginal community. As Fay Gale noted:

> It is not uncommon to find an Aboriginal household in Adelaide consisting of an extended family. The dominating character in such a household is often a grandmother. Her establishment may consist of daughters with their children and with or without spouses. Very often one or more single male relatives, sons, brothers and cousins may be attached to, rather than part of, the household (Gale, 1972:165).

Similar situations are to be found with respect to Aboriginal families throughout urban Australia.

Aboriginal identification

Aboriginal people are invariably interested in finding out where a person is from as a first step toward placing a person whom they do not know correctly into their own universe. Quite often when Aborigines meet for the first time the situation is characterised by a high degree of diffidence. In 1981 John von Sturmer recorded his account of two Aboriginal people meeting for the first time:

> I recall travelling with an Aboriginal man, Mickey, from Edward River. We stopped at Mareeba to buy some food. Mickey remained in the vehicle. I observed an Aboriginal man walk past him along the footpath. He was clearly intrigued to find out who Mickey was,

and Mickey was equally curious. The man walked backwards and forwards several times. Finally he came up to the vehicle and the conversation went something like this:

> *Mareeba man*: Where you from?
> *Mickey*: I'm Edward River man. Where you from?
> *Mareeba man*: I'm Lama Lama man ... do you know X?
> *Mickey*: No. Do you know Y?
> *Mareeba man*: No. Do you know Z?
> *Mickey*: Yes. She's my aunty.
> *Mareeba man*: That old lady's my granny. I must call you daddy.
> *Mickey*: I must call you boy. You give me cigarette.
> (von Sturmer, 1981:13).

Of course this type of approach is possible even between Europeans and Aborigines, especially if the European already knows a number of Aborigines who have fitted him/her into the kinship system. People can search for relations whom they share and then establish their relationship on that basis. Presentation of a cigarette—an almost standard device—or another small gift may seal this preliminary transaction as it did on the occasion in Mareeba.

Aboriginal people often express the view that history gives them something to identify themselves by and to know that they do have a family. When they are with fellow Aborigines they feel a certain bond, a certain magic; they feel part of their family. It is a wonderful feeling, actually—a feeling of joy, a feeling of pride.

The younger generation of Aborigines are keen to find out to whom they are related. They use their family tree to see how the whole family is related. Some are worried about who they may marry. They are interested in identifying their different cousins on the tree and determining how they are related. Many others feel they need to know to be sure of their identity. For those who were removed from their family at birth or soon after, being given access to their genealogy gives them a feeling for their historical place in Aboriginal society. It is difficult to be proud of your Aboriginal heritage if you do not know your ancestry.

The National Inquiry into the removal of Aboriginal and Torres Strait Islander children (Human Rights and Equal Opportunity

Commission, 1997:20) found many such children lost their heritage and have been left with nowhere to belong, no sense of identity.

Aboriginal people have, since 1973, been required by the Federal Government to meet its definition of Aboriginality. It has three conditions, all of which must be met to participate in specific Government initiatives for Aborigines and Torres Strait Islanders. An individual must:

- be of Aboriginal or Torres Strait Islander descent.
- identify as being of Aboriginal or Torres Strait Islander descent.
- be recognised by the community as being a person of Aboriginal or Torres Strait Islander descent.

For an Aboriginal person who can not identify/describe their genealogy there is some insecurity as to whether they meet the government definition. A knowledge of their genealogy makes an Aboriginal person feel more secure, while also enabling a person to know the location of their ancestral lands and the history of their people.

Conclusion

Some Aboriginal people can draw strength from their traditional culture. They still practise their ceremonies, songs and dances and speak the language of the group to which they belong. Others do not have such ready access. Often they do not know their language group, cultural traditions or family history and, consequently, many of the traditional practices have been lost or severely modified. This is particularly true for those forcibly removed from their families.

Generally, the more urbanised Aborigines have not lost their sense of Aboriginality; they feel themselves to be, and identify themselves as, Aboriginal Australians. Nor does their identification necessarily depend upon physical features or skin colour. Rather, it has to do with shared experiences, sharing the same relatives (even on a national basis), stories, background, history, oppression, discrimination and a host of other factors. For most it provides a comfortable feeling of belonging and pride based on a knowledge of an ancient cultural heritage. Kinship provides a conceptual framework which allows people's humanism to come to the fore.

Some Aboriginal people who do not have dark skin, hair or eyes face a dual problem—acceptance of their Aboriginality by some Aboriginal and non-Aboriginal people alike. A Tasmanian woman who spoke to the 1986 Aboriginal Women's Task Force on this issue said that "the battle is made even harder when state governments—past and present—maintain there are no Aboriginal people in the State". While the National Inquiry into the removal of children was told "you spend your whole life wondering where you fit. You're not white enough to be white and you're not black enough to be black either". Social and economic conditions today also put many Aboriginal people under stress. Mixed marriage partnerships, for example, sometimes place pressures on the Aboriginal partner to conform to non-Aboriginal values and way of life and to reject their Aboriginal identity.

When Aborigines refer to their family they invariably mean their extended family which might include parents, several children, numerous aunts, uncles and cousins, and grandparents. These family members can be both genetic and classificatory. It is the kinship ties which determine a person's rights, responsibilities and behaviour.

Aboriginal kinship ties, values, beliefs, identity and language are maintained by the family. The continuance of Aboriginal society is dependent on keeping Aboriginal families strong and healthy both physically and culturally.

References

Aboriginal Women's Task Force (1986). *Women's Business*. Canberra: AGPS.

Barwick, D (1974). "The Aboriginal family in South-Eastern Australia and the family in Australia". In *Australian Families,* edited by J Krupinska and A Stoller. Sydney: Pergamon.

Beckett, Jeremy (1964). "Aborigines, Alcohol and Assimilation". In *Aborigines Now*, edited by Marie Reay. Sydney: Angus and Robertson.

Bell, James, H (1964). "Assimilation in New South Wales". In *Aborigines Now*, edited by Marie Reay. Sydney: Angus and Robertson.

Berndt, CH and RM (1978). *Pioneers and Settlers*. Carlton: Pitman.

Berndt, CH and RM (1988). *The World of the First Australians.* Canberra: Australian Studies Press.

Edwards, WH (1988). *An Introduction to Aboriginal Societies.* Wentworth Falls: Social Science Press.

Edwards, Coral and Read, Peter, editors (1989). *The Lost Children.* Moorebank, NSW: Doubleday.

Gale, Fay (1972). *Urban Aborigines.* Canberra: ANU.

Human Rights and Equal Opportunity Commission (1997). *Bringing Them Home: A Guide to the Findings and Recommendations of the National Inquiry into the Separation of Aboriginal and Torres Strait Islander Children From Their Families.* Sydney: Human Rights and Equal Opportunity Commission.

Keen, Ian (1988). Kinship. In *Social Anthropology and Australian Aboriginal Studies: A Contemporary Overview*, edited by RM Berndt and R Tonkinson. Canberra: Aboriginal Studies Press.

Macdonald, Gaynor (1998) "Continuities of Wiradjuri Tradition". In Edwards, WH, editor. *Traditional Aboriginal Society.* Second edition. South Yarra: Macmillan.

Maddock, Kenneth (1974). *The Australian Aborigines: A Portrait of their Society.* London: Allan Lane The Penguin Press.

Mattingley, C and Hampton, K (1988). *Survival in Our Own Land.* Adelaide: Wakefield Press.

Myers, Fred R (1986). *Pintupi Country, Pintupi self: sentiment, place and politics among Western Desert Aborigines.* Canberra: Aboriginal Studies Press.

Radcliffe-Brown, AR (1952). *Structure and Function in Primitive Society.* London: Cohen and West.

Read, Peter (nd). *The Stolen Generation* (Occasional paper number 1). Sydney: Ministry of Aboriginal Affairs.

Tonkinson, R (1987). "Mardudjara Kinship". In *Australians to 1988*, edited by DJ Mulvaney and JP White. Fairfax: Syme and Weldon Associates.

von Sturmer, J (1981). AIAS newsletter no. 15. Canberra: AIAS, pp 13-30.

Wafer, J (1982). *A Simple Introduction to Central Australia Kinship Systems.* Alice Springs: Institute for Aboriginal Development.

Williams, Don (1981). *Exploring Aboriginal Kinship*. Canberra: Curriculum Development Centre.

Chapter 7

Australian Languages: Our Heritage

Rob Amery and Colin Bourke

Australian Languages

Aboriginal and Torres Strait Islander languages are the indigenous languages of Australia. Accordingly, they are correctly referred to as Australian Languages (Dixon, 1980). Australian languages share certain typological features and are distinguished from other languages spoken outside Australia by virtue of their sound systems and grammars. They constitute Australia's unique linguistic heritage.

English is **not** an Australian language, even though it is Australia's national language and is used as a *lingua franca*, or common language, by speakers of Aboriginal and Torres Strait Islander languages from different parts of the country.

Multilingualism[1] was widespread in the pre-contact period as there was no common Aboriginal language which was understood across all the country. Some 600 dialects belonging to in excess of 270 different languages were spoken throughout the continent at the time of the invasion (House of Representatives Standing Committee on Aboriginal and Torres Strait Islander Affairs, 1992:1). However, non-Aborigines are generally ignorant of the linguistic richness of the indigenous Australians. This ignorance is reflected in questions like *Can you speak Aboriginal?* or *What's the Aboriginal word for_____?* Some books written as late as 1990s, are being sold that contain words drawn from Australian languages where the words are glossed simply as *An Aboriginal word for_____* even though the source language is known and the information is readily available. The Macquarie Library publication *Macquarie Aboriginal Words* (Thieberger and McGregor, 1994) attempts to address this situation with the publication of wordlists in 17 selected languages from different parts of Australia. Each vocabulary list is prefaced with a short introduction placing the language within its geographical, historical and social context. Unfortunately the spin-off publication, *Macquarie Aboriginal Naming Book* (1996) is a retrograde step, again lumping together words from different languages and downplaying the association between a language, its territory and speakers. No advice is given to the reader of this latter publication about choosing local words and the need to consult with the relevant Indigenous language community.

Census statistics and language policies often lump all Aboriginal languages together, even though the same documents distinguish between other minority languages.

The current status and distribution of Australian languages

Only a small proportion of the 270 or so languages once spoken in Australia remain as fully viable languages, that is, they are still being acquired by children and spoken "right through", and used, in all areas of contemporary life. Some 20 languages, including Pitjantjatjara, spoken in the northwest of South Australia, are in this category (Schmidt, A, 1990:1). Map 7.1 is a guide to the distribution of strong Aboriginal languages.

It is reasonable to speculate that all of Australia's languages are threatened. In fact, one linguist warns that:

> If nothing is done about it, almost all Aboriginal languages will be dead by the year 2000. Even the two most likely groups to survive, the Yolngu languages of north-east Arnhem Land and the Western Desert language may not last long beyond that date (McConvell, 1991:143).

Once the domains or areas of life in which the language is constructed and used are invaded and restricted, then there is cause for concern. A language might be used only at home or just with the older generation or exclusively for traditional matters. Even the strongest languages like Pitjantjatjara are undergoing radical changes. Some domains of vocabulary, for example, names of stars or fine distinctions in the meaning of closely related words, are falling into disuse and are not known by the younger generation. All languages change, new words are invented and some words are lost. That is a natural progression. However, the rate of change in most Australian languages is so rapid and the influence of English so strong that the very integrity of the languages is threatened.

KEY

1.	Warlpiri	3,000 +	9. Kaitej	200
2.	Arrente dialects	3,000 +	10. Maung	200
	—Western, Eastern Arrente		11. Burarra	400-600
	—Anmatjirra		12. Ndjebbana	200-
	—Alyawarra		13. Yindjibarndi	500-600
3.	Western Desert, eastern	3,000+	14. Nyangumarta	700-800
	—Pitjantjatjara		15. Jaru	250
	—Pintupi-Luritja		16. Western Destert, western	1,000+
	—Yankunytjatjara		—Manjiljarra	
4.	Murrinh-Patha	900+	—Yulparija	
5.	Tiwi	1,400	—Martu Wangka	
6.	Dhuwal-Dhuwala dialects (Yolnu)		—Gugaja	
	—Gupapuyngu	1,700-2,000	—Ngaanyatjara	
	—Djambarrpuyngu		17. Wik Mungkan	900-1,000
	—Gumatj		18. Kala Lagaw Ya	3,000-4,000
7.	Gunwinggu	900	19. Thayore	500
8.	Anindilyakwa	1,000+	20. Kuku Yalanji	300

Map 7.1: Distribution of Strong Aboriginal Languages

Source: Schmidt, A (1990)

A number of languages in the Pilbara, Kimberley, Northern
Territory and northern Queensland have just one or a handful of older
speakers remaining. Once those older speakers die, much of those
languages will be lost. It is important that as much recording and
documentation of Aboriginal and Torres Strait Islander languages as
possible is done now, while these speakers remain. Some languages
have been lost almost without trace. In other cases a short word list
remains; for some only the name remains. Undoubtedly some
languages have disappeared without trace. Map 7.2 shows the distribution of severely threatened Aboriginal languages.

Map 7.2: Distribution of Severely Threatened Aboriginal Languages

Source: Schmidt, A (1990)

Table 7.1 Severely Threatened Languages and numbers of Speakers

1	Walmajarri	1000	36	Koko Bera	50
2	Guugu Yimithirr	400	37	Oykangand	50
3	Nunggubuyu	300-400	38	Yir Yoront	50
4	Dhangu dialects	350	39	Lardil	50
5	Kija	300	40	Mudbura	50
6	Ritharngu	300	41	Yuwarliny	50-
7	Dijinang	200-300	42	Kurrama	50-
8	Gurindji	250	43	Marithiyel	50-
9	Garawa	200+	44	Marri Ngarr	30-50
10	Dharlwangu	200	45	Wageman	50-
11	Warumungu	200	46	Mangarayi	50-
12	Bardi	100-200	47	Wardeman	50-
13	Meriam Mir	100+	48	Nyigina	20-50
14	Wik Nganthana	100-200	49	Dyirbal	40
15	Jawony	100+	50	Alawa	30
16	Ngalkbun	100-200	51	Yawuru	30
17	Iwaidja	180	52	Ngardi	30
18	Ngarinman	170	53	Djamindjung	30
19	Rembarrnga	150	54	Adnyamathanha	20+
20	Ngarluma	100	55	Banjalang	20+
21	Wik Nganjara	100	56	Karajarri	20
22	Gunbalang	100	57	Worrorra	20
23	Ngaliwuru	100	58	Wunambal	20
24	Marri Jabin	100	59	Malngin	20
25	Gooniyandi	100	60	Nyungar	20
26	Ngarinyin	100-	61	Djingili	20
27	Umpila	100-	62	Gungoragone	20
28	Ngankikurungkurr	100-	63	Ngalakan	20
29	Nakara	75-100	64	Mangarla	20-
30	Bunaba	501-00	65	Miriwoong	10-20
31	Kaiadilt	70	66	Ngarla, Nyamal	10
32	Yanyuwa	7-100	67	Madngele	10?
33	Watjarri	50	68	Maramanindji	10?
34	Panyjima	50	69	Batyamal	10?
35	Wanyjirra	50	70	Malak Malak	10?
				Maranungku	??

Source: Schmidt, A (1990).

Note: These speaker numbers are very rough estimates and not final. They are provided to give some indication of the radically low number of speakers for each language. These figures are based on Black and Walsh (1982), Thieberger (1987), McGregor (1989), advice from communities and scholars in each region, and my own observations during the course of this project. Only languages with more than 10 fluent speakers are listed. This list is not exhaustive. It is the best estimate possible based on available information at the time of writing this report. All comments and corrections are welcome.

In the literature many Aboriginal languages, including Kaurna, the language of the Adelaide Plains, have been referred to as "dead" or "extinct". For instance, Schmidt (1990:2) classifies 160 of Australia's 270 languages, that is 59%, as "extinct". But zoological metaphors do not apply well to languages. The language may cease to be spoken "right through" or cease to be spoken as a first language, but, typically, memories of a language linger on and remain for many years afterwards. For instance, a number of words of Tasmanian languages are still remembered and used within the Palawa[2] community there. Invariably the languages are still of considerable significance to the descendants of their speakers. This is certainly the case in Tasmania where Tasmanian Aborigines have obtained considerable funds under the Aboriginal Languages Initiatives Program to retrieve and reclaim their linguistic heritage. A composite language, known as *Palawa Karni,* is, according to Gaye Brown (1995), "being successfully revived and taught around Tasmania".

In some cases, with access to old written records, knowledge in the community can be increased considerably. The Kaurna language of the Adelaide Plains is an interesting case to consider. It is believed that Kaurna ceased to be spoken as a mother tongue back in 1929, or perhaps even earlier, with the death of Ivaritji (Gara, 1990:66). Nungas in Adelaide are now reclaiming that linguistic heritage and some are beginning to relearn the language. The programs are drawing primarily on early descriptions of the language, especially Teichelmann and Schürmann (1840).

Throughout the 1990s, Kaurna language programs have been introduced at all levels of education, including within early childhood, primary, secondary, adult and tertiary programs. Kaurna was first introduced within a Songwriter's workshop in 1990, then taught in workshops of one or two weeks duration held just once a year. On the strength of this, Kaurna was introduced as the school language program at Kaurna Plains School in 1992 and is taught to students across all year levels. In 1994 it was added as a compulsory component to the Cultural Instructors and Tourism course at Tauondi, the Aboriginal Community College in Port Adelaide and later that year introduced to Year 11 at the then Elizabeth City and Elizabeth West campuses of Inbarendi College. In 1997 the Kaurna language was taught as a component of the compulsory Aboriginal Studies program taught to all Year 8 students at Fremont-Elizabeth City HS and a course in Kaurna linguistics has been developed and is being taught at the University of Adelaide.[3]

The reclamation of Kaurna is still in its infancy. However, greetings such as *Ninna marni?* (Are you good?) and leave-takings such as *Nakkota or Nakkiota!* (Will see [you]!) along with relationship terms such as *ngarpadla* (aunty) and *kauwawa* (uncle) have come back into common usage, within that school community and to some extent within the wider Kaurna community. Children within the school programs are now using longer expressions, such as *Kudnawodlianna padniai?* "May I go to the toilet?" and are beginning to use the language amongst themselves.

Many songs and stories have now been written in the Kaurna language. Nursery rhymes and European stories have been translated into Kaurna and new terms have recently been developed in Kaurna. For example, *padnipadnitti* (car), *karrikarritti* (aeroplane), *mukamuka karndo* (computer, from brain + lightning), since shortened to *mukarndo, turraturrarndiappetti* (photocopier), *warraityatti* (telephone), *turraityatti* (television) and other terms have been coined by drawing on productive word-forming processes that are described or evident in the early descriptions of the language (see Amery, 1993). The Kaurna language is also being used increasingly to deliver speeches at public meetings, a practice that is becoming part of protocol at Indigenous and other events held in Adelaide and elsewhere in Kaurna country.[4] Hence one must ask: Is Kaurna really "dead" or "extinct"?

The revival of Kaurna goes hand in hand with reclaiming Kaurna heritage, especially sites of significance, and a revival of other aspects of Kaurna culture. The language is helping to forge a stronger sense of Kaurna identity, as distinct from Nunga identity, and is contributing to the rebuilding of Kaurna society.

There is growing interest throughout Australia in reviving and reclaiming Aboriginal linguistic heritage. In addition to Kaurna and the Palawa Karni, revival programs are operating in Nyungar at Bunbury, south of Perth and in Djabugay, Dyirrbal and other languages in northern Queensland which are no longer spoken in everyday life. A number of languages in New South Wales including Bandjalang, Gumbaynggir, Paakantji, Ngiyampaa, Wangkumara and Gidabul have also been introduced into schools. Yorta Yorta was introduced into Worawa College on the outskirts of Melbourne, whilst Ganai is now taught at a Koorie school in Gippsland, Victoria. Larakiya and Kungarakany have been taught in recent years in a Darwin high school. In a number of communities and schools across Western Australia and the Northern Territory where language use has been restricted to the older generations, revitalisation programs have been implemented to increase knowledge and use of the language within the younger generations. The revival of Aboriginal languages is nation-wide.

Despite the emphasis on the maintenance of viable languages inherent in *Australia's Languages: The Australian Language and Literacy Policy* (1991), the majority of Aboriginal Languages Initiatives Programs identified in that policy is in fact going to support languages other than those deemed to be viable.

The nature of Australian languages

The working assumption among practicing linguists is that almost all the languages of Australia are genetically related, sharing a common ancestor (Walsh, 1991:33). It is not certain, however, that the languages of Tasmania are part of this language family. At the same time there is nothing to suggest that they are not related.

Within Australian languages, there is a basic division between the languages of the north and north west of Australia and the languages of the rest of the continent. The languages of the north and north west of Australia are *prefixing* (and *suffixing*) while the languages of the rest of the continent are strictly *suffixing*. See map 7.3 on the following page for an illustration of the classifications of Australian Languages. Schmidt (1919), working with limited data, first proposed this north versus south division. The boundary between these two groups of languages was repositioned by Capell (1956) and revised later by Hale (1964).

The vast majority of Australian languages are thought to belong to the suffixing Pama-Nyungan[5] language family while the prefixing (and suffixing) non-Pama-Nyungan languages are thought to be distributed across 20 to 30 language families. While there is undoubtedly a fairly strict division on typological grounds, the genetic basis of the Pama-Nyungan versus non-Pama-Nyungan dichotomy has been questioned recently. More detailed work is needed to clarify the situation.

There is a remarkable similarity of sound systems of Australian languages in all but a few phonologically deviant languages of the Cape York Peninsula, which have markedly different sound systems. The grammars of Australian languages, too, show marked similarities across the continent, yet there is considerable diversity within the vocabulary of the languages. The phonological similarity plus grammatical similarity combined with a diversity in vocabulary provides a contrast with the way diversity is managed in literate societies.

Map 7.3: major classifications of Australian Languages

Source: Dixon, RMW (1980).

Key to the major classifications of Australian Languages

Alawa 100
Alyawarra 84
Andegerebina 83
Anguthimri 5
Anindilyakwa 105
Anmatjera 85
Arabana 132
Aranda 82
Arandic sbgp 82-6
Atampaya 3
Awabakal 49
Awngthim 5
Baagandji 72
Balyku 150
Banjalang 42
Banyjima 150
Baraba-Baraba 68d
Bardi 140
Bariman Gutinhma 14
Bidyara 40c
Biri 36
Biyaygirri 33
Bunaba 126
Bungandij 71
Burarra 109
Burduna 151
Daly River sbgp 119-21
Darkinyung 50
Dhalandji 151
Dharawal 52
Dharuk 51
Dhuduroa 59
Dhurga 55
Dhuwala/Dhuwal 107
Diyari 129
Djapu 107
Djaru 138
Djinah 108
Djingili 97
Dyangadi 47
Dyirringany 56
Eastern Torres Straits
Language 2
Gabi 38
Gadang 48
Gamilaraay 61
Garadyari 143
Gariyarra 148
Girramay 30
Gog-Nar 24
Gugada 133i
Gugu-Badhun 32
Gugu-Wara 21

Gagu-Yalanji 22
Gulhay 30
Gumbaynggir 45
Gunbalang 115
Gundungura 53
Gunggari 40d
Gunggay 29
Gungoragone 112
Gunibidji 111
Gunwinygu 114
Gunwinygu sbgp 113-15
Gunya 40b
Gupapuyhu 107
Gureng-Gureng 37
Gurindji 137
Gurrama 147
Guugu Yimidhirr 23
Guwa 81
Guwamu 40c
Jab Wurrung 68c
Jabugay 28
Jaitmathang 59
Jaja Wurrung 68f
Jirrbal 30
Jirru 30
Kaititj 36
Kala Lagau Langgus 1
Kalkatungu 89
Keramin 74
Kitja 127
Koko-Bera 19
Kolijon 69
Kukatj 26
Kuku-Thaypan 18
Kunggari 80
Kurnu 72
Kuuku-Ya'u 9
Kuurn Kopan Noot 70
Lama-Lama 17
Lardil 95
Linngithigh 7
Madhi-Madhi 68b
Malak-Malak 120
Malyangapa
Mamu 30
Mangala 142
Mangarayi 99
Mantjiltjara 133c
Mara 101
Maranunggu 121
Margany 40a
Maric sbgp 32, 36, 40, 81
Maung 116

Mbabaram 27
Mbara 31
Mbiyoom 8
Mpalitjanh 4
Mudbura 137
Muk-Thang 60
Murawari 41
Murinypata 122
Nakara 110
Ngaanyatjara 133c
Ngajan 30
Ngaliwuru 123
Ngamini 131
Ngandi 103
Nganyaywana 46
Ngarigo 54
Ngarla 145
Ngarluma 148
Ngarndji 98
Ngawun 35
Ngayarda sbgp 145-50
Ngayawung 76
Ngiyambaa 63
Nhanda 154
Nhuwala 149
North Kimberly sbgp 124-5
Northern Paman sbgp 3-8
Ntra'ngith 5
Nunggubuyu 104
Nyamal 146
Nyanganyatjara 133g
Nyangatjatjara 133h
Nyawaygi 44
Nyigina 141
Nyungal 22
Olgolo 20
Oykangand 16
Pallanganmiddang 58
Peek Whurrong 70
Pintupi 133d
Pitjan(tja)tjara 133f
Pitta-Pitta 87
Rembarrnga 113
Ritharhu 106
Tanganckald 77
Thargari 152
Thawa 57
Tiwi 118
Tycraity 119
Umbuygamu 13
Umpila 9
Ungarinyin 125
Uradhi 3

Waga 39
Wagaman 22
Wakoora 22
Walmatjari 139
Wambaya 92
Wangaaybuwan 63
Wangganguru 132
Wangkumara 79
Wari 30
Warlmanpa 136
Warlpiri 135
Warluwarra 90
Warndarang 102
Warnman 134
Warrgamay 33
Warumungu 91
Warungu 32
Wathawurrung 67
Wemba-Wemba 68a
Wergaia 68c
Western Desert 133
Western Torres Straits
Language 1
Wik-Me'nh 12
Wik-Muminh 11
Wik-Munkan 10
Wiradhuri 62
Worora 124
Wuywurrung 66
Yabula-Yabula 64
Yadhaykenu 3
Yalarnnga 88
Yandruwanhtha 130
Yanyuwa 96
Yaralde 77
Yawuru (Yauor) 141
Yaygir 44
Yidiny 29
Yinggarda 143
Yinwum 6
Yinyjibarnrdi 147
Yir-Yoront 15
Yitha-Yitha 73
Yiwaja 117
Yolhu sbgp 106-8
Yota-Yota 65
Yugambal 43
Yukulta 94
Yulbarija 133b
Yuwaalarraay,
Yuwaaliyaay 61
Yuyu 75

Note: A single number is used for each language; the location of dialects is shown only for Margany, Wemba-Wemba and Western Desert.

The matter of vocabulary difference is intriguing. Linguists have pointed to the high rate of vocabulary replacement, contributed to by taboos on the use of names (or words sounding similar) of recently deceased persons and borrowing from other groups as possible causes. The Reverend Bill Edwards records that when he first lived with the Pitjantjatjara, *kapi* was the word for water. It is actually a Yankunytjatjara word. It was replaced by *mina* and still later by *kumpili*.

The lexical competence of the average speaker of an Aboriginal language is equivalent to that of the average speaker of other languages. The vocabularies of Aboriginal languages allow their speakers to express their mythology, culture, thoughts and feelings. Working vocabularies in excess of 10,000 words are common. Aboriginal languages belong to different cultures with different values and belief systems to English-speaking cultures. They are rich in ritual vocabulary and in words which express understanding of spirituality. In some cases language and vocabulary are taught through ceremony and ceremonial knowledge is a reflection of hierarchical stratification.

Aboriginal vocabularies reflect an intimate knowledge of the physical and social environment. Fine distinctions are made between vocabulary relating to flora, fauna and seasons. Desert groups, for example, have various words for different types of sand and for plants and animals at different stages of development. When referring to plants, reptiles and insects, speakers of Aboriginal languages typically employ specific species names. Unlike plant names in English, such as *blackberry,* or *ghost gum*, plant names in Aboriginal languages usually consist of a single word that is totally unrelated to other words in the language.

Aboriginal languages, like other languages, have complex and intricate grammatical structures. A typical Australian language has nine or ten parts of speech including nouns, verbs, pronouns, adverbs and, frequently, adjectives. Some parts of speech such as indefinite articles (words like *a* and *an* in English) are absent, but Aboriginal languages have their own complexities.

Some languages, such as Pitjantjatjara, have a set of independent pronouns, as in English, used alongside pronoun suffixes or bound pronouns that are attached to other parts of speech (for example, verbs). Compare the following Pitjantjatjara sentences:

> *Ngayulu nyuntunya nyangu.* (I saw you.)
> *Nyangunanta.* (I saw you.)
> (where the suffix -na = *ngayulu* 'I' [subject] and -nta = *nyuntu* 'you' [object]).

Australian languages typically employ suffixes or endings, known as a *case system,* instead of prepositions such as *in, to, from, by* and so on. Consider the following words in Yolngu Matha from north east Arnhem Land:

rangingura	*on* the beach
ranginguru	*from* the beach
rangikurru	*along* the beach
rangilili	*to* the beach
rangipuy	*associated with* or *belonging to* the beach
miyalkthu	*by the* woman (subject: Ergative case)
miyalknha	the woman (object: Accusative case)
miyalkkungu	*from/by* the woman
miyalkkala	*to/with* the woman

Australian languages are referred to as *ergative* languages by linguists (along with Basque, Hindi, Fijian). Ergativity is a fundamental concept in Aboriginal languages but is peripheral in English, restricted to constructions such as causatives.

In an ergative language, the subject of a *transitive* verb (for example, hit, see, hold) is marked differently to the subject of an intransitive verb (for example, sit, stand, sleep). In fact, usually the object of a transitive verb takes the same form as the subject of an intransitive verb. Consider for example the Yolngu Matha sentences:

> Miyalkthu weti lukana. *(The woman ate wallaby.)*
> Miyalk wandina. *(The woman ran.)*
> Weti wandina. *(The wallaby ran.)*

Note the suffix *-thu* on *miyalk* (woman) in the first sentence. This indicates that the woman, *miyalk,* is the subject and the one "eating" something. The patient or object is *weṯi* (wallaby). The suffix *-thu* is defined as the *ergative case suffix*.

English and most other languages use fixed word order to indicate which participant in the sentence is the subject and which is the object. Because Aboriginal languages have case suffixes,[6] this allows considerable flexibility of word order. In fact, any ordering of the constituents in the sentences above is possible.

Aboriginal languages exhibit many structures that make them difficult for English speakers to learn. Typically Australian languages have pronoun systems that differentiate between singular, dual and plural pronouns. Pronouns, too, take different forms depending on their case, that is, depending on their function within the sentence.

Note the following sentences in Kaurna and their English translations, which illustrate thirteen different forms for which the second person pronoun "you" is required in English:

Ninna tikkandi.	You (one) are sitting.
Niwa tikkandi.	You (two) are sitting.
Na tikkandi.	You (many) are sitting.
Nindo ngai nakki.	You (one) saw me.
Ngatto paru ninnanni yunggi.	I gave (to) you (one) meat.
Ngatto paru niwanni yunggi.	I gave (to) you (two) meat.
Ngatto paru nanni yunggi.	I gave (to) you (many) meat.
Pa nindaitya padni.	He/she went to you (one).
Pa niwadlitya padni.	He/she went to you (two).
Pa naalitya padni.	He/she went to you (many).
Pa nindaityangga tikki.	He/she sat/stayed with you (one).
Pa niwadlityangga tikki.	He/she sat/stayed with you (two).
Pa naalityangga tikki.	He/she sat/stayed with you (many).

In English there is just one second person pronoun *you* which remains the same whether it is referring to one, two or more people and whether the referent is the subject or object of the sentence. In Kaurna one would have to choose between *ninna* (you: *one*), *niwa* (you: *two*), *na* (you: *many*), *nindo* (you: *one as agent*), *ninnanni* (to you: *one*), *niwanni* (to you: *two*), *nanni* (to you: *mob*), *nindaitya* (towards you: *one*), *niwadlitya* (towards you: *two*), *naalitya* (towards you: *mob*), *nindaityangga* (with you: *one*), *niwadlityangga* (with you: *two*) and *naalityangga* (with you: *mob*). to translate the English word "you". Similarly, there are many words which translate as "you" or "yours".

Despite the fact that relatively few number terms are employed, a feature shared by many Aboriginal languages, Kaurna has distinctive birth order names[7] for the first, second, third, fourth child, right up to the ninth born child. These birth order names are also differentiated for gender.[8]

	Female	*Male*
First born	*Kartanya/Kartiato*	*Kartamerru*
Second born	*Waruyu/Warriarto*	*Warritya/Yerraitya*
Third born	*Kudnato*	*Kudnuitya*
Fourth born	*Munato*	*Munaitya*
Fifth born	*Midlato*	*Midlaitya*
Sixth born	*Marruato*	*Marrutya*
Seventh born	*Wanguato*	*Wangutya*
Eighth born	*Ngadlaato*	*Ngadlaitya*
Ninth born	*Pauane/Pouarna*	*Pauane/Pouarna*

These terms appear to have been frequently used. Birth order names are also used in some other SA languages, for example, Nukunu, Adnyamathanha.

Australian languages have many more relationship or kinship terms than English and the kinship systems are organised along somewhat different principles to English. Typically, terms which would most readily translate as *mother* and *father*, for example *ngunytju* (mother) and *mama* (father) in Pitjantjatjara, in fact refer to a number of people. *Mama* (father) refers to father's brothers and others in that "father" relationship to the individual, while *ngunytju* (mother) also refers to one's mother's sisters and others in a "mother" relationship. Some terms are not easy to translate into English but they are still basic terms within Australian languages.

Many Aboriginal words have no equivalent English meaning. The Pitjantjatjara word *tjukurrpa*, for instance, is often translated as "dreaming". But this does not really capture the essence of the term. *Tjukurrpa* is glossed in Goddard's dictionary as *Dreaming, Law (often, and appropriately, spelt with a capital letter in this usage). Note that there seems to be an emerging Aboriginal preference for this use of the word not to be given an English equivalent at all* (Goddard, 1987:145).

Place names, in particular, generally cannot be translated from Aboriginal languages into English.

Forms of communication

Prior to the invasion in 1788, Australian languages were not written, though the precursors of writing existed in the symbols used in message sticks, drawings or bark and sand paintings. The writing systems used today were first developed by missionaries and linguists. The Kaurna language of the Adelaide Plains was first written down in the 1830s and first described by Teichelmann and Schurmann (1840). One of the first recorded documents in an Australian language, written by Aboriginal people, was a letter written in Kaurna to Governor Gawler in 1841 by Kaurna children who attended the Native Location School or Piltawodli. This letter appeared just five years after the proclamation of the colony of South Australia. By contrast, the slow spread of European settlement into the more arid areas meant that Pitjantjatjara was not recorded in a written form for another century, until a mission was established at Ernabella in 1937 (Gale, 1992).

In Central Australia and, undoubtedly, in other areas as well, sand painting or ground drawings were used to reinforce verbal communication. They were used to illustrate stories told to children, stories related to the group's activities, Dreaming stories and ceremonies. Interestingly, a number of today's coffee table books on Aboriginal art contain illustrations or photos of sand paintings, along with an explanation in English or the language of the artist or both. Hence, Aboriginal people are adjusting to new ways of communicating.

In Alice Springs Aboriginal people have set up their own media services in Central Australian Aboriginal Media Association Radio and IMPARJA TV. Both CAAMA and IMPARJA produce programs in a number of Central Australian languages.

As well as speaking aloud, Aboriginal people used handsigns or gestures to communicate. This happened when people were hunting and didn't want their prey to hear, when gossiping, if endeavouring to be secretive or when ritual demanded silence be enforced.

Australian languages typically have highly conventionalised sign languages, highlighting complexity in this area. Nowadays, sign languages provide a very useful medium for conducting a conversation while travelling in a noisy vehicle.

Secret/sacred languages are limited to certain audiences. In parts of Central Australia, newly initiated boys are secluded from the main group and are required to use a special set of words. In many parts of Australia, for example Dyirrbal in north-east Queensland, separate vocabularies are used between a woman and her son-in-law. Other special vocabularies consist of words for sacred matters known only to fully initiated men or words revealed at different periods in a man's life as he progresses through rituals. Women also have their own vocabularies for their own cultural activities and rituals.

Trading routes criss-crossed the continent. Trade was facilitated by multilingualism or knowledge of a number of languages. These trading routes facilitated the spread of vocabulary across the continent. Terms for new concepts spread from one language to another. It is interesting to consider the terms for *horse* in the languages of Australia. Two terms are widespread. *Yarraman* (horse), originally from around Sydney, spread across eastern Australia and up into north-east Arnhem Land. It seems that the word had been absorbed into some languages even before the first appearance of horses into the region (Dixon, Ramsom and Thomas, 1990:231). *Nantu* (horse), from *nanto* (kangaroo) in Kaurna, the Adelaide language, spread up through South Australia into the Centre and parts of Western Australia.

Pidgins, creoles and Aboriginal English

In some parts of Australia new languages, *creoles*, have developed (Mühlhäusler, 1991). Where speakers of different languages have been brought together and need to communicate with each other, a *pidgin* will sometimes emerge. A pidgin language is a simplified code with a reduced vocabulary and a simplified grammar. A pidgin is nobody's first language. It is used for restricted purposes. When a pidgin becomes acquired by children as a first language it rapidly increases in complexity and its vocabulary expands. This new complex language is called a *creole*.

Linguistically, creoles are on a par with any other language. Australian creoles draw words from a number of languages, though the majority originate from English. However, they are not readily understood by English speakers. They have their own grammar and structure. With more than twenty thousand speakers, there are now more speakers of Kriol[9], spoken across the Kimberleys, the cattle country of the Northern Territory and into Queensland, than of any other contemporary Australian language. Torres Strait Islanders have developed their own creole referred to as Broken or Torres Strait Creole.

While the majority of urban Aboriginal people speak English and often have little knowledge of their ancestral languages, they are still typically linguistically distinct in that they may speak a variety of English in their family situations and social networks that is not shared and is often poorly understood by other Australians. Aboriginal English varieties spoken in urban settings are social dialects and are linguistically distinct from standard Australian English (see Malcolm and Kaldor, 1991). They may reflect grammatical structures and features of the sound systems of their ancestral languages which have long ceased to be spoken. They may also incorporate words from those ancestral languages or use English words in different ways or with changed meanings. In some places Aboriginal English varieties are diverging from Australian English spoken in the same urban centre. The speech of urban Aboriginal people may range from standard English through to varieties of Aboriginal English which on occasion may not be understood by non-Aboriginal Australians. Many urban Aboriginal people are adept at switching between standard English and Aboriginal English varieties, depending on the context and to whom they are talking.

Language policy and language education

Australian society generally is poorly informed about the existence of Australian languages, of their value, and uniqueness, and also about the fragile and endangered state of some of many, if not all, of them. As these languages are central to Aboriginal identity, it follows that non-Aboriginal Australians are generally ignorant of the expressed needs, aspirations and cultures of Aboriginal people.

Many Aboriginal people use their languages to fulfil all their needs. Knowledge about Aboriginal languages and the ways languages are used is vital to the appreciation and understanding of Aboriginal cultures.

Colonisation of Australia caused drastic social changes which have resulted in actual or imminent extinction for many Australian languages. The early missionaries and government officials suppressed the use of Aboriginal languages because they were a major expression of Aboriginal identity. While Aboriginal people continued to speak their own languages, they were also regarded as heathen rubbish, and such use was seen as a threat to imposed authority. The speaking of Aboriginal languages was often viewed by authorities as a sign of failure to conform and assimilate. This was sufficient, in some cases at least, for children to be separated from their parents if they were caught using their own languages.

However, recent Government policies (eg Department of Employment, Education and Training, 1991:90-96) have supported initiatives which assist the preservation, use and reconstruction of Aboriginal languages. Australian Aboriginal language issues are matters of national significance with respect to Australian heritage and identity. Australian language heritage should be important to all Australians. It is a unique national treasure. It can provide a key to understanding the continent in which Australians live. Australian languages are obviously of even more significance to Aboriginal and Torres Strait Islander people. The continued active use and recording of Aboriginal languages is fundamental to the survival of Aboriginal cultures and identity. Therefore, language maintenance programs for Aboriginal children are necessary for the survival of those Aboriginal languages still being used on a daily basis.

Aboriginal and Torres Strait Islander people live in a range of socio-cultural settings throughout Australia. The term *traditionally-oriented* is used to characterise Aboriginal people who follow their own customs and use their own language rather than English in their family situations. Many Aboriginal people in this category are multilingual. They may speak more than one Australian language as well as English. In addition, they may use an Australian creole.

The proper provision of government services to traditionally-oriented Aboriginal communities requires appropriate translating and interpreting services. Professional translating and interpreting services will ensure that non-English speaking Aboriginal people are able to deal with the wider community and are ensured access to information and services which might otherwise not become known to them. These services exist in Alice Springs and are coordinated by the Institute for Aboriginal Development.

In the Northern Territory, bilingual education programs were implemented in the early 1970s with the primary aim of facilitating the learning of English by establishing early conceptual development at school and literacy skills in the child's first language. In more recent times, language maintenance has been increasingly identified as the reason for implementing bilingual programs. Currently, 21 official bilingual programs operate in 17 languages in Northern Territory schools.

Yipirinya is an independent Aboriginal school in Alice Springs, established so that Aboriginal children learn "both ways", that is, to read and write in the Aboriginal way and the non-Aboriginal way. The school's curriculum offers a bilingual and bicultural program, with both Aboriginal and non-Aboriginal curriculum components. Hartman and Henderson eds. (1994) and McKay (1996) provide excellent descriptions of language programs in schools and in communities in a range of settings.

Generally, Aboriginal and Torres Strait Islander languages have suffered in the past under both government and non-government education systems. They have seldom been taught as first or second languages in schools or universities. Despite a clearly identifiable need that has been recognised for some time, it wasn't until 1994 that an Australian language was taught at senior secondary level in an accredited course. Prior to this, in excess of thirty languages other than English had been accredited by senior secondary assessment authorities around Australia, but not one Australian language was included. The House of Representatives Standing Committee on Aboriginal and Torres Strait Islander Affairs in *A matter of survival* (1991:51) noted that:

> The committee finds it intolerable that while most migrant children with a first language other than English have been able to study that language up to matriculation level, most Aboriginal and Torres Strait Islander children cannot study their language at high school.

The Australian Indigenous Languages Framework was a federally funded national curriculum initiative, implemented from 1993 to 1996 sought to address these needs. In 1994, several Australian languages, including Eastern Arrernte in Alice Springs, Pitjantjatjara/Yankunytjatjara in Port Augusta, Antikirinya in Ooodnadatta, Gupapuyngu at Worawa College near Melbourne and Kaurna in Adelaide were taught for credit in senior secondary schools for the first time.

The project recognised the diversity among Australia's languages and the different historical experiences that each of these languages has undergone. The framework (AILF, 1996a; 1996b; 1996c) is flexible enough to accommodate all Australian languages and linguistic heritage, whether the language is spoken by entire communities and still acquired by children or whether it is no longer spoken. The project aims to teach all Australians about the nature of Australian languages and their importance to both Aboriginal Australians and the wider community. While recognising the loss of linguistic heritage the main focus is to celebrate the survival of Aboriginal and Torres Strait Islander languages and their continuing and increasing importance in Australian society.

Furthermore, the study of Australian languages serves to increase the standing and status of these languages within Australian society, which in turn impacts positively on their long term survival. Positive attitudes to languages are fundamental to their maintenance and continued use and vitality.

Language centres

Language centres were initially established in the Kimberleys and Pilbara in Western Australia and in Alice Springs and Tennant Creek in the Northern Territory where they have been particularly active. Aboriginal language centres have now been established around the country to provide maximum access with limited resources. Language recording, research and publication facilities are made available to a range of language groups within the one centre. These centres are funded from a variety of sources, including Commonwealth funds under the Aboriginal and Torres Strait Islander Languages Initiatives Program (ATSILIP). A review of this program was conducted recently (NLLIA, 1995) and a second commissioned report into language maintenance and development needs (McKay, 1996) contain the most up to date information on activities within Aboriginal language centres.

Work on Australian languages has shifted away from the production of esoteric linguistic descriptions and analyses of languages written primarily for other linguists to the development of more "hands-on" materials for the lay person and school use. The Australian Institute for Aboriginal and Torres Strait Islander Studies (AIATSIS) has coordinated an Aboriginal Dictionaries Project, resulting in the production of 20 dictionaries in 1992/93. A further 20 or so dictionaries are in production. Many of these dictionaries concern languages, such as Dharuk from Sydney, Nukunu from Port Augusta, Wiradjuri from the Riverina in NSW and Wamba Wamba[10] from northwest Victoria, which are no longer spoken fluently as a first language. Nick Thieberger whilst at AIATSIS produced a set of Hypercard stacks on Australian languages which provides information stacks on the distribution, vocabulary, writing systems, pronunciation and other aspects of Aboriginal languages, providing an excellent resource for schools and the general community. Many local initiatives are also producing multimedia resources in specific languages within community-based and school-based programs.

Aboriginal language centres, the Australian Institute of Aboriginal and Torres Strait Islander Studies (AIATSIS) in Canberra or universities offering studies in Australian linguistics, can provide more detailed information on the languages of Australia. The University of South Australia offers three subjects in Pitjantjatjara language as part of its undergraduate awards within its Aboriginal and Islander Studies program. The Institute for Aboriginal Development in Alice Springs offers courses in a number of central Australian Languages and the Centre for Aboriginal and Islander Studies at the Northern Territory University in Darwin offers courses in the Yolngu languages from north-east Arnhem Land. Monash University is still teaching Bundjalung at its Gippsland Campus and, as of July 1997, the University of Adelaide offers a course in Kaurna language and linguistics.

Conclusion

Australian languages are a fundamental part of Australia's national heritage. As such they are of importance to all Australians, but especially to Aboriginal and Torres Strait Islander people. Indigenous Australians are the custodians of this heritage. All the languages of Australia are important. There are, however, many languages which are still spoken, sometimes by just a handful of speakers, which are in need of assistance. It is a matter of national urgency to assist those communities to maintain, revive and reclaim their linguistic heritage should they desire to do so. It is their basic human right to reclaim and maintain that heritage.

References

Amery, Rob (1993). "Encoding new concepts in old languages: a case study of Kaurna, the language of the Adelaide Plains". *Australian Aboriginal Studies,* no. 1, pp 37-47.

Amery, Rob (1996). "Kaurna numbers, maths and the quantification of time" (a draft discussion paper). *Kaurna Language and Ecology* Readings, vol. 1, pp 157-163. University of Adelaide.

AILF (1996a). *Australia's Indigenous Languages Framework.* Wayville: Senior Secondary Assessment Board of South Australia.

AILF (1996b). *Australia's Indigenous languages in practice.* Wayville: Senior Secondary Assessment Board of South Australia.

AILF (1996c). *Australia's Indigenous Languages.* Wayville: Senior Secondary Assessment Board of South Australia.

Blake, Barry J (1991). *Australian Aboriginal Languages: a General Introduction.* 2nd edition. St Lucia, Qld: University of Queensland Press.

Brown, Gaye (1995). "Nina tunapri mina karni? Do you understand what I'm saying?". *Alive andDeadly.*

Capell, A (1956). *A new Approach to Australian Linguistics.* Sydney: Oceania Linguistic Monographs.

Department of Employment, Education and Training (1991). *Australia's Language: The Australian Language and Literacy Policy.* Canberra: Australian Government Printing Service.

Dixon, RMW (1980). *The Languages of Australia.* Cambridge: Cambridge University Press.

Dixon, RMW, Thomas, WS and Thomas, Mandy (1990). *Australian Aboriginal Words in English: Their Origin and Meaning.* Melbourne: Oxford University Press.

Edwards, WH (1988). *An Introduction to Aboriginal Societies.* Wentworth Falls, NSW: Social Science Press.

Gale, Mary-Anne (1992). *Dhangum Djorra'wuy Dhäwu: the Development of Writing in Aboriginal Languages in S.A. and the N.T. Since Colonisation.* Masters of Education thesis. Darwin: Northern Territory University.

Gara, Tom (1990). "The life of Ivaritji ('Princess Amelia') of the Adelaide Tribe". In *Aboriginal Adelaide.* Special issue of the *Journal of the Anthropological Society of South Australia,* vol. 28, no. 1, pp 64-104.

Goddard, Cliff (1987). *A Basic Pitjantjatjara/Yankunytjatjara to English Dictionary.* Alice Springs: Institute for Aboriginal Development.

Hale, Ken (1964). "Classification of the Northern Paman Languages, Cape York Peninsula, Australia: a research report". *Oceanic Linguistics,* vol. 3, nos. 248-65.

Hartman, Deborah and Henderson, John (1994). *Aboriginal Languages in Education.* Alice Springs: Institute for Aboriginal Development Press.

House of Representatives Standing Committee on Aboriginal and Torres Strait Islander Affairs (1992). *Language and Culture—a Matter of Survival. Report of the Inquiry into Aboriginal and Torres Strait Islander Language Maintenance.* Canberra: Australian Government Printing Service.

McConvell, Patrick (1991). "Understanding language shift: a step towards language maintenance". In *Language in Australia,* edited by S Romaine. Cambridge: Cambridge University Press.

McKay, Graham (1996). *The Land Still Speaks: Review of Aboriginal and Torres Strait Islander Language Maintenance and Development Needs and Activities.* National Board of Employment, Education and Training commissioned report, no. 44. Canberra.

Macquarie Library (1996). *Macquarie Aboriginal Naming Book*. Sydney: Macquarie Library. Macquarie University.

Malcolm, Ian G and Kaldor, Susan (1991). "Aboriginal English—an overview". In *Language in Australia*, edited by S Romaine. Cambridge: Cambridge University Press.

Mühlhäusler, Peter (1991). "Overview of the pidgin and creole languages of Australia". In *Language in Australia*, edited by S Romaine. Cambridge: Cambridge University Press.

NLLIA (1995). *Backing Australian Languages: Review of the Aboriginal and Torres Strait Islander Languages Initiatives Program*. Canberra: National Languages and Literacy Institute of Australia Limited.

Social Change Media (1995). *Alive and Deadly: Reviving and Maintaining Australian Indigenous Languages*. DEET funded project. Leichardt, Sydney: Social Change Media.

Schmidt, Annette (1990). *The Loss of Australia's Aboriginal Language Heritage*. Canberra: Aboriginal Studies Press.

Schmidt, W (1919). *Die gliederung der Australischen sprachen*. Vienna.

Teichelmann, CG and Schürmann, CW (1840). *Outlines if a Grammar, Vocabulary and Phraseology of the Aboriginal Language of South Australia*. Facsimile edition 1982. Largs Bay: Tjintu Books.

Thieberger, Nicholas. Editor (1995). *Paper and Talk: a Manual for Reconstituting Materials in Australian Indigenous Languages from Historical Sources*. Canberra: Aboriginal Studies Press.

Thieberger, Nicholas and McGregor, William. Editors (1994). *Macquarie Aboriginal Words*. Sydney: Macquarie Library, Macquarie University.

Walsh, Michael (1991). "Overview of indigenous languages of Australia". In *Language in Australia*, edited by S Romaine. Cambridge: Cambridge University Press.

Yallop, Colin and Walsh, Michael (1993). *Language and Culture in Aboriginal Australia*. Canberra: Aboriginal Studies Press.

Endotes

[1] Multilingualism is defined as the use of a number of different languages within the same speech community.

[2] Words drawn from Aboriginal languages are often used in preference to *Aborigine* or *Aboriginal*. No universal term is accepted. Different groups have their own in-group terms to refer to themselves. *Palawa* is used in Tasmania, *Koori* in New South Wales, Victoria and until recenlty in Tasmania. *Nunga* in the south of South Australia, *Nyungar* in the south west of Western Australia and *Yolgnu* in the north of the Northern Territory and so on. These terms are used when referring to people from those specific areas.

[3] A set of language learning tapes and accompanying tape transcripts have been produced and books of course readings compiled.

[4] More than 150 Kaurna speeches have been given durng the period 1991-1997, and the number given each year is increasing exponentially. The number of Kaurna people delivering the speeches is also increasing year by year.

[5] Pama-Nyungan languages extend across most of the continent from Cape York Peninsula where the word for man/person is *pama*, to south-western Australia where *nyungar* for man/person is found.

[6] By contrast English employs prepositions such as *in, at, on, by, for, to, through* etc. where Aboriginal languages typically employ case suffixes or endings attached to the noun in a similar fashion to Latin.

[7] The roots of these birth order names, together with words such as *irka* 'heap'; *parto irka* 'big heap'; *tauatta* 'many' and *wiwurra* 'multitude', have been used to develop a Base-10 number system which is able to count up into the millions (Amery 1996).

[8] In the table below, terms are drawn from several Kaurna sources, but especially Teichelmann and Schürmann(1840) and Eyre (1845).

[9] Kriol is the name given to a particular creole language spoken in the Northern Territory and Western Australia.

[10] Throughout the *Chapter* some Aboriginal words are spelt more than one way, for example, Wamba Wamba is also written as Wemba-Wemba.

Chapter 8

Living Wisdom: Aborigines and the Environment

Olga Gostin and Alwin Chong

Introduction

This chapter explores Aboriginal attitudes towards the environment
with special emphasis on indigenous systems of knowledge and
their relationship to local technologies and science. These aspects of
Aboriginal cultures have perhaps been the least understood or most
misinterpreted by Europeans, whose own attitudes to the
environment, science and technology are cast in a completely
different mould. The Aboriginal world view is essentially *inclusive*
or *holistic*. Humans and all aspects of human endeavour, as well as
nature and all natural phenomena, including animals and plants in
all their diversity, are seen as equal manifestations of a timeless
spiritual or cosmic order. The origins, meaning and integrity of
these cultural codes are not open to challenge.

Thus the Kaurna people of the Adelaide Plains of South
Australia have a markedly different perception of their world order
and their very interpretation of the environment is different to that of
non-Aborigines. For example, the Mount Lofty Ranges represent
the body of the ancestral hero Urabilla. It forms the boundary
between Kaurna and Peramangk territory. Based on an expression of
their personal belief system, the Kaurna, therefore, see the Mount
Lofty Ranges differently from non-Aboriginal people for whom the
ranges are a geological feature that has no necessary personal
connection to anybody at all (P Clarke, 1990, 1991).

The European world view tends to separate the spiritual, natural
and human domains whose characteristics and attributes are ever
open to challenge, debate and reinterpretation. In this lies another
important distinction between the two cultural traditions as
expressed in attitudes towards knowledge. In the Aboriginal world
view, knowledge is an extension of the cosmic order and comprises
the accumulated wisdom of the group since time immemorial,
handed down from generation to generation by word of mouth. This

does not mean that the body of knowledge is changeless or finite, but rather that changes and additions become incorporated into the collective wisdom of the group. The individual acquires this knowledge progressively and cumulatively during a lifetime punctuated by periods of intense learning now described in many parts of Australia as "going through The Law". Knowledge is acquired both by imitation in day to day contact with peers and older persons, and by bestowal by specialist older persons. In the latter instance, knowledge is often transferred in a highly charged ritual setting which excludes those who are not undergoing the same experience. It does not invite debate or challenge. The individual progresses through stages of specialised learning and graduates with a different status, new knowledge, new privileges and new responsibilities. This change in status is universally accepted by the group whose acceptance enforces the person's new role and responsibilities derived directly from having tapped into the ancient wisdom of the group. The diversity of Aboriginal Australia is such that not all Aboriginal people necessarily access the same sources of knowledge. Even so, the role of older persons and kin groups in passing on knowledge is universally acknowledged.

The European quest for knowledge, by contrast, is markedly different in character. It is essentially an individual search driven by specialist interests backed by open access to the accumulated knowledge of past generations stored in written form. The cosmic order has itself been secularised and the quest is to establish verifiable facts and theories in an atmosphere of detached critical analysis and intellectual debate.

This impersonal academic tradition is a far cry from the highly ritualised bestowal of knowledge upon a neophyte by the custodians of ancient wisdom. The end product of the two traditions results in a very different reading of the environment and a different perception of what, in the West, is identified as science and technology, and in Aboriginal culture is celebrated as ancient wisdom and traditional skills. This is not to say that Aboriginal people did not or can not think about the environment in a scientific or rational way. They can and do (Lewis, 1993; Hunn, 1993; Healey, 1993).

Adapting to environment

Aboriginal Australians have indeed proved successful in adapting to their environments—which range from the tropical island habitat of the Torres Strait to the desert of the Centre; from the rain forests of the tropical north to the temperate rain forests of Tasmania; from the riverine basin of the Murray Darling to the lacustrine environment of Lake Eyre.

The successful adaptation and survival of Australian hunting and gathering communities in this vast continent was firmly founded on a detailed understanding of nature and natural phenomena. This knowledge was integrated into socio-economic structures which facilitated successful adaptation to a variety of environments. This approach was very different from the attitude towards the environment which evolved over centuries in Europe. It was characterised by the notion that humans are dominant over nature and that "progress" lies in being able to evade, if not control, the vagaries of climate, environmental adversity and other natural phenomena.

Adaptation in the Pleistocene[1]

Versatility and adaptability are indeed the most striking feature of Aboriginal cultures, not only in historical times but extending to the very earliest periods of Aboriginal settlement of Australia. Geological evidence suggests that for the last 100,000 years, during the so called late Pleistocene period, Australia experienced several glacial peaks about 100,000, 60,000, 40,000 and 18,000 years ago. During these times, sea levels fell by up to 140 metres, creating the greater Australian land mass known as the Sahul, which included Papua New Guinea and Tasmania in a continuous land mass one-seventh larger than present day Australia.

During the inter-glacial periods, when the polar ice caps melted due to global warming, the ocean levels rose again, flooding areas which had hitherto sustained human occupation. Aboriginal people not only coped but thrived in these highly changeable periods, populating the continent and the extended coastal areas during the ice ages and retreating inland or to the new coastal margins as the sea levels rose.

This would have had implications for economic systems as people moved into new ecological areas. No doubt there would have been political and demographic implications too, as the flooded coastal people encroached upon the inhabited hinterland. The social and spiritual adaptations which ensued are open to speculation. The constant factor was the need to adapt to each successive period of change. The latest flooding of Bass Strait about 10,000 years ago, isolated the Tasmanians from mainland Australia, and left them to develop their culture in unprecedented isolation from outside influences (Flood, 1995).

The formation of the Torres Strait Islands

The Torres Strait was flooded about 8,000 years ago and the people of the Sahul plains between Papua New Guinea and the Australian mainland found themselves retreating to the higher points in their territory—now the islands of the Torres Strait. Here the new maritime society developed a uniquely vibrant culture blending features of their Melanesian neighbours to the north and cultural attributes of the Aboriginal people to the south (Arthur, 1992; Smith, Spriggs and Fankhauser, 1993).

The Strait covers a total area of over 40,000 km2 made up mostly of open ocean. Some 100 islands and islets dot this vast continental shelf habitat which has been described as one of the most ecologically complex areas in the world (Nietschmann, as quoted by Mulrennan, 1992). Four separate island groups can be distinguished, as shown in the map on page 148.

The four separate island groups of the Torres Strait:

- A western group of high islands of acid volcanic and granitic rocks characterised by a mixed economy of fishing and gardening. The main islands here include Badu, Moa and Mabuiag. Thursday Island, the administrative centre for the Torres Strait, forms part of the Prince of Wales group of islands which falls within the geographic boundaries of the western group.
- A central group of low coral cays surrounded by coral reefs whose inhabitants depend almost totally on fishing as there is very little soil that can cultivated. These include Coconut, Warraber (Sue), Yorke and Yam Islands.

Map 8.1: map of Torres Strait Islands

Source: Beckett, J (1987).

- An eastern group of high islands with fertile volcanic soils derived from the eroded remnants of volcanic cones. These include Mer (home of the famous Mabo land claim), Erub (Darnley) and Stephens Island. The islanders here enjoy a mixed economy based on fishing, pig husbandry and gardening.
- The north western islands of Boigu, Saibai and Dauan lie close the Papuan mainland and consist of low lying mangroves swamps and peats. The people on these islands survive by trading with their neighbours.

The inhabitants of these four island groups show subtle cultural adaptation to the limitations of resources provided by their different island habitats.

According to the 1996 Australian Census some 6,300 Islanders reside on 16 inhabited islands in the Strait and two communities (Seisia and Bamaga) on the tip of Cape York. In addition, another 22,000 Islanders live on the Australian mainland where they maintain links with their home islands, particularly at times of communal ritual importance such as mourning feasts which culminate in the unveiling of tombstones (Australian Bureau of Statistics, 1997; Beckett, 1987).

Megafauna[2]

Just as the Torres Strait Islands with their distinctive culture emerged as a result of the dramatic rise in sea levels at the end of the last ice age, other parts of the continent also experienced vast environmental changes as a result of associated climatic shifts.

For example, the Lake Eyre Basin was once part of a large inland water system which sustained humans and unique Pleistocene animals known as *megafauna,* creatures such as Diprotodon, Procoptodon and Zaglossus, corresponding to giant wombats, kangaroos and echidnas (Quirk and Archer, 1983; Vickers-Rich, 1991). These large animals, which were also found in other parts of Australia and which were unique to this continent, became extinct in Central Australia about 35,000 to 40,000 years ago, yet lingered around the coastal margin till as recently as 14,000 years ago.

The circumstances of their extinction are still debated. Some scientists argue that megafauna were victims of changes in climate which led to marked changes in habitat and hence to the demise of

Short-faced giant kangaroo
Procoptodon pusio

Diprotodon optatum

Zygomaturus trilobus

Marsupial lion
Thylacoleo carnifex

Palochestes azeal

Giant wombat
Phascolonus giges

Common wombat
Vombatus ursinus

Human
Homo sapiens

Eastern grey kangaroo
Macropus giganteus

Figure 8.1: megafauna with human scale

Source: Smith, J (1986).

the large herbivores. Others have taken the view that Aboriginal hunting practices were responsible (Flannery, 1994), while others still have sought an explanation in a combination of climatic factors, habitat changes and human impacts such as hunting and firestick farming (Horton, 1980; Kohen, 1995). The fact remains that the megafauna disappeared but Aboriginal people survived the vagaries of climate and habitat change with characteristic versatility.

Lake Mungo

Two examples highlight the contrasting adaptation of Aboriginal people to the challenge of climatic and environmental changes. In both incidents technological skills and detailed knowledge of the environment ensured survival and the development of a prosperous lifestyle. The first example refers to Lake Mungo in western New South Wales about 100 km north east of Mildura. It is one of a series of lakes making up the Willandra Lakes system. Over the last 50,000 years Lake Mungo has undergone periodic rises and falls in water level, corresponding to changes of climate over the continent. They culminated with the lake totally drying out about 15,000 years ago. When the Willandra Lakes were full they provided a resource-rich environment which saw the flowering of a civilisation featuring ceremonial burial practices rating among the oldest recorded on Earth (Bowler, 1990; Flood, 1995).

It was here that Mungo Lady was buried after being cremated about 26,000 years ago. Some 500 metres from this site an even older burial shows a fully extended recumbent adult male whose body had been anointed with ochre. Dated at 36,000 years, Mungo Man conclusively shows that Aboriginal people were engaged in metaphysical thinking and elaborate burial practices far earlier than conventional thinking had suggested.

More importantly, the uniform size of fish remains (as noted by the otoliths or ear bones) found in 30,000 year old hearths not far from the burial sites, suggests that the Mungo people engaged in gillnet fishing. This implies that a fairly sophisticated technology of making string and nets was in place at that time. When the lake finally dried up 15,000 years ago, the local Aboriginal people adapted from a lacustrine resource-rich economy to one focussed on the grass plains involving a mixed economy based on hunting game

and harvesting native grasses and local produce (Balme, 1991).
Today, the Mutthi Mutthi, Barkindji and Ngyiampaa groups form a
living link with this ancestral place and are directly involved in
passing on knowledge to the younger generation. The vital
importance of Lake Mungo in world human evolution was
recognised in 1981 when it was placed on the World Heritage List
(Gostin, 1993; World Heritage Australia, 1996).

Lake Condah

A second example of successful technological adaptation by
Aboriginal people occurs at Lake Condah in western Victoria. Here
the Kerrup-Jmara people turned the eruption of Mt Eccles about
6,000 years ago to their advantage by arranging volcanic basalt
boulders into an elaborate system of weirs, channels and stone walls
which effectively regulated the flow of the local Darlot River. This
complex of structures described by archaeologists as a "marvellous
piece of prehistoric hydro-engineering" ensured the harvesting of a
steady supply of fish and migratory eels (Coutts, Frank and Hughes,
1978). This enabled the local populace to live semi-permanently in
the area as shown by the circular (3m in diameter) foundations of
some 200 stone houses. Some controversy surrounds the
interpretation and usage of smaller stone circles (1m in diameter).
Builth (1996) suggests that these might have been eel storage
facilities used by the local people, in the tradition of similar
practices in Europe and among some Native Americans groups.
Anne Clarke (1994) on the other hand, suggests that these stone
circles are merely caused by natural processes. The debate underlines
the continuing ambivalence of European scholars in interpreting the
diversity and cultural complexity of classical Indigenous Australian
groups (Lourandos, 1995).

Firestick farming[3]

Aboriginal people have shown versatility in the face of major
climate and environmental changes. While some environmentalists
have promoted Aboriginal people as model conservationists, it must
be remembered that the original Australians had an impact on the
continent for tens of thousands of years. To some extent it would be
true to say that the whole of Australia is an Aboriginal artefact

(Langton, 1995). The reference here, of course, is to *firestick farming* which Aboriginal people have practised from the earliest times. This involved systematic burning of the countryside in a chequered or mosaic pattern which had the multiple effect of flushing out game, rejuvenating plant growth and attracting animals once new regrowth started. Such burning was founded on precise knowledge of seasonal and local weather patterns as well as on botanical knowledge of what plants were pyrophyllic (fire loving) and what plants were not fire tolerant (Latz, 1995; B Rose, 1995b; D Rose, 1995).

Burning was controlled and "safety zones" surrounded places of special ritual importance and areas vegetated by plants which disliked regular burning. On the other hand, burning helped stimulate the simultaneous fruiting of *macrozamia* plants of the cycad family to the extent that ceremonies could be planned months ahead in expectation of a bountiful supply of food from this plant. The use of macrozamia as a food raises the question of how and why it became a food staple given that in its natural state the fruit is highly toxic and has to be treated by elaborate soaking and leeching procedures before it can be safely eaten. In fact, archaeological evidence suggests that macrozamia became part of the Australian diet only as recently as 5,000 years ago (Flood, 1995).

It is possible that the long term effect of firestick farming changed the plant succession in the continent from Casuarina dominance to Eucalyptus and other fire-loving plants as early as 100,000 years ago. This remains a contentious issue and awaits confirmation if and when human occupation is proved at this early time (Blainey, 1978; Singh et al, 1981; Smith, 1986).

In any case, Aboriginal people, while managing their resources, were actively engaged in modifying the landscape. Systematic burning on a regular basis, resulted in low intensity fires which gave rise to an open landscape favouring the proliferation of herbivores like kangaroos. Ironically, the original Australians thereby set the scene for the pastoral invasion of the British settlers.

From the earliest days of contact, the British commented on the "burning continent" and the firestick practices of the Aboriginal people (Hallam, 1975). As the European frontier extended inland and Aboriginal land management practices were forcefully repressed, the plant succession hitherto managed by firestick burning was radically modified (Smith, 1992b). Clearings gave way to a tangle of undergrowth. When burning occurred, whether by design or by accident, this gave rise to devastating high intensity fires which destroyed both the undergrowth and the tall tree canopy. The scene was thus set for plant destruction and soil erosion on an unparalleled scale.

Technology and science

In the past, and to some extent, even today, Westerners have tended to pass judgement on Aboriginal cultures and peoples by regarding their level of technological sophistication and achievements in material culture as the gauge of so-called cultural advancement. In the words of George Taplin, missionary among the Ngarrindjeri of South Australia:

> Man, in order to get his living, must have an implement...In this very necessity lies all the capacity for unlimited advances in human condition. The improvement of the human race has its origin in this necessity for the use of an implement. The 'zero of humanity' will be the tribe which has fewest and rudest tools, the most imperfect weapons, and which obtains its subsistence most from the spontaneous productions of the country where it lives (Taplin, 1879:9).

Such an equation, based on only one aspect of culture, the technological or material, completely misses the spiritual, ethical and social dimensions of living as expressions of the quality of life.

Advanced technology and scientific thinking are not the exclusive prerogative of the West, even though science has evolved there, as a specific methodology characterised by highly specialised disciplines operating in a reductionist, analytical and experimental framework. For indigenous cultures, scientific thinking is incorporated into a total body of knowledge, the collective wisdom of the elders of a particular group. Scientific principles do inform these traditional forms of knowledge, as well as many practices of indigenous cultures. The distinguishing factor is that Aboriginal cultures make no firm demarcation between so-called scientific thinking, social values and beliefs, technology and other aspects of culture. Indigenous cultures have evolved a detailed and profound knowledge of nature and humankind seen as an inseparable whole, expressed in ritual and song cycles, oral traditions, ceremonies and practices which do not necessarily conform to conventional scientific norms yet embody a wealth of often precise and detailed verifiable knowledge. It is important to emphasise that such knowledge is localised and that Aboriginal knowledge systems (unlike their western counterparts) do not seek to universalise (D Rose, 1996).

The integration of mythical beliefs and natural phenomena is exemplified in the following example. Looking at the night sky, the Western Desert people will focus on the dark patches in the Milky Way and discern the outline of an emu with the head approximately in the area of the Southern Cross. At different times of the year the night sky emu will be fully extended as though running, or compactly "sitting". This corresponds in real life to the time when emus may be hunted or when they are nesting and should not be disturbed (C Cameron, 1992, pers.comm). Similar associations apply to seasonal cycles, the life cycle of animals, the fruiting of plants, though it must be noted that not all groups have access to the same knowledge about the Sky Beings.

Among the Ngeamba people of western New South Wales for example, the "sky country" is the home of their creative beings. In the words of Fred Biggs, a Ngeamba man:

> There's Ngintu, with his dogs, who guards the skins
> of Everlasting Water in the sky.
> And there's the Crow-man, carrying on his back
> the wounded Hawk-man. There's the serpent, Thurroo,
> glistening in the leaves. There's Kapeetah.
> the Moon-man, sitting in his mia-mia.
>
> And there's those Seven Sisters, travelling
> across the sky. They make the real cold frost.
> You hear them when you're camped out on the plains.
> They look down from the sky and see your fire
> and 'Mai, mai, mai,' they'd sing out as they run
> across the sky. And, when you wake, you find
> your swag, the camp, the plains, all white with frost
> (Robinson, 1970:25).

The Indigenous Australians have also had a long association with technology and their understanding of the environment and natural processes has stood the test of time. Changes in world view and attitudes to the environment no doubt can and did occur, but always in the context of a hunter-gatherer lifestyle. For Aboriginal people, technology is an extension of everyday living, an extension of the self. In such a society there is no redundancy, no mass production and no impersonal manufacturing.

Classical (pre-1788) Aboriginal cultures can be popularly described as Stone Age in the sense that stone tools were the basic implements which, in turn, helped to fashion wooden tools as well as bone and shell implements. Archaeologists vary in their categorisation of the stone tool sequence, though most would agree that the oldest tools tend to be larger, and of the so-called *core tool* and *scraper* tradition, while a more distinctive small tool assemblage made up of geometric points appeared about 6,000 years ago (Flood, 1995; Mulvaney, 1975). These tools were carefully selected, shaped and fashioned into spearhead-like shapes. Other tools, such as adzeheads, were hafted or attached to wooden handles with spinifex resin, wax, animal sinew and/or string made from bark or human hair. An interesting feature of Aboriginal technology is that modern media were incorporated into the traditional tool kit very soon after first contact and sometimes even ahead of actually meeting the first Europeans (Reynolds, 1981:7). Thus, beautifully worked glass tools can be found, as well as implements using steel. Later still, hub caps, bicycle spokes, crow bars and beer cans were fashioned into functional tools such as digging implements and scoops.

Some non-Aboriginal people today make blanket generalisations about Aboriginal technology without understanding the degree of specialisation of individual tools or the extent of regional diversity across the continent. For example, the boomerang and the didgeridoo are promoted as ubiquitous Aboriginal symbols. In fact the distribution of these artefacts was localised and their use determined by gender and/or limited to certain members of a community. The boomerang was not found in all parts of Australia and varied greatly in size and mode of use. Some were returning, most were non-returning (P Jones, 1996). Likewise, the didgeridoo originated in the north of the continent as a strictly male artefact though its diffusion as a commercial tourist artefact has greatly diversified its role (Barwick, 1997).

Altogether some 120 distinct artefacts have been recorded on mainland Australia ranging from the beautiful and intricate basketry of the Ngarrindjeri of the Coorong of South Australia to the multifunctional, highly specialised *woomera* or spear thrower of the Western Desert people. The eastern seaboard people used complex fishing equipment including bone hooks, while the Murray-Darling dwellers fished from their bark canoes with the aid of fire at night to attract the fish. In the Torres Strait the outrigger canoe, possibly an innovation adapted from Macassan traders, gives stability to hunt sea turtles and the dugong and facilitates safe movement in the open sea. Other artefacts include digging sticks, carrying dishes (*coolamon*) which double up as water dishes and/or scoops, clubs and spears. The characteristic feature of these artefacts is that they were portable, generally multi-functional and an expression of the identity of their owner/maker. Some tools because of their size (eg. grinding stones) or because of their ritual uses were not transported but kept in special places.

In European countries, technology has assumed an impersonal dimension characterised by anonymous mass production and is no longer necessarily related to simplicity, function or even usefulness. In a general way, technological know-how, as expressed through the proliferation of material goods, has become the criterion for gauging so-called cultural development. Starting from this Western point of view, Rhys Jones raises a contentious issue in his film, *The Last Tasmanians,* when he identifies a tool kit of only twenty-two artefacts and argues that this so-called decline in technological skill is an indication that the Aboriginal Tasmanians were in a process of cultural degeneration when compared to the richer cultures of the mainland.

It could, however, be argued that the Tasmanians had refined their management of resources and satisfaction of needs to the point that they needed only minimal technology (Flood, 1995; Ryan, 1996). Even so, it remains a mystery why Tasmanians appear to have abandoned the making of bone tools and the eating of scaly fish some 3,000 years ago (Allen, 1979; R Jones, 1977). Whatever the reason, it in no way detracts from the remarkable achievements of the Tasmanians whose hand stencils in Kutikina Cave, dated at some 20,000 years ago, testify to their presence at the peak of the last glacial period. At that time, the Tasmanians represented the southernmost point of human occupation on earth.

Aboriginal practices revisited

Human impacts on the Australian environment have greatly accelerated since the arrival of the Europeans some 210 years ago. Careless farming practices, deforestation, over-fertilising, the practice of monoculture and over-stocking have resulted in land degradation and soil erosion across the continent, indicating major environmental mismanagement. It is only in comparatively recent times that non-Aboriginal people have turned to the management practices of the original Australians as a method of possible alternative land use. Thus, regular low intensity burning has been re-introduced at Kakadu National Park (Birckhead et al, 1992; Lewis, 1989). The joint management of parks is increasingly being regarded as the ideal means of combining indigenous knowledge and land care practices with the management skills and technical know-how of non-Aboriginals (B Rose, 1995a).

Permaculture[4] is also finding acceptance and respectability as a more sustainable form of land use (Mollison and Holmgren, 1984). In effect this mirrors the Aboriginal practice of harvesting a variety of crops in a sustainable way in the natural environment. One of the benefits of this new-found respect for Aboriginal botanical knowledge and land management skills is a re-discovery of Aboriginal pharmaceutical and medicinal practices (Low, 1990, 1991; Aboriginal Communities of the Northern Territory of Australia, 1988). Many of these are firmly based on verifiable scientific facts and have generated a flurry of activity to retrieve and safeguard this knowledge lest it be lost to humankind.

The same point is made in the ABC TV series *Bushtucker Man* which explores the rich diversity of the Australian environment and, most importantly, reveals the depth of knowledge and understanding of the natural environment of the original Australians. However, many Aboriginal people believe that the series would have been more appropriate with Aboriginal persons identified as the focal and unifying point. As it stands, the series is regarded as a form of cultural appropriation. While they are proud of the belated recognition given to the richness of their cultures, Aboriginal people resent the way aspects of their ancient knowledge and wisdom were recorded and interpreted and are handled today. More recently, leading Aboriginal academics such as Marcia Langton (1993) and Wendy Brady (1997) have been most outspoken against cultural appropriation and commercialisation, seen as the latest expression of colonial dispossession. The associated issues of intellectual property rights, cultural appropriation, copyright and ethical considerations are now being integrated into protocols dealing with Indigenous Australian groups. This will undoubtedly affect the nature and context of research in Aboriginal cultures.

Conclusion

Against the current anxiety over environmental issues, it could be argued that a re-orientation and re-assessment of nationwide attitudes to land use and land management is essential. It should be clear from this exploration of Aboriginal wisdom and attitudes to the environment, that a more enlightened way lies ahead in the blending of western and indigenous systems of knowledge. The collective wisdom of both cultures could then ensure a more holistic approach to everyday life. In an ideal setting, science, technology and the environment would no longer be discrete units, but vital connections between human beings and the natural environment in which they live.

References

Aboriginal Communities of the Northern Territory of Australia (1988). *Traditional Bush Medicines: An Aboriginal Pharmacopoeia.* Richmond Victoria: Greenhouse Publications.

Allen, H (1979). "Left in out in the cold: why the Tasmanians stopped eating fish". *The Artefact,* vol. 4, pp 1-10.

Arthur, W (1992). "Culture and economy in border regions: the Torres Strait case". *Australian Aboriginal Studies,* vol. 2, pp 15-33.

Australian Bureau of Statistics (1997). *1996 Census of Population and Housing Australia.* Canberra: Australian Government Printers.

Balme, J (1991). "The antiquity of grinding stones in semi-arid western NSW". *Australian Archaeology*, no. 32, pp 3-9.

Barwick, L (1997). "Gender 'taboos' and didjeridus". In *The Didjeridu: from Arnhem Land to Internet*, edited by Karl Neuenfeldt. Sydney: John Libbey and Company.

Beckett, J (1987). *Torres Strait Islanders: Custom and Colonialism*. Melbourne: Cambridge University Press.

Birckhead, J; De Lacy, T and Smith, L (1992). *Aboriginal Involvement in Parks and Protected Areas*. Canberra: Aboriginal Studies Press.

Blainey, G (1978). *Triumph of the Nomads: a History of Ancient Australia*. Melbourne: Sun Books.

Bowler, J (1990). "Human occupation and environmental change: the ancient records of the Willandra Lakes". In *The Mallee Lands: a Conservation Perspective*. Proceedings of the National Mallee Conference, Adelaide—1989, April. Edited by JC Noble, J Joss and GK Jones. Melbourne: CSIRO.

Brady, W (1997). "Australian indigenous rights in education". *Campus Review* [Special Report on Indigenous Education] June 25 - July 1, 1997, pp 15-16.

Builth, H (1996). *Lake Condah revisited: archaeological constructions of a cultural landscape*. BA Honours Dissertation. Adelaide: University of South Australia.

Clarke, A (1994). "Romancing the stones: the cultural construction of an archaeological landscape in the Western District of Victoria". *Archaeology in Oceania*, 29, pp 1-15.

Clarke, P (1990). "Adelaide Aboriginal cosmology". *Journal of the Anthropological Society of South Australia*, 28 (1 and 2), pp 1-9.

Clarke, P (1991). "Adelaide as an Aboriginal landscape". *Aboriginal History*, 15 (1), pp 54-73.

Coutts, P; Frank R and Hughes, P (1978). "Aboriginal engineers of the Western District, Victoria". *Records of the Victorian Archaeological Survey*, vol. 7.

Dargin, P (1976). *Aboriginal fisheries of the Darling-Barwon Rivers*. Brewarrina: Brewarrina Historical Society.

Flannery, T (1994). *The Future Eaters: an Ecological History of the Australasian Lands and People*. Chatswood: Reed.

Flood, J (1995). Revised edition. *Archaeology of the Dreamtime*. Sydney: Angus and Robinson.

Gostin, O (1993). *Accessing The Dreaming: Heritage, Conservation and Tourism at Mungo National Park*. Adelaide: Aboriginal Research Publications.

Hallam, S (1975). *Fire and Hearth: a Study of Aboriginal Usage and European Usurpation in South-western Australia*. Canberra: Australian Institute of Aboriginal Studies.

Healey, C (1993) "The significance and application of TEK". In *Traditional Ecological Knowledge: Wisdom for Sustainable Development*, edited by N M Williams and G Baines. Canberra: Centre for Resource and Environmental Studies, Australian National University, pp 21-26.

Horton, D (1980). "A review of the extinction question: man, climate and megafauna". *Archaeology and Physical Anthropology in Oceania*, vol. 15, pp 86-97.

Hunn, E (1993) "What is traditional ecological knowledge?" In *Traditional Ecological Knowledge: Wisdom for Sustainable Development*, edited by N M Williams and G Baines. Canberra: Centre for Resource and Environmental Studies, Australian National University, pp 13 -15.

Jones, P (1996). *Boomerang: Behind an Australian Icon*. Adelaide: Wakefield Press.

Jones, R (1969). "Firestick farming". *Australian Natural History*, vol. 16, no. 7, September 1969, pp 224-228.

Jones, R (1977). "The Tasmanian paradox". In *Stone Tools as Cultural Markers: Change, Evolution and Complexity*, edited by R Wright. Canberra: Australian Institute of Aboriginal Studies.

Kohen, J (1995). *Aboriginal Environmental Impacts*. Sydney: University of New South Wales Press.

Langton, M (1993). *Well, I Heard it on the Radio and I saw it on the Television* (italics). Sydney: Australian Film Commission.

Langton, M (1995). "Wilderness—the European cult". *Land Rights Queensland*, December 1995, p 13.

Latz, P (1995). *Bushfires and Bushtucker: Aboriginal Plant use in Central Australia*. Alice Springs: IAD Press.

Lewis, H (1989). "Ecological and technological knowledge of fire: Aborigines versus park rangers in Northern Australia". *American Anthropologist*, vol. 91, pp 940-961.

Lewis, H (1993). "Traditional ecological knowledge—some definitions". In *Traditional Ecological Knowledge: Wisdom for Sustainable Development*, edited by NM Williams and G Baines. Canberra: Centre for Resource and Environmental Studies, Australian National University, pp 8 -12.

Lourandos, H (1985). "Intensification and Australian prehistory". In *Prehistoric Hunter-gatherers: the Emergence of Cultural Complexity*, edited by Douglas Price and James Brown. Sydney: Academic Press.

Lourandos, H (1997). *Continent of Hunter-gatherers: New Perspectives in Australian Prehistory*. New York: Cambridge University Press.

Low, T (1990). *Bush Medicine: a Pharmacopoeia of Natural Remedies*. North Ryde: Angus and Robinson.

Low, T (1991). *Bush Tucker: Australia's Wild Food Harvest*. North Ryde: Angus and Robinson.

Mollison, B and Holmgren, D (1987). *Permaculture one: Practical Design for Human Settlements*. Tyalgum, NSW: Tagari

Mulrennan, M (1992). *Coastal Management: Challenges and Changes in the Torres Strait Islands* (Discussion paper no. 5). Darwin: North Australian Research Unit.

Mulvaney, D (1975). *The Prehistory of Australia*. Ringwood: Penguin.

Quirk, S and Archer, M (1983). *Prehistoric Animals of Australia*. Sydney: Australian Museum.

Reynolds, H (1981). *The Other Side of the Frontier*. Townsville: James Cook University.

Robinson R (1970). *Altjerringa and Other Aboriginal Poems*. Sydney: Reed.

Rose, B (1995a). *Aboriginal Land Management Issues in Central Australia*. Alice Springs: Central Land Council.

Rose, B (1995b). *Land Management Issues: Attitudes and Perceptions Amongst Aboriginal People of Central Australia*. Alice Springs: Central Land Council.

Rose, DB, editor (1995). *Country in Flame: Proceedings of the 1994 Symposium on Biodiversity and Fire in North Australia.* Australian National University: Department of the Environments, Sports and Territories.

Ryan, L (1996). *The Aboriginal Tasmanians.* St Leonards: Allen and Unwin.

Singh, G; Kershaw, AP and Clark, R (1981). "Quaternary vegetation and fire history in Australia". In *Fire and the Australian Biota*, edited by AM Gill, RH Groves and IR Noble, Canberra: Australian Academy of Science.

Smith, J (1986). "Biogeography of Australian flora and fauna". In *A Natural Legacy: Ecology in Australia,* edited by H Recher, D Lunney and I Dunn. Sydney: Pergamon Press.

Smith, J (1992a). "The burning bush". In *The Unique Continent: an Introductory Reader in Australian Environmental Studies,* edited by J Smith. St Lucia: University of Queensland Press.

Smith, J (1992b). "The ecology and history of bushfires in Eastern Australia". In *The Unique Continent: an Introductory Reader in Australian Environmental Studies,* edited by J Smith. St Lucia: University of Queensland Press.

Smith, M, Spriggs, M and Fankhauser, B (editors) (1993). *Sahul in Review: Pleistocene Archaeology in Australia, New Guinea and Island Melanesia.* Canberra: Australian National University.

Taplin, G (1879). *Manners, Customs and Languages of the South Australian Aborigines.* Adelaide: Government Printer.

Vickers-Rich, P; Monaghan, JM; Baird, RF and Rich, TH, editors (1991). *Vertebrate Palaeontology of Australia.* Lilydale, Victoria: Pioneer Design Studio in cooperation with the Monash University Publications Committee, Melbourne.

World Heritage Australia (1996). *Sustaining the Willandra: Plan of Management.* Canberra: Department of the Environments, Sports and Territories.

Endnotes

[1] Pleistocene: Geological period characterised by ice ages covering the last two million years, but excluding the last ten thousand years known as the Holocene.

[2] Megafauna: Large animals, which in Australia were distinctive and became extinct during the late Pleistocene period.

[3] Firestick farming: Term coined by Rhys Jones (1969) referring to systematic and deliberate seasonal burning practised by Aboriginal people as a form of land management.

[4] Permaculture: A system of crop production based on a variety of perennial plants which are compatible and self-sustaining.

Chapter 9

Education: The Search for Relevance

Howard Groome

Introduction

Many colonial powers saw education as an essential aspect of their dealings with Indigenous peoples. Schools and schooling were regarded as tools by which they could control and transform the societies which they were supplanting. They used education in a variety of ways. It could be forced on Indigenous children, or it could be withheld from them; it could be delivered in second rate ways which denied these children real opportunities for development. All of these patterns can be seen in the history of the education provided for Indigenous Australians.

For Indigenous people themselves the struggle has been to find and achieve relevance; to find educational experiences for their children which both recognise their cultural background and assist them to take their place as full citizens in Australian society.

In this brief survey we will consider the three major phases in the history of Indigenous education before discussing some current issues. As a starting point however it is essential to consider the education practised by Indigenous people in Australia prior to colonisation.

Education and socialisation in Indigenous Australia

In pre-colonial Australia education was the responsibility of everybody and learning went on all the time. From an early age children were taught to closely observe every aspect of the world around them. They saw skills being modelled and were expected to replicate these, often with expert tuition. They listened to, and were expected to retain, the stories and songs which taught the moral principles of the Law. As they participated in family life they learnt the web of relationships to others around them. Part of that web was their own role as teachers, they were expected to pass on what they had leant to others younger than themselves.

The concern of the adults was to develop in the children practical skills of survival as well as social skills of living in harmony with others. They were expected to learn how to balance their own needs against those of others. The personal skills they gained were only of value if they enhanced the life of the group (Nganyintja Ilyatjari in Edwards, 1998:1-5).

As the children grew older the learning became more rigorous. In their teenage years the boys (and to a lesser degree the girls) were taken away from their family by elders. They entered into an intensive learning situation in which they were taught skills, knowledge, values in a setting which some Aborigines have compared to a residential university. This was just the beginning of a lifelong learning of advanced survival skills coupled with the complex spiritual knowledge and values of their people (Coombs et al, 1983).

The colonists, with very few exceptions, were totally unaware of the existence of these sophisticated learning systems and the values and lifestyles which underpinned them.

Early government schools 1830s and 1840s

Indigenous adults demonstrated from an early stage that they were not prepared to abandon their established culture and adopt that of the newcomers. The colonists therefore turned to their children as the ones through whom they would transform Indigenous society. The children became artefacts in a program of re-education. There was a naive belief among the colonial authorities that, with a little training, the children would gladly forsake their cultural roots. Schools for Indigenous children were opened in the early years of most early settlements. Some were day schools but, as Matthew Moorhouse, the Protector of Aborigines in South Australia, indicated in 1849, the preference was for boarding schools where contact with their families could be minimised.

> Our chief hope now is decidedly in the children; and the complete success as far as regards their education and civilisation would be before us, if it were possible to remove them from the influence of their parents (in Rowley, 1972).

The parents were reluctant to allow their children to attend and heavy bribery was frequently used to get the children to school.

> The children's attendance is procured in various ways–some will come into the School because they prefer a regular supply of food to an irregular one and especially in the winter season; others are sent by the parents on condition that they receive a blanket for three months' attendance and others again are sent by the police if found begging about town. No healthy adult is entitled to receive a blanket on the Queen's birthday unless he have a child in school (Moorhouse, in Mattingley and Hampton, 1988:100).

The schools were seen as an essential part of the colonising mission. The basic motives were reformist and assimilationist. The colonists believed that they had a God given task to "civilise and Christianise" the children of a people who they regarded as living in total degradation. The schools themselves were modelled on overseas practices, introducing a pattern which was to recur frequently in Indigenous education. Two influences were evident: strategies which had proved successful in colonising the Pacific Islands, and those developed in Britain itself. The British model was the school system developed in the Industrial Revolution. It had been designed to transform the redundant peasantry into the disciplined workforce needed in the new factories. This model gives a clue to the aims which the colonial powers had for Indigenous young people, to take their place in society at the lower level as a source of cheap labour.

There was little understanding of Indigenous culture, and no recognition of it in the schools. Bi-lingual schools which taught the children in their mother tongue as well as English were begun in Western Australia and South Australia in the 1830s. However public opposition forced them to stop educating in the mother tongue (Broome, 1982).

The colonists themselves were not blind to the tensions and contradictions about the fate of the Indigenous peoples. Newspapers contained many spirited debates about Indigenous issues, especially on the topic of education. Some of the writers, such as James Bonwick, understood the Indigenous position very clearly:

> We teach [the Aboriginal lads] to read, and their fathers want to instruct them in woodcraft. We show them how to handle the pen,

and they want to guide their arm with the spear. We give them light upon other countries, and they are losing time in learning the haunts of birds, the retreat of the wombat, and ways of the emu. We can train them in the elements of astronomy, but cannot give them the practical arts of the forest—the means of their life, and the source of high animal enjoyment. We cultivate their mental faculties, but dwarf their physical capabilities. The old warrior finds the schoolboy less fleet in the chase, less cunning on the trail, and less merry in the leafy glades as they despise the training we give the lads (Bonwick, 1862:127).

There is evidence from several of these schools that the Indigenous children were good learners. Some achieved results superior to those of contemporary white students (Woods, 1994:27). However, as time passed Indigenous parents began to increasingly resist these moves to educate their children. They were finding that, despite the promises made by colonial leaders, those children who had gained European skills were not successful in achieving worthwhile permanent work or acceptance in white society. They were learning too, as many of their descendants were to learn, that education was no guarantee against the prejudices of endemic racism.

These early schools closed as they were boycotted by parents. By the end of the 1850s there were no government schools for Indigenous children anywhere in Australia. Governments passed the responsibility for the "protection" of Indigenous people to churches and other groups. For the next 100 years provision for the needs of Indigenous families in most states would be on the "missions" run by these groups. Governments however were to retain, and even increase their control over the lives of individual Indigenous children.

Indigenous schooling 1850 to 1960

Indigenous missions and reserves were established extensively throughout Australia from the middle of the 19th Century on. They offered sanctuary to dispossessed Indigenous families, but at a price. In modern terms they can be described as indoctrination and re-education centres. Missionaries saw their task as being to provide opportunities for Indigenous people, especially the young to become "useful" in society. They believed that their role was to carry out a "process of reclamation" by training the children in habits of "industry, cleanliness and order" (Attwood, 1989). Schools were the central agents in this process. School programs emphasised Christian activities, supplemented with basic literacy and numeracy, and with farming and trade training for the boys and domestic training for the girls. Health and hygiene were strongly emphasised. Charles Rowley (1972) has called this process *civilisation by tuition*. There was a basic contradiction at the heart of these institutions. They functioned as places of segregation, where Indigenous people could be kept away from white society. At the same time the children were supposed to be being trained to enter that society. In the end the powerful racist barriers to Indigenous people being accepted in Australian society prevailed and few Indigenous children ever gained skills to enter fully into the dominant society.

There was no place for Indigenous cultures in these schools. It was seen as a threat to all that they stood for. On most missions use of the mother tongue was outlawed and children were often savagely punished for using it. On many missions the children were isolated in dormitories to keep them away from the "harmful influences" of their families and to overcome their "wildness" (Reynolds, 1989). Conditions were very harsh in most dormitories. In 1950 one dormitory was described as being "indistinguishable from slavery". Children were severely restrained and subject to excessive physical punishment for trivial misdemeanours (Trigger, 1988). Dormitories still existed on some missions in the 1970s.

Rowley comments that, "the missions attempted to split the generations and wreck the traditional pattern of socialisation in order to save the soul of the child" (1972:102). George Taplin, the missionary at Pt McLeay demonstrates the typical outlook of the time.

> Their parents were very averse to the hair-cutting process for the bigger boys. It is the custom of the natives to let a youth's hair grow from the time he is ten years old until he is sixteen or seventeen–that is until he is made a young man, or narumbe ... But I insisted that my pupils must have their hair cut, and after some scolding from their mothers I carried the point.

The schoolboys are glorying in the fact that they have done several things in defiance of native customs, and have received no harm. They have eaten wallaby, and yet have not turned grey. They have eaten tyere (fish), and have no sore legs. They have cooked ngaikunde (fish) with palye, and yet there are plenty more (Mattingley and Hampton, 1988:101).

Mission schools varied considerably in the quantity and quality of education they provided. The majority appear to have been ineffective, erratic in both their hours of opening and in the quality of instruction. This was a period when there was a shortage of trained teachers throughout Australia; the persons employed as teachers on Indigenous missions were frequently untrained and incompetent. The prevailing attitude among many mission staff has been described by Loos (1988) as a blend of concern and contempt towards Indigenous people. Jimmy Barker recalls being told by a teacher that as an Aboriginal he was the lowest form of humanity (in Broome, 1994). There were occasional exceptions. For example, an inspector's report on the school at Ramahyuck Mission in Victoria stated "This school has again passed an excellent examination. This is the first case since the present result system has been enforced that one hundred percent of marks has been gained by any school in the colony" (Harris, 1990:203). Some Indigenous adults who grew up on the missions have warm memories of at least one teacher whom they remember for showing genuine concern (Mattingley and Hampton, 1988). The school on the Presbyterian mission at Ernabella continually sought to respect both the culture and the integrity of the Pitjantjatjara children in its care.

Education departments in some states had a watching brief over these schools but their influence was not positive. They often followed policies which ensured that literacy and numeracy skills among Indigenous children were kept lower than those in mainstream schools (Broome, 1982:149). Very few students were allowed to gain skills which they could use to gain permanent employment. They lacked too the skills of independent living and self-management within the dominant society. One of the women whom testified to the Stolen Generations report described her frustrations at being blocked from achieving her ambitions on the basis of her Aboriginality.

I wanted to be a nurse, only to be told that I was nothing but an immoral black lubra, and I was only fit to work on cattle and sheep properties...I strived every year from grade 5 up until grade 8 to get that perfect 100% mark in my exams...which I did succeed in, only to be knocked back by saying that I wasn't fit to do those things...Our education was really to train us to be domestics and take orders (Wilson, 1997:171).

These kinds of experiences were common among children attending mission schools but have also been reported by Indigenous children and their parents in schools in current times (Groome and Hamilton, 1995).

Some Indigenous families avoided being drafted onto missions. Their children met with mixed fortunes. Several States had a policy of not allowing Indigenous children to attend government schools if local white parents objected. When in the 1930s, the Colebrook home in Quorn wanted to involve Aboriginal children in town life, including attendance at the local school, the local community protested, arguing that they were a threat and a moral menace to white children (Jacobs et al, 1988:149).

Those children who were allowed to attend their local state schools were usually segregated from other students. They had separate areas for play and in the classroom usually sat together in a Black kids section at the back or on the "dark side" of the room. These conditions were still being reported in some Australian schools in the 1970s. In addition to the segregation they frequently suffered harassment from white peers and discrimination from teachers.

The stolen generations

In the early years of the 20th century all mainland states and the Northern Territory introduced *protectionist legislation* which gave them control over Indigenous people. They claimed to be protecting the "full blood" people, who were assumed to be dying out, from the worst effects of white society; and also promoting the absorption of the growing numbers of indigenes of mixed descent into the dominant society. It was believed that these children were likely to be easily absorbed, that children with "white blood" had more intelligence (Markus, 1990:22). They were also seen as being a useful source of cheap labour (Wilson, 1997:29). Jacobs et al (1988) comment that this was part of a deliberate project to weaken Indigenous culture and "breed out" Indigenous people. It was a massive piece of social engineering, described in the Human Rights and Equal Opportunity report (Wilson, 1997) as genocide.

The Protection Acts focussed on Indigenous children. Chief Protectors of Aborigines were made the legal guardian of every Indigenous child under 21 years of age. These officials had the power to make any decision regarding these children without consulting with their parents. The existing practice of forcibly removing Indigenous children, especially girls, from their mothers was strengthened. The practice was especially severe in Queensland and New South Wales where it is estimated that one sixth of all Indigenous children were taken into "care" (Pettman, 1992).

Up until the 1970s many thousands of Indigenous children throughout Australia were taken from their parents and committed to an institution or a private home, often many hundreds of kilometres from their homes, for "care, control and training". In most places there was an excess of control, very little care and minimal training. Conditions were frequently harsh; physical and mental punishment was common, as were starvation and deprivation. Few of these children gained anything positive from this experience. The majority lost their Indigenous identity and all self-confidence. The vacuum of their lost homes and families was rarely filled. Many of them experienced emotional trauma which fostered alcoholism and destructive behaviours. Only a few gained acceptance in the white world. The effects of these forced separations have had a profound effect on generations of Aboriginal children. Deprived of effective parenting themselves and often suffering on-going mental and emotional trauma from their experiences, members of the Stolen Generation have found it hard to effectively parent their own children. Many find it hard to support their children in school after their own negative experiences (Wilson, 1997). The experiences related below are typical:

> ... I never told anyone for years and years. And I've had this inside me for years and years and years. I've been sexually abused, harassed, and then finally raped, y'know, and I've never had anyone to talk to about it...nobody, no father, no mother, no-one. We had

no-one to guide us. I felt so isolated, alienated. And I just had no-one. That's why I hit the booze. None of that family bonding, nurturing—nothing. We had nothing (Evidence to the Stolen Generation Inquiry (Wilson, 1997:184)).

Scientists and Indigenous children

In the early years on the nineteenth century psychologists became interested in the imagined differences between the mental abilities of different cultural groups. Stanley Porteus in particular carried out series of tests on Aboriginal children. His findings, which are now discredited, were that these children were intellectually inferior to non-Aboriginal children, their brain size was smaller and their intelligence more limited and stunted (Markus, 1990).

The work of Porteus and others has had long term effects on the education of Indigenous children. His work was used in the 40s and 50s to support policies of deliberately limiting Indigenous students to lower levels of achievement. His views have influenced many teachers into believing that Indigenous students are intellectually inferior and should not be expected to perform to the level of their white peers.

Throughout the hundred years between 1850 and 1950 the approach to the education of Indigenous children was unchanged. The basic motive remained to "improve", "civilise" and assimilate children who were seen as being members of a backward and inferior "race".

New beginnings in Indigenous education

During the 1970s and 1980s educators and others began to realise the magnitude of the disaster which surrounded Indigenous students and their education. The distinctive field of expertise now known as Indigenous Education began to emerge. This was due to several factors:

- With the passing of the 1967 referendum, in which Indigenous people gained recognition as citizens of Australia, long held attitudes towards them began to be challenged.
- The control of missions passed from churches and welfare agencies to community members. Education Departments began

to take responsibility for the schools and this led in most cases to improvements in the quality of teaching.

- As employment opportunities reduced in rural Australia, Indigenous families moved into major cities in increasing numbers.
- The Indigenous birth rate continued at a high rate, creating a population with a large juvenile sector.
- Australia began to be influenced by worldwide emphases on the educational needs of children from minority and Indigenous groups.

The influential *cultural deficit* and *deprivation* theories arrived in Australia from the United States and Britain in the 1960s. These theories focussed on the social and cultural settings of under achieving children. The failure of minority group children to achieve was explained by the *disadvantaged* or *deprived* nature of their homes and communities. The belief was that as their homes lacked stimulating learning and language, these children were unable to benefit from schooling to the same degree as children whose homes were *enriched*.

The influence of these theories was felt in many aspects of Indigenous education, most noticeably in the various programs funded by the Van Leer Foundation in the 1960s and 70s (Teasdale and Whitelaw, 1981). These programs aimed to create the development experiences which these children were believed to have missed due to their "deficient" home backgrounds. To achieve their goals these programs generally carried out far reaching intervention into the lives of the children and their families.

While these programs were welcome in that they focussed attention on Indigenous children they still worked from an assimilationist assumption. In most of them there was little recognition of the distinctive cultural background of the children. The fact that they might come to school with strong values and attitudes and have their own rich learning patterns and languages was not understood.

In this period however the seeds of future major change were sown as Indigenous people began to enrol in teacher training courses.

The current situation: issues and needs

The latter years of the twentieth century have seen the most significant developments in Indigenous education. There are however still significant problems. While in theory there is now nothing to prevent Indigenous students from attending schools there is still a significant group who are not participating. These include students living in remote areas who do not have a primary or secondary school near to their home and the significant numbers of Indigenous children who are refusing to attend their local school. This latter group includes many children, some of whom are very young. This pattern of school refusal can be found in both rural and urban areas. Of those who do attend numbers are now succeeding in school, but they are still only a minority. The bulk of Indigenous students are still not achieving as well as their peers. On a national basis approximately only a third of all Indigenous students continue on to Year 12.

The achievement patterns are not an indication of lesser ability but show a general disenchantment with schooling which is reflected in the low attendance rates of Indigenous children. The average Indigenous student loses between two and four years of schooling in their school going years (Groome and Hamilton, 1995:3).

There is now a better understanding of the nature of the problems which need to be addressed if Indigenous students are to gain maximum benefit from their education. The challenge to Australian educators at all levels is to take the needs of Indigenous students seriously and make the modifications which are needed so that the education they provide is more relevant to their needs.

Racism in schools

Despite the work that has been done in this area, racism remains as a major negative and destructive factor in the lives of many Indigenous children. Racism is manifested by direct or hidden harassment of Indigenous students by both peers and teachers. Few schools are successful in overcoming racism. Only rarely is it recognised for the destructive force that it is and treated in the same way as other issues such as smoking and violations of the uniform codes. Racism creates pressures and strains which sidetrack Indigenous children away from their aspirations to achieve, lowers their positive participation in school life, and frequently leads into a marginalised position. It can be a major factor contributing to decisions by Indigenous students to leave school prematurely. Many Indigenous parents become pre-occupied with assisting their children to cope with racism in all its various forms, and in preventing them from becoming defeated by it.

In addition to the reality of verbalised racism there is a hidden or institutionalised racism in schools. One aspect of this is the failure by schools and teachers to recognise the distinctive cultural needs of Indigenous children in their organisation, teaching and management policies (Groome and Hamilton, 1994).

Failure to recognise the needs of Indigenous children

The range of cultural differences among contemporary Indigenous people are being increasingly documented, as are the ways in which these affect the schooling experiences of their children (Malin 1990).

Recent research has highlighted differences between the values and behaviours which are emphasised in many Indigenous homes and those emphasised in the majority of Australian classrooms. Many Indigenous families follow patterns of socialisation which reflect, in varying degrees of intensity, those practised in Indigenous communities prior to white arrival. Malin (1990) has shown how the autonomy and affiliation emphasised in many Indigenous families frequently conflict with the expectations of many junior primary classrooms. Indigenous children frequently find that in their schools their family values are denied, their language and communication strategies are challenged and their identity and self-confidence is threatened (Eades, 1985; Christie, 1985).

Many recognise that if they are to survive they have to learn new strategies. They have to learn to handle the shame of being invisible as an individual person and yet highly visible racially. They have to cope with the negativity they meet because of their racial identity and also their comparatively lower level of performance. Some face the dilemma that if they improve their academic level they may face rejection by their Indigenous peer group. Some learn survival strategies and succeed. But too many others learn only to expect failure. This inevitably affects their academic achievement. In the sorting and grading process of school many Indigenous children find themselves continually losing ground, until often prematurely, they leave, with inadequate social, academic or economic skills.

It is possible to identify the elements which contribute to this situation; it is far harder to achieve an improvement. Behind it lies the colonising attitude described by Mulvaney (1989) as a mixture of contempt, fear, total lack of understanding, and guilt. The product of this is a *suffocation of conscience* which has made the history of Indigenous education, as much as that of the nation, one of indifference.

The reality of poverty

There is a complex relationship between education and poverty among Indigenous Australians. As the chapter has already demonstrated the education offered to Indigenous people in the past has rarely been effective; at best it prepared them to enter the work force at the lowest levels. When Australia had a large unskilled and semiskilled labour market, especially in rural areas, job opportunities were plentiful for Indigenous people, especially males. However over the past four decades, with the collapse of this labour market segment, Indigenous people have experienced increasing difficulty in gaining employment. As a result Indigenous people as a group within Australia now have the highest levels of poverty (Choo, 1990). There is no easy resolution of this problem. Once an individual or family is trapped in the cycle of poverty it is hard to escape.

Indigenous young people, boys especially, have few models of success and regular employment to encourage them. They realise at an early age that few of their peers of relatives have achieved good jobs. They can become convinced that school is a waste of time and that it is not relevant to their lives. These perceptions increase their lack of confidence and inferiority and lead to a further reduction in effort. This situation can be aggravated by racial prejudice in the school. Many students develop a hostility to society which is expressed by an increasing reluctance to participate in school. They may develop anti-social behaviour and persistent non-attendance which will serve to aggravate the conflict with school staff and tend to reduce their chances of receiving support (Groome and Hamilton, 1994).

Poverty and unemployment is a breeding ground for family dislocations which can make regular sustained schooling difficult. There is a high level of mobility among many Indigenous family living in poverty and a high level of single parenting.

Poverty in the home adds considerably to the difficulties of Indigenous children seeking to cope with schooling. Many Indigenous families have difficulty in supporting their student children in matters such as regular attendance, homework and wearing of school uniform (Choo, 1990). As a direct result of poverty many Indigenous children suffer from acute health problems which affect their ability to learn and their attendance at school. Vision and hearing difficulties occur very commonly and Indigenous children are very susceptible to a broad range of infectious diseases (Choo, 1990).

For these and other reasons Indigenous children are frequently irregular attenders at school. They also tend to have a high level of mobility between schools which further disrupt their learning.

Poverty is a structural problem at the heart of Indigenous Australia which reflects the failings of education systems to meet the needs of Indigenous students, and also acts to block their overcoming these problems.

The gulf between Indigenous people and schools

The problems described above are not easily overcome because of the lack of communication which frequently exists between Indigenous people and the educators of their children.

The nature of the education provided for Indigenous people for many generations has left a negative legacy. Many Indigenous parents view schools in the light of their own experiences and communal perceptions. Because of their experiences on missions, reserves and in fostering institutions, many older people have no tradition of needing or respecting European education. The close association between education and the management of the institutions made schooling an unpleasant controlling and limiting experience rather than an empowering one. School became just another aspect of white domination, something to be avoided. This long history of negative experiences fostered a persistent mistrust of schooling among many families. This in turn has lead to an ignorance of how schools operate and the ways in which they can effectively support their children in schools.

Many teachers are ignorant about contemporary Indigenous people, their cultures, values and lifestyles. The House of Representatives Select Committee (1985) found that many teachers did not understand the attitudes and motives of Indigenous students and were unresponsive to their needs. Until, very recently teachers have not received guidance in their training on how to work with Indigenous students. In most States of Australia preservice teacher training now includes sensitisation to the needs of Indigenous students. In addition inservice training programs are being offered more widely.

The way ahead in Indigenous education

Despite the problems which have been described there are currently positive signs in Indigenous education. An increasing number of schools are providing an education which is genuinely responsive to the needs of Indigenous students. These schools are characterised by staff committed to meeting more effectively the social, emotional and educational needs of Indigenous students. There is growing recognition of the need to include Indigenous Studies in the curriculum at all levels and to teach it with accuracy and understanding. There is an increasing involvement of Indigenous people in the education of their children, at all levels. There are increased numbers of Indigenous children going on to matriculation. In 1992 there were 5,105 Indigenous students enrolled in universities. The ultimate measure of success will be if the quality of education for all Indigenous students is seen to improve.

Indigenous involvement in schools

The majority of Indigenous parents still value education as being essential for their children if they are to achieve a better future. Many have a concept of what is a good education and are idealistic about schools. Many are concerned that their children develop in "both ways"; that they develop a strong sense of Indigenous identity as well as developing strong academic skills.

This outcome will only be achieved if teachers are culturally responsive and find ways of incorporating the values and language styles of Indigenous children into their classrooms. To do this effectively they need to establish close working relationships with Indigenous parents. Over the past 20 years there has been an increasing involvement of Indigenous people in the education of their children, both at the parental level and as teachers, aides and advisers. They have played a vital liaison role between their communities and the schools.

The National Aboriginal Education Committee (NAEC) was formed in 1977. It rapidly became a major agenda setting body, establishing policy and practice and continually presenting Indigenous viewpoints on education until it was dissolved in 1988. One of the major achievements of the NAEC was to launch the successful program for the training of 1,000 Indigenous teachers. While this goal was achieved many of the graduates found their careers in administration rather than in teaching. There is still a pressing need for Aboriginal teachers in classrooms to provide Aboriginal perspectives and models for Aboriginal children.

At the present time there is no national group reflecting Indigenous education needs. Consultative Committees (AECGs) in each state advise their respective education ministers on all aspects of Indigenous education. Their work covers a wide field as significant numbers of Indigenous students are now enrolled in TAFEs and universities as well as the majority of state primary and secondary schools. In many states the leadership of Indigenous education planning is in the hands of Indigenous educators, but programs still have to function within the constraints of the system.

In 1989 the Commonwealth launched the National Aboriginal and Torres Strait Islander Education Policy. This comprehensive policy, designed to bring about substantial improvements in Indigenous education, was a response to the earlier report by Aboriginal educator Dr Paul Hughes. Hughes had found that on a range of educational criteria, "Aborigines remain the most severely educationally disadvantaged people in Australia" (Woods, 1994:31).

There have been some successful outcomes from the policy. The most notable has been the formation of local action groups and parents committees in schools with significant Indigenous enrolments. Among the initiatives developed by these committees are after hours homework centres organised and supervised by parents.

In their 1995 report to the Ministerial Council on Education Employment Training and Youth Affairs (MCEETYA) the Taskforce for the education of Aboriginal and Torres Strait Islander Peoples identified the priorities which needed to be addressed for Australian Indigenous peoples to gain maximum benefits from education. Pursuing a goal of self-determination for Indigenous people in education, they believe that Indigenous people need to be more strongly represented within education, as professionals and as decision makers. For Indigenous children to gain higher achievement they need improved access to, and participation in, education. Indigenous cultures and languages need to be promoted, maintained and supported in schools. There has been some progress towards these aims.

In some areas Indigenous parents have taken the initiative to gain complete control of the education of their children. Yipirinya school at Alice Springs was begun by local parents who despaired of their children gaining an effective education in the existing schools in the town.

Other Indigenous communities, notably in Western Australia, have also started their own independent schools in recent times. At the current time there are approximately a dozen independent Indigenous schools in the country. These range from schools in remote communities to the prestigious Worowa College in the Dandenong ranges.

There are variations on this theme. The Pitjantjatjara and Yankunytjara people of the Western desert have gained a form of management over education in their homelands through the establishment of the Pitjantjatjara Yankunytjara Education Council (PYEC). They work with the State governments, who continue to fund and staff the schools.

There are several government schools such as Yirrkala and Millingimbi in the Northern Territory which have a majority of Indigenous staff, including principals. They are beginning to reflect community concerns more closely in their curriculum and teaching strategies.

The challenge that faces all these groups is to develop schools which will enable Indigenous students to take their place in Australian society without losing pride in their identity as an Indigenous person. There is considerable debate about how this can be achieved.

One approach, practised by the Yirrkala school, is that there must be an integration of Indigenous and European knowledge and values into the one curriculum. They believe that it is possible to have "both ways" working together. They have already achieved this in the difficult area of mathematics curriculum.

An alternative view, represented currently in the Pitjantjatjara schools, maintains that integration is not feasible and that the two domains of European and Indigenous learning must be kept separate in all aspects of the children's experience.

Some of the most significant developments in Indigenous education in recent years have come in the post-secondary area. Over the last fifteen years there has been an explosion in the number of Indigenous students enrolling in TAFE Colleges and universities across a wide range of courses. Many universities are now offering specific training opportunities to Indigenous students in education, health, law and other professional areas. The University of South Australia, Edith Cowan University (Mt Lawley) and Monash University have the longest history of dedicated Indigenous courses and research. As a result of these initiatives Indigenous people are now entering professions and skilled trades at a higher rate than ever before.

There are a range of institutions, many of which are Indigenous controlled, which seek to meet the educational needs of mature age Indigenous students, providing specialised instruction ranging from para-professional training to short term preparatory courses for university entry. Among these are Tranby College in Sydney, Tauondi College in Adelaide and the Institute for Aboriginal Development in Alice Springs.

Batchelor College in the Northern Territory is an independent Indigenous TAFE institution which offers teacher training and a range of other specialised courses such as media, health and management.

Conclusion

In many aspects education for Indigenous people in Australia has changed greatly since its first beginnings in small schools on the outskirts of the embryonic colonial towns. Schools are now available for almost all Indigenous children. There is now theoretically no limit to their progress through the schooling system and on into higher education. Systems and schools are gradually beginning to recognise the needs of Indigenous students and are catering for them more. Indigenous parents and communities are gaining influence, and in some cases control, over the education of their children.

Yet the basic question of what constitutes an appropriate and relevant education for Indigenous children is far from resolved. Within both the Indigenous and non-Indigenous communities there is still debate about the exact nature of the education which these children need. The spectrum of opinion held within both groups ranges from what may be called assimilationist ideas to those of an education which closely reflects traditional Aboriginal values and skills. It is apparent that different communities will seek their own preferred solution. The challenge to the systems, schools and teachers is to be open to hear Indigenous voices and to work with their local communities to provide an education which is locally appropriate and relevant.

References

Attwood, B (1989). *The Making of the Aborigines*. Sydney: Allen and Unwin.

Bonwick, J (1862). *Rides out and About, Rambles of an Australian School Inspector*. London: Religious Tract Society.

Broome, Richard (1994). *Aboriginal Australians*. 2nd edition. Sydney: George Allen and Unwin.

Choo, C (1990). *Aboriginal Child Poverty*. Melbourne: Brotherhood of St Laurence.

Christie, M (1985). *Aboriginal Perspectives on Experience and Learning: the Role of Language in Aboriginal Education*. Geelong: Deakin University Press.

Coombs, H; Brandl, M and Snowden, W (1983). *A Certain Heritage*. Canberra: CRES, Australian National University.

Eades, D (1985). "You gotta know how to talk: information seeking in SE Queensland Aboriginal society". In *Cross Cultural Encounters: Communication and Miscommunication,* edited by J Pride. Melbourne: River Seine.

Edwards, WH, editor (1998). *Traditional Aboriginal Society.* Second edition. South Yarra: Macmillan.

Groome, H (1988). *Relationships Between Aboriginal Parents and Schools.* Adelaide: University of South Australia.

Groome, Howard and Hamilton, Arthur (1995). *Meeting the Educational Needs of Aboriginal Adolescents.* NBEET Commissioned report, no. 35. Canberra: AGPS.

Harris, John (1990). *One Blood. 200 years of Aboriginal Encounter with Christianity: A Story of Hope.* Sutherland: Albatross Books.

House of Representatives Select Committee (1985). *Aboriginal Education.* Canberra: AGPS.

Hughes, P (1981). *Report of the Aboriginal Education Policy Task Force.* Canberra: Department of Employment, Education and Training.

Jacobs, Jane; Laurence, Caroline and Thomas, Faith (1988). "Pearls from the deep". In T Swain and DB Rose, editors. *Aboriginal Australians and Christian Missions.* Bedford Park: Australian Association for the study of religions.

Loos, Noel (1988). "Concern and contempt". In T Swain and DB Rose, editors. *Aboriginal Australians and Christian Missions.* Bedford Park: Australian Association for the study of religions.

Malin, M (1990). "The visibility and invisibility of the Aboriginal child in an urban classroom". *Australian Journal of Education,* vol. 34, no. 3.

Markus, Andrew (1990). *Governing Savages.* Sydney: Allen and Unwin.

Mattingley, C and Hampton, K, editors (1988). *Survival in our Own Land, Aboriginal Experiences in South Australia Since 1836.* Adelaide: Wakefield Press.

Ministerial Council on Education Employment Training and Youth Affairs (1995). *A National Strategy for the Education of Aboriginal and Torres Strait Islander Peoples 1996-2002,* Canberra.

Mulvaney, DJ (1989). *Encounters in Place*. St Lucia: University of Queensland Press.

Pettman, Jan (1992). *Living in the Margins; Racism, Sexism and Feminism in Australia*. Sydney: Allen and Unwin.

Read, P (1982). *The Stolen Generations: the Removal of Aboriginal Children in New South Wales, 1883 to 1969* (Occasional paper no. 1). Sydney: NSW Ministry of Aboriginal Affairs.

Reynolds, H (1989). *Dispossession, Black Australians and White Invaders*. Sydney: Allen and Unwin.

Rowley, C (1972). *The Destruction of Aboriginal Society*. Ringwood: Penguin Books.

Teasdale, G and Whitelaw, A (1981). *The Early Childhood Education of Aboriginal Australians*. Melbourne: ACER.

Trigger, David (1988). "Christianity, domination and resistance in colonial social relations". In T Swain and DB Rose, editors. *Aboriginal Australians and Christian Missions*. Bedford Park: Australian Association for the study of religions.

Wilson, Sir Ronald (1997). *Bringing Them Home, Report of the National Inquiry into the Separation of Aboriginal and Torres Strait Islander Children from Their Families*, Canberra, AGPS.

Chapter 10

Health: An Holistic Approach

Jenny Burden

Introduction

In 1986 the Better Health Commission stated that good health is dependent upon:

> a variety of material and non material factors: adequate shelter, suitable nutrition, companionship, income and a healthy environment (Saggers and Gray, 1991a:82).

To this can be added the many prerequisites for good psychosocial adjustment. These include a firm sense of individual identity and group belonging; a sense of security, purpose, personal involvement, satisfaction and achievement; the knowledge and skills to allow an individual to function effectively in society; the freedom to make choices of benefit to self and others, as well as a sense of control over important aspects of one's life. These conditions were, according to Boyden (1987), amply provided for in hunter-gatherer societies, such as those that occupied pre-colonial Australia.

However, in Australia, as the lives and lifestyles of Aboriginal people were radically altered by encroaching Europeans, very few if any, of the conditions necessary for the maintenance of physical and psychological health survived intact. Not surprisingly, Aboriginal health began to deteriorate, until today the health status of Aboriginals throughout Australia is a cause for grave concern.

> Indigenous Australians [today] suffer a higher burden of illness and die at a younger age than non-Indigenous Australians, and this is true for almost every type of disease or condition for which information is available (McLennan and Madden, 1997:1).

Aboriginal health prior to colonisation

In order to understand the complex nature of Aboriginal health problems today, it is essential that an historical perspective be taken and that the contemporary pattern of ill health should be analysed within the context of the lifestyle changes that have occurred for Aboriginal people throughout Australia since 1788.

While there is scant information recorded regarding the health of Aboriginal people with little or no alien contact, all the indices are that their health prior to European invasion was good. Reports from early European explorers and settlers often stated that when first encountered Aboriginal people appeared to be in good health and free from disease.

This view of pre-contact health status is supported by contemporary evidence (Lee and De Vore, 1968) which suggests that traditional hunter-gatherer societies throughout the world provided for their members' lifestyles which, prior to European contact, *were ... enviable in terms of health, nutrition and leisure* (Saggers and Gray, 1991a:19). Within such societies:

> the existence of an effective psychological support network, a certain amount of creative behaviour and situations which promote a sense of personal involvement ... are (also believed to have been) conducive to human health and well being (Boyden, 1987:40).

There is no evidence to suggest that the hunter-gatherer societies within Australia, prior to 1788, in any way departed from these generalisations.

For pre-contact Aboriginal people daily life was lived within small, close knit groups of kin whose size varied according to the availability of water and other essential resources. Generally, these small kin-based groups followed a seasonal pattern of movement within a known and defined territory, to which they had deep spiritual ties. Periodically they would congregate in larger numbers for ceremonial purposes or when a seasonal abundance of some food source drew them to a particular site.

Kinship was the organising principle around which social life revolved and prescribed each person's relationships and responsibilities to others within the local group and the larger language group of which it was a part. These social responsibilities and obligations were inculcated from childhood and *the individual was much aware of his or her responsibilities to the community* (Boyden, 1987:73).

From a psychological perspective, the social links between the people within the larger language group were of significance, for they not only ensured that people lived their lives within a known and "expectable" social environment but also "allowed for greater social harmony at times of congregation and for interdependence between groups during periods of scarcity" (Morice, 1978:25). In addition, "the ease with which individuals could be accepted into other groups, by virtue of the ... (prescribed) ... relationships, enabled the resolution of conflict and tension by fission to occur" (Morice, 1978:75). When serious tensions or conflicts arose within a group, it was possible for members to leave their local group temporarily and join a neighbouring group. As Morice (1978) and others have pointed out, this mitigated against the deleterious effect of prolonged stress which is so often a concomitant of unresolved interpersonal conflict and tension.

For Aboriginal children:

> psychological development was attuned to both the physical and social environment. The infant Aborigine was reared in an atmosphere which stressed physical contact and immediate gratification. Throughout childhood years permissiveness was the rule, so that when adolescence was entered, the average Aborigine could have been expected to have developed a sense of basic trust, autonomy, initiative and an absence of inferiority. The stage of adolescence was marked by a series of ... rites of passage, through which the young person was prepared for, and accepted into, the spiritual and secular life of the tribe (Morice, 1978:25).

This formalised process of identity formation provided the basis for the development of a strong sense of individual identity and group belonging (Morice, 1978).

In relation to physical well being, the hunter-gatherer lifestyle dictated frequent exercise which minimised the risk of obesity and associated health problems. In addition, the environment provided a wide range of naturally occurring plants and a great diversity of animal life which allowed for a well-balanced, nutritious diet of protein and plant foods, high in fibre and low in salt, sugar and fat.

The actual composition of the pre-contact diet was, of course, dictated by regional and seasonal variations in the availability of food. In coastal and riverine areas fish and shell fish provided a dietary addition not available in the riverless inland areas of Australia and larger, more permanent settlements were possible. Within the most arid regions of Australia, such as Ooldea on the Transcontinental line and the Western Desert region of Western Australia, the range and variety of food was more limited than in more fertile regions and the population was, of necessity, more widely dispersed across the country. However, even in these harsh and arid environments there were still many different varieties of plant and animal food available to provide a nutritionally adequate diet.

In 1941, the anthropologists, Ronald and Catherine Berndt (1988:109) recorded some indigenous foods which could be easily obtained in the spinifex area immediately around the Ooldea Soak and Mission station. The list included 18 varieties of mammals and marsupials, 19 birds, 11 reptiles, 8 insects, 17 varieties of seeds, 3 vegetables, 10 fruits and berries, 4 other plants and fungi, as well as a variety of eggs. Berndt and Berndt (1988) considered this a very conservative list with many varieties of plants and animals not recorded.

Similarly, in the Western Desert region, Gould (1980) recorded "a minimum number of 37 staple plant species and 48 animal species ... (and) ... reported that even in times of extreme drought, the people were assured of a regular, if sometimes monotonous, diet" (Saggers and Gray, 1991a:28, 41).

As is typical of hunting and gathering communities which follow a more or less nomadic life style, most Aboriginal groups were spread sparsely over the continent. This mitigated against the spread of disease. Many contagious and infectious diseases cannot take hold in a population as sparsely spread and relatively isolated with defined group territory, as was the case with pre-contact Aboriginal society. Hygiene was not a problem.

Diseases indigenous to Aboriginal people appear to have been few. Dental disease was relatively rare and, according to Abbie (1976:75-77), smallpox, influenza, measles, whooping cough, tuberculosis, leprosy and syphilis were unknown. The common cold, yaws and some skin diseases were probably endemic. Trachoma may also have been present.

This pre-contact situation is in sharp contrast to the situation which developed after the arrival of the First Fleet.

Aboriginal health after colonisation

People do not become ill or die simply because they are Aboriginal. Poor Aboriginal health is traced to 200 years of oppression and limited opportunity following European settlement (AHC and SAHC, 1994:9).

From the beginning of European occupation, Aboriginal people have been subjected to pressures which have had disastrous consequences with respect to their health and also led to a decimation of the population. The economic historian and demographer, Noel Butlin, in 1983 estimated a 1788 pre-contact population of over 1,000,000 people which had been reduced to 150,000 by 1850.

This drastic population decrease resulted, in large part, from the devastating effect of introduced diseases to which the Aboriginal population had no immunity and which, in epidemic proportion, began their sweep when smallpox ravaged the Aboriginal population around Sydney Cove in 1789.

Watkin Tench gave the first account of a smallpox outbreak in 1788. He recorded that boat parties exploring the foreshores found the bodies of 'Indians' (meaning the Aboriginals) in many of the coves and inlets of the harbour. Pustules, like those caused by smallpox, were spread thickly on their bodies. Tench could not understand how a disease, to which the natives seemed strangers, could have been introduced and spread so quickly. [He] ... did not realise that the disease had been introduced by the settlers themselves. Many of them were carriers and although they did not develop the disease themselves, they had spread it among the Aboriginals (McEwan, 1979:66).

Disease spread ahead of European settlement, so that Sturt, on his riverine journeyings in 1828, commented on the piles of bones seen and the evidence of pox marked faces as testament to the fearful toll taken on Aboriginal communities (Butlin, 1983). The evidence of venereal diseases was not so easy to recognise, but its scourge was already wreaking silent havoc. Other infectious diseases such as measles, tuberculosis, typhoid, diphtheria and influenza began ravaging the Aboriginal population. "Traditional treatment did not work against new diseases and widespread illness began to affect Aboriginal life" (AIIC and SAIIC, 1994:9).

Violence was another potent factor responsible for population reduction, but, as Reynolds (1982) has pointed out, its importance has been seriously underplayed in official accounts of the history of settlement.

As settlement spread on the Eastern seaboard and in other areas of European occupation, conflict developed. Aboriginal resistance in defence of land, lifestyle and society was seen by authorities and settlers alike as deviant hostility, to be put down with the strongest possible force. Punitive expeditions of Europeans formed genocidal bands, moving along the ever widening frontier in bloody retribution for perceived villainies and imagined wrongs. Systematic killings took place, sometimes under military leadership, with self-righteous justification the answer to any qualms of conscience from more humane members of the wider public. *Settler justice* ruled the frontier.

The death toll resulting from this conflict has been estimated by Reynolds (1982) to have been at least 20,000 with massacres continuing well into this century. The *Bulletin*, in 1880, reported on the situation in Queensland:

> The blacks have been murdered by thousands ... there is ... wholesale massacre of human beings; a relentless violation of women. [I have] seen the brains of an infant dashed out against a tree after the mother had been murdered. This is not a fiction but the statement of one who, not three years ago, saw in Queensland scrub the sunburned corpses of men and women and children who had been murdered by officers of 'justice' and left for the crows (cited in Pollard, 1968:24).

The rapid decline in population resulting from disease and violence had a dramatic effect on the ability of Aboriginal groups to maintain themselves as social entities. With the death by violence of many adult males and the loss of countless numbers of people through disease, Aboriginal societies were shattered by generational disruption. These factors, in conjunction with the forced dispossession from homelands, dealt a fatal blow to Aboriginal life as it had been prior to 1788.

Dispossessed from their land, the dispirited and disoriented remnants of broken tribes were forced into unfamiliar and often alien territory. Many were relocated on missions and reserves where traditional ceremonies and language were forbidden. Some lived as fringe dwellers on the outskirts of European towns, newly sprung up on traditional land, or worked on sheep and cattle stations in order to remain close to their own country. Most Aboriginal people lived in squalid conditions, far removed from their traditional lifestyle.

The once vibrant hunter-gatherer societies were reduced to little more than collections of sick, impoverished and undernourished mendicants, forced to eke out an existence on the fringes of European settlement, cut off from their country, their sacred sites and their religion. The essence of their life had been taken from them.

For those forced to live on missions and reserves, likened by many to prisons or reformatories (Stanner, 1979; Nathan and Japanangka, 1983), the experience was one of almost total loss of freedom[1]. They were virtual prisoners, totally at the mercy of whichever local or official government policy happened to be in place at the time.

In many instances, as well as experiencing the confusion, grief and trauma resulting from loss of country and kin, Aborigines were forced to live together, under mission or reserve control, with people from totally different language groups. They thus lost not only their land and their freedom but had to endure the stress of discord and violence frequently generated in such situations.

In all areas of their lives, too many Aboriginal people lost the right to self-determination and became a subjugated people. Not even their family life was safe, as many children of mixed ancestry were forcibly removed from their mothers and reared in isolation from their kin (the Stolen Generation). The majority of these children were placed in institutions, with the intent of training them to become domestic servants or farm workers in the non-Aboriginal community. In most instances, the conditions under which they lived were extremely poor with resources which were "insufficient to keep children properly clothed, fed and sheltered ... [where] the education provided ... was essentially a preparation for menial work ... [and where] excessive physical punishments were common" (Human Rights and Equal Opportunity Commission, 1997:15-16). Many never saw their parents again. Others did so, but only after years of heartbreaking search.

The effects of this policy, which was relentlessly pursued until 30 years ago, left a significant proportion of Aboriginal people with a severe emotional handicap and a debilitating identity crisis.

The psychological trauma which accompanied this massive disruption of Aboriginal family, social and cultural life was frequently accompanied by a deep sense of despair. Feelings of hopelessness, powerlessness and helplessness—of life empty of meaning and purpose—resulted in widespread apathy among the Aboriginal population. All too often escape into alcoholic oblivion became a panacea for the psychological pain experienced by vast numbers of Aboriginal people. It remains so for many to this day.

Physical as well as psychological well-being suffered. Cut off from natural food sources, Aboriginal people were forced to exist on meagre and nutritionally inadequate rations of tea, flour and sugar, with the occasional addition of meat.

In some instances, those living on missions or reserves in the Northern Territory were subjected to the ultimate indignity of having their daily food provided for them through communal kitchens, with the menus dictated by the white authority. This mass feeding arrangement was bitterly resented, for it removed from the parent generation one of their primary and few remaining responsibilities—the provision and preparation of food for themselves and their children.

Those living on cattle stations fared no better. The adult able-bodied men were expected to work as stockmen and the women as domestic servants, but were not necessarily paid until the 1960s.

Many commentators have drawn attention to the plight of *station blacks* in the earlier part of this century. Markus says of the situation in the 1920s-1930s that most of the station owners were not concerned with the condition of "their" *camp blacks* and even with those who had previously been employed, but were now too old or sick to work, "generally the only food they received ... (was) the offal of the beasts on killing day" (1990:63). For these people there was nothing to be gained by moving to government ration depots, as the Aboriginal people living at such depots were also undernourished and emaciated.

In the 1930s Dr Charles Duguid found a similar situation on cattle stations around Alice Springs. He described government rations as a "ludicrous diet for people who, in tribal days, lived largely on raw natural foods" (Duguid, 1972:101) and reported that the ration for the Aboriginal working men was grossly inadequate with insufficient calories for the work they had to do. The women and children were even worse off and many older people simply starved to death.

In 1945, Ronald and Catherine Berndt (1988) found no improvement in the Northern Territory. Writing of conditions at some outstations they reported that Aboriginal people were faced with conditions of near starvation (Berndt and Berndt, 1988). In 1974 Frank Stevens published a similar account of living conditions on cattle stations in the Northern Territory:

> ... while the masters at some stations sat down to dine in virtual baronial splendour, being waited upon by up to as many six highly trained [Aboriginal] domestics, occasionally decked out in monogrammed aprons and caps, the husbands and children of the maids sat in the dust picking at the offal from their disgusting pottage, and eventually crawling into 'dog kennel-like' structures to sleep (Stevens, 1974:108).

Other factors, besides malnutrition, took their toll. Forced into a sedentary lifestyle of inactivity and purposelessness, with inadequate housing and little or no provision for the sanitary disposal of human and other waste, illness and infection became widespread.

The severity of the situation with respect to housing was highlighted by the 1976 Senate Select Committee on Aboriginal and Torres Strait Islanders (SSCATSI) reporting that:

> visits to local communities undertaken during four years of inquiry impressed on the committee time and again the fact that housing conditions for Aboriginal families are appalling .. (with) an estimated minimum of 4455 Aboriginal families throughout Australia ... living in humpies, shacks, abandoned car bodies, and

> other makeshift shelter and ... thus in dire need of adequate
> accommodation .. (with) an even larger number of families living
> in substandard and overcrowded accommodation. (SSCATSI,
> 1976:169)

In such situations, with high density sedentary populations living
without basic amenities in unsatisfactory accommodation, hygiene
became a major problem. A population which was once protected
against infectious and other diseases by its low density and semi-
nomadic lifestyle became susceptible to such diseases in the
settlement environment. With inadequate nutrition and living under
appallingly unhygienic and overcrowded conditions, the deterioration
in health was inevitable. Under such conditions, Aboriginal people
became susceptible to all manner of illness to which they had not
previously been vulnerable (Saggers and Gray, 1991b).

This summary of the enforced change from hunter-gatherer to
impoverished sedentary mendicant highlights the disastrous
consequences for both the physical and psychological health and
well-being of Aboriginal people.

Aboriginal health in the 1990s

> The health disadvantage of Indigenous Australians begins early in
> life and continues throughout the life cycle (McLennan and Madden,
> 1997:1).

Despite some notable improvements in the last 20 years, the health
status of Aboriginal people in the 1990s remains a matter of
considerable concern.

In many instances, the health status of Aboriginal people is
comparable to that of poorer third world countries. However, while
the people of the third world are, in the main, victims of the
"diseases of poverty" (acute infectious diseases, malnutrition and
parasitic diseases etc), the irony of the situation for Aboriginal
people is that they carry a double burden of disease. They suffer not
only the "diseases of poverty" but, increasingly, the degenerative
"lifestyle" diseases characteristic of developed countries
(cardiovascular disease, chronic lung disease, hypertension, diabetes
and cancer).

Aboriginal people are also seriously disadvantaged in terms of health, when compared with Indigenous minorities in other 1st world countries who (like Aboriginal Australians) suffered invasion and dispossession as well as substantial depopulation as a result of introduced diseases and settler violence.

Some 30-40 years ago, Indigenous minorities in the United States of America, Canada and New Zealand experienced extremely poor health status, similar to that within the Indigenous population in Australia. However, in the intervening years, substantial improvements have occurred for these Indigenous populations. Their mortality rates have fallen, as have their infant and maternal mortality rates and their life expectancies have increased with about a three year discrepancy between Indigenous and non-Indigenous people in the United States of America and about 8 years in Canada and New Zealand (Kunitz, 1994).

There has not been a matching improvement in Aboriginal health in this time period, with the death rate from all causes remaining at a consistently higher level than within the total Australian population, and life expectancy in the 1990s up to 20 years less than that of the total Australian population.

That the life expectancy at birth among Aboriginal people in the 1990s is "lower than for most countries in the world with the exception of Central Africa and India" (McLennan and Madden, 1997:5) and is comparable to that found among Indigenous minorities in North America and New Zealand in the 1950's, is indicative of the plight of Aboriginal Australians in relation to health.

In the 1990s, infant mortality rates within the Aboriginal population remain unacceptably high, being two to four times greater than that found in the total Australian population. While a significant reduction in Aboriginal infant mortality occurred in the 1970s, due, in large part, to specific programs which targeted infant and maternal health and well being, this level of improvement in Aboriginal infant mortality was not sustained during the 1980s. Having reached a plateau, Aboriginal infant mortality has remained consistently higher than that in the total Australian population from the early 1980s.

In addition to high infant mortality rates, a greater proportion of Aboriginal infants are considered to be at risk than non-Aboriginal infants because of the prevalence of low birth weight (less than 2,500 grams) in the Aboriginal population.

Maternal mortality, a relatively uncommon event in the total Australian population, remains unacceptably high among Aboriginal women.

While living conditions and patterns of disease vary from region to region, it is, nevertheless, the case that *throughout* Australia the health status of Indigenous Australians is extremely poor.

In all age groups, the Aboriginal death rates are far in excess of the corresponding total Australian death rates. The greatest difference between the two populations, however, occurs between the ages of 25-54 years. In this age bracket, the Aboriginal population experiences a disproportionately high percentage of deaths compared with the total Australian population.

Indeed, over the last 25 years, spiralling death rates among young to middle-aged Aboriginal adults have offset the improvement that has occurred in infant mortality and child health in the same period. A recent Western Australian report shows that diseases of the circulatory system are now the leading cause of death, a trend that is not confined to WA but has also been noted in other states and territories. One very disturbing aspect of this increase in diseases of the circulatory system is that among young to middle-aged Aboriginal adults, deaths from this cause "occur at 10 to 20 times the expected rates for other Australians" (Western Australian Health Department, 1992:61).

While in the 1990s, diseases of the circulatory system account for about 25% of *all* Aboriginal deaths, other leading causes of death within the Aboriginal population include diseases of the respiratory system; external causes (injury, suicide and murder); cancer and diabetes (Anderson et al, 1996).

The most recent figures available (1992 - 1994) show that Aboriginal deaths from diseases of the respiratory system occur with a frequency of 7-8 times that in the Australian population as a whole, while deaths resulting from external causes (including injury from motor vehicle and other accidents, poisoning, suicide, homicide and other interpersonal violence) occur almost four times as frequently with in the Aboriginal population as in the Australian population generally (McLennan and Madden, 1997).

In this latter category, suicide assumes a particular importance as a cause of death among 15-29 year old Aboriginal people, while alcohol related motor vehicle accidents and interpersonal violence also take a heavy toll in terms of mortality and morbidity (Kamian, 1993; AHC and SAHC, 1994).

Cancer is another leading cause of death within the Aboriginal population, with the death rate amongst Aboriginal women "70% higher than expected when compared with Australian women generally" (Bhatia and Anderson, 1995:18). Diabetes mellitus, while not one of the four leading causes of death among Aboriginal Australians, is nevertheless a major health problem within the Aboriginal community, accounting for disproportionately high rates of morbidity and mortality within the Aboriginal population. Between 1992 and 1994 the Aboriginal death rates from diabetes increased and were "12 times higher from men and nearly 17 times higher for women than rates for other Australians" (AIHW, 1996:21).

While about 75% of all Aboriginal deaths are attributable to one of these five "disease" factors, the disproportionately high death rates from infectious and parasitic diseases, with Aboriginal mortality rates up to 17 times greater than in the Australian population generally (Anderson et al, 1996) make this a disease category which cannot be ignored. Similarly, deaths arising from mental disorders are disproportionately high in the Aboriginal population (Bhatia and Anderson, 1995).

While it is the "lifestyle" diseases which, in the main, affect disproportionate numbers of the adult Aboriginal population, it is the acute infectious diseases that inflict major illness and suffering on Aboriginal infants and young children. Among this group *preventable* diseases, such as gastroenteritis and acute respiratory disease, are serious cause for concern, as is the high rate of chronic ear disease which leaves a significant proportion of Aborigines with a marked hearing deficit, and has serious consequences in relation to education among children and employment prospects among teenagers and young adults.

Many possible explanations have been advanced by researchers in the field to account for the plight of Aboriginal people in relation to health status. Factors such as the physical and psychological effect of dispossession, poverty, high levels of unemployment, unsatisfactory and overcrowded living conditions, alcohol and other substance abuse, faulty diet and malnutrition, as well as lack of appropriate medical services, have all been implicated as causative or contributory factors.

While it is generally acknowledged that there are many causes for the high morbidity and mortality rates within the Aboriginal population, researchers differ in "the relative importance they attach to each of these causes" (Saggers and Gray, 1991a:17). The argument presented in this chapter seeks to draw attention to the fact that as these factors rarely (if ever) occur in isolation, it is their cumulative and interactive affect that has to be considered.

Factors contributing to Aboriginal ill health

Medical services

Despite the serious deterioration in health which occurred from 1788 onwards, very little real attempt was made to provide comprehensive medical services to the Aboriginal population. Up until the 1960s the special provisions for Aboriginal health were primarily directed at protecting the white Australian population from the ravages of infectious disease sweeping through the Aboriginal population (Saggers and Gray, 1991b) with responsibility for such "health care" in the hands of the police or government officials.

> Aboriginal people remember health care being delivered by officials who also controlled or abused Aboriginal people and took away land and children. This led to distrust of mainstream services, reinforced by cultural mores which put reliance on extended families for support and assistance and which makes hospitalisation a distressing experience (AHC and SAHC, 1994:11).

Nathan and Japanangka (1983) report that the enforced treatment programs, hospital admissions and house searches and the use of violence by the police "protectors" in carrying out their caretaker role has left a deep impression on Aboriginal people. As late as the

1980s, many recalled how "the police used to force people into hospital ... for ... checkups ... If people left the hospital, they'd get the police onto it. They'd be under police guard all the time" (Nathan and Japanangka, 1983:29).

The situation improved only marginally when, more recently, government doctors took over the role of "protector". In this role, doctors had "enormous power over their wards ... and many Aboriginal people ... experienced feelings of intimidation and humiliation in a health care setting" (Mobbs, 1991:315).

In the light of these highly aversive experiences, it is little wonder that many Aboriginal people have, over the years, shown a marked reluctance to make use of the mainstream health services. These health services were unacceptable because of the impersonal nature of the clinic or hospital setting and the presence of an exclusively non-Aboriginal nursing and medical staff, who were perceived by Aboriginal people to be either indifferent to their plight, patronising in their approach, or demonstrably racist in their attitudes.

This under-utilisation of available health services often exacerbated the health problems, as all too often minor ailments, which were left untreated, developed into serious illnesses.

In the late 1960s-early 1970s, recognition was finally given to the fact that Aboriginal health needs warranted special attention, when it was found that Aboriginal mortality and morbidity rates were significantly higher than for non-Aborigines. Not only was Aboriginal health status found to be significantly worse than that of non-Aborigines, it was also realised that Aboriginal health "showed little or no improvement over that of the last century" (Reid and Lupton, 1991:23).

The specific health strategies introduced in the late 1960s and early 1970s (targeted in particular at maternal and infant health problems) were, however, based on the culturally alien and inappropriate Western biomedical model of health care. As Nathan and Japanangka (1983) have pointed out, the authorities at the time did not question the appropriateness of mainstream services in relation to Aboriginal health care and acted upon the assumption that Western medicine had all the knowledge and technical skills necessary to rectify Aboriginal health problems. All that was needed, it was believed, was an injection of funds to provide a proper system of health care, with "highly qualified practitioners, clinical settings and medical equipment and systematic research" (Nathan and Japanangka, 1983:2). In the event, however, apart from achieving an initial dramatic decline in infant mortality rates, these special provisions failed to have an impact on Aboriginal health and "provided little more than 'bandaid' curative services" (NAHSWP, 1989:59).

One of the major deficiencies with the biomedical model of health care is that it is primarily interested in the recognition of treatment of disease and defines health negatively, as an absence of infirmity or disease. It has been criticised, generally, for its mechanistic, curative approach and for focussing too narrowly on biological malfunction as a cause of illness while paying too little attention to the psychological, social and environmental factors which affect health in *any* population, not just the Aboriginal population (Powles, 1979; Sobel, 1979; Taylor, 1986).

Aboriginal conceptions of health are radically different from this disease oriented biomedical perspective. Health to Aboriginal people is a much broader concept and relates not simply to the "physical well-being of the individual—but [encompasses] the social, emotional, and cultural well-being of the whole community ... a whole-of-life view" (NAHSWP, 1989:X). Such a perspective places health and well-being within a wider context that relates to:

> all aspects of their life including control over their physical environment...dignity...community self esteem...and justice. It is not merely a matter of the provision of doctors, hospitals, medicines or the absence of disease and incapacity (NAHSWP, 1989:IX).

Western medicine has not only failed to come to grips with the conceptual gulf which exists between its own philosophy and Aboriginal traditional beliefs with respect to health matters, but has also failed to address the complex web of factors which affect Aboriginal health status.

Psychosocial factors

Among the many factors responsible for the high rate of morbidity and mortality in the Aboriginal population today, the psychological factors already discussed are of particular importance. These include the trauma and social dislocation associated with loss of land, the powerlessness associated with loss of autonomy, the dependency which has accompanied institutionalisation and the inertia and "general anomie that ... [has] so widely characterised Aboriginal life during their association with us" (Stanner, 1979:235). To this must be added the psychological effects of overt and covert discrimination and the immediate and ongoing trauma associated with the enforced removal of children of mixed descent from their families. The guide to the report into the removal of Aboriginal and Torres Strait Islander children from their families, *Bringing Them Home* states that:

> For the majority of witnesses to the inquiry, the effects have been multiple, continuing and profoundly disabling.
>
> The trauma of separation and attempts at 'assimilation' have damaged their self esteem and well being, and impaired their parenting and relationships.
>
> In turn their children suffer. There is a cycle of damage people find difficult to escape unaided (Human Rights and Equal Opportunity Commission, 1997).

The overwhelming trauma and stress associated with such enforced separation and with the excessively high rates of illness, hospitalisation and premature death, which characterise contemporary Aboriginal society, must all be considered in relation to the impact they have on psychological well being and physical health. In particular, the loss and grief associated with suicide and other untimely, traumatic or violent deaths, which occur with a much greater frequency within the Aboriginal community than in the general community, must be profound. "The trauma associated with many such causes of death ... is likely in and of itself to contribute to psychiatric morbidity, for instance post traumatic stress disorder" (Swan and Raphael, 1995:25).

The importance of such psychological stress factors in the aetiology of disease is now widely acknowledged (Gatchel et al, 1989; Sibthorpe, 1988; Boyden, 1987).

In addition to these psychological factors, the depressed socio-economic status of most Aboriginal people is also a major factor in relation to poor health status.

In the 1990s, the level of employment among Aboriginal people remains low and a high proportion of the Aboriginal population continues to subsist on welfare payments, with the result that the majority of Aboriginals "living in an otherwise affluent Australia, are still trapped in a vicious cycle of poverty and powerlessness from which they feel they can never hope to escape" (Franklin and White, 1991:3).

This level of poverty has important implications for health as it frequently acts as a barrier to achieving adequate nutritional status essential for good health. With the provision of a nutritionally adequate diet dictated as much (if not more) by availability and affordability as personal choice, "the economic disadvantage of Indigenous Australians means that Indigenous people throughout Australia can not always afford the most healthy foods" (McLennan and Madden, 1997:22).

Those living in remote areas have the additional problem of limited availability of healthy foods compounded by the higher cost of foods in the more remote areas of Australia. As a greater proportion of the Aboriginal population than the non-Indigenous population live in rural or remote areas, Aboriginal people are more likely to suffer disadvantage in this respect than non-Indigenous Australians.

The problem is a serious one as many Aboriginal children are failing to thrive. The severity of the problem has been highlighted by Matthews (1993) who found "that the nutritional status of Aboriginal children was considered to be deteriorating rather than improving with 20% satisfying the WHO definition for malnutrition, a factor likely to affect physical and intellectual growth and development" (Swan and Raphael, 1995:23). It is also believed that such childhood malnutrition can predispose to diseases such as diabetes, heart disease and hypertension in adult life.

For Aboriginal adults, nutritional status is also an important factor in relation to health, as diet is believed to be a contributing factor in relation to obesity, hypertension, diabetes and cardiovascular disease (Lester, 1994), all of which are major causes of illness and death among adult Aborigines.

Alcohol and other substance abuse

Alcohol is a major health risk factor in the Aboriginal population and excessive consumption of alcohol has serious consequences, leading, amongst other things, to death from alcohol related cirrhosis of the liver, alcohol dependence syndrome and foetal alcohol syndrome (McLennan and Madden, 1997).

It is frequently a contributing factor in relation to injury or death from motor vehicle and other accidents, interpersonal violence, homicide and suicide and leads to disproportionately high rates of illness and death among Aboriginal people (Unwin et al, 1994).

Alcohol misuse is also a serious social problem and is associated with physical, social and emotional disruption in many Aboriginal communities.

A recent study conducted in the Kimberley region of Western Australia reported that "there is a consensus that alcohol has had a major, and generally damaging impact on Aboriginal traditional life, family structure, health and capacity for self determination" (Hunter et al, 1991:5).

While studies have shown that a smaller proportion of Aboriginal adults consume alcohol than is the case in the Australian population generally, of those who do consume alcohol, a high percentage drink to excess.

A 1991 report from the Northern Territory notes that while a majority of Aborigines in the Territory do not drink alcohol (60% of Aborigines compared to 24% of the non-Indigenous population in the Northern Territory), it is nevertheless the case that of those who do drink, 80% drink at what is considered dangerously excessive levels (AIHWJ, 15(1):1991). A similar finding has been reported from the Kimberley region of Western Australia (Hall et al, 1993).

Smoking is another health risk factor within the Aboriginal population, with Aboriginal people almost twice as likely to smoke as members of the Australian population generally. Associated with diseases such as lung cancer, emphysema, chronic bronchitis and cardiovascular diseases, it leads to higher rates of smoking related illness and death among Aboriginal people than among Australians generally (McLennan and Madden, 1997).

Whilst it is "clearly an important factor in the heavy burden of chronic disease and premature death suffered by Indigenous Australians" (McLennan and Madden, 1997:40), the failure among Aboriginal people to perceive the health risk associated with smoking suggests that they are unlikely to change their habits in this respect unless some intensive educational programs are instigated.

Environmental living conditions

> On a range of indicators of environmental health, such as the break down of utilities, crowding and the availability of suitable water, Indigenous people have high levels of disadvantage and these are likely to impact on their health and wellbeing in a negative way (McLennan and Madden, 1997:19).

The importance of environmental living conditions in relation to health and well-being is widely recognised (McLennan and Madden, 1997). Despite this and the high priority given to environmental health by the House of Representatives Standing Committee on Aboriginal Affairs in 1979, environmental living conditions continued to play a significant role in Aboriginal ill health in the late 1990s, with a majority of Aboriginal people throughout Australia continuing to live under conditions that are wholly unsatisfactory.

Without basic facilities which other Australians take for granted—without adequate housing or disposal systems for refuse and human waste, or safe and reliable water supplies; without facilities for bathing, washing clothes, blankets and eating utensils—it is virtually impossible for *any* sedentary population to remain healthy. Aboriginal people are no exception.

For remote communities the situation is particularly bad, especially in relation to water supplies. In 1992 the ATSIC Housing and Community Infrastructure Needs Survey found that of the 838 separate communities covered in the survey in Western Australia, South Australia, Northern Territory and Queensland "water in 306 of the centres was ... unfit for human consumption" (McLennan and Madden, 1997:18). In some instances in remote regions the problem lies not simply with the adequacy of *good quality* water supplies but rather, with the availability of *any* water at all, regardless of quality.

In remote and rural communities where a water supply and other essential services have been provided, it is often the case that the residents are little better off than those without such facilities. Too often the facilities provided are inappropriate for the prevailing conditions and for the level of technical sophistication within the community. Problems frequently arise, in fact, because residents in such communities do not understand the operating principles of the sewerage or water reticulation systems with which they have been provided (NAHSWP, 1989). The systems, once broken, often remain inoperative until outside assistance can be obtained to service, repair or replace them.

In the mean time, the blocked drain, the broken pipe or sewerage system can all too easily become a serious health hazard through contamination of the environment; a non-functioning water supply system has its own hazards in relation to basic hygiene.

In communities where housing has been provided, it is frequently just inappropriate or inadequate and overcrowded (Reid and Lupton, 1991). All too often, housing designs reflect the cultural baggage of the non-Aboriginal architect or housing authority, rather than the needs and wishes of the Aboriginal recipients.

Frequently the houses are too small for the number of people needing to be accommodated. The health hazards associated with such overcrowding are manifold and include not only the risk of infection but also the very real possibility that too many people living in one house can cause the plumbing system to break down completely.

Such overcrowded living conditions, environmental contamination, lack of facilities for personal and domestic hygiene and unsafe water supplies are important factors in the aetiology of disease, and are often implicated in the disproportionately high incidence of infectious and parasitic diseases, including infections of the respiratory system and kidneys, as well as diarrhoeal diseases, hepatitis B and gastro-intestinal infections.

The situation regarding essential services in Aboriginal communities would not be tolerated if it occurred in the Australian population generally. The wider Australian community expects and receives an adequate provision of essential services.

However, this is unlikely to be achieved within Aboriginal communities in remote and isolated rural localities, until the different levels of government and different government departments collaborate to define their respective responsibilities and coordinate their efforts with respect to the funding, provision and maintenance of essential services and housing for the Aboriginal population.

Conclusion

If significant improvement is to occur in the health status of Aboriginal people, it is essential that the underlying causes of Aboriginal ill health be addressed and that a preventative, holistic—rather than a curative—approach be adopted. It is also imperative that medical authorities take cognisance of the Aboriginal perspective with respect to health and well-being and accept that in:

> contrast to the more focussed clinical and disease oriented approach of non-Aboriginal health professionals, Aboriginal people's collective concerns are to regain their land, to ensure that their children have tucker and to be able to undertake social obligations including ceremonial duties. Health business includes all of these as well as access to reasonable housing, freedom to have their babies 'on the land' and having good water to drink (SA Health Commission, 1993:3).

As early as 1978, Hollows expressed the view that Aboriginal health problems would only be resolved when Aboriginal people regained control over their lives and their land.

Regaining control—community controlled health services

Since the early 1960s Aboriginal and Torres Strait Islander initiated political action has brought about a situation where today Aboriginal Australians have a greater degree of control over their lives and destiny than at any time since 1788. Starting with the Yirrkala bark petition in 1963, the push for civil rights led onto the

Gurindji political action beginning in 1966 with the Walk-off from Wave Hill Cattle Station; the 1967 referendum which gave Aboriginal people citizenship; the 1972 Tent Embassy in Canberra; the 1976 Northern Territory Land Rights Act; the 1981 Pitjantjatjara Land Rights Act; the 1992 High Court Mabo decision which removed the fiction of terra nullius and the 1996 Wik decision. This political action is indicative of the increasing militancy within the Aboriginal and Torres Strait Islander population in the last 35 years, and of their unwillingness to continue to accept the role historically cast for them within the wider (white) Australian society.

The emergence of Aboriginal controlled health services in the early 1970s was another manifestation of this militancy. Frustrated by the lack of health services which were appropriate to their cultural needs and imbued with a new sense of autonomy following the 1967 referendum, Aboriginal people took matters into their own hands.

In 1971 the first Aboriginal community controlled health service was established at Redfern. Other communities followed and in the ensuing years set up their own health services—in Fitzroy in 1973, Perth in 1974 and in Alice Springs the Central Australian Aboriginal Congress was established in 1974.

By the end of the 1980s there were more than 60 Aboriginal community controlled health services in existence with an additional 91 centres awaiting funding to establish their own health services. In 1990-91, following the recommendation of the National Aboriginal Health Strategy (1989), the Commonwealth Government allocated $6.74 million to fund 67 additional health projects. Some new health services were included among these projects. In the late 1990s there are in excess of 200 organisations (overwhelmingly community controlled) funded by the Commonwealth, to provide Aboriginal health or health related services throughout Australia (personal communication, C. Banks, Organisation of Aboriginal and Torres Strait Islanders Health Services, 1997).

The Aboriginal controlled health services are based on a broad, holistic concept of health which takes into account the wider social, economic and political issues affecting Aboriginal life and lifestyles. Throughout Australia, Aboriginal controlled health services—such as the Central Australian Aboriginal Congress—in addition to providing medical care, have sought to address the political, social, economic and environmental factors that underlie so much Aboriginal illness. Their aim is to improve the *quality* of life at both the individual and community level. Saggers and Gray (1991b) believe that the community development functions of these health services are probably as important as those of health care delivery.

The real strength of these alternative and culturally appropriate health services lies in the fact that they are community owned and community controlled—they are run *by* the local community *for* the community. The philosophy of community control on which Aboriginal health services are based is of singular importance. Aboriginal people believe that in order for improvement in health status to occur, "they must be able to control their own destiny and ... (assume) responsibility for their own decision making" (NAHSWP, 1989:XIII).

Community control gives Aboriginal people the opportunity to exercise such rights, and to be active participants in the restoration and promotion of health and well-being in Aboriginal communities. Such active community participation is as vital an element today as it was in pre-contact Aboriginal society, where responsibility for health and well-being was a shared community responsibility. Today, it allows Aboriginal communities to be involved not only in defining the health related problems facing the communities and identifying their own solutions but also in shaping the services to meet the specific health needs of their particular community.

These community controlled health services, in conjunction with other Aboriginal controlled organisations, such as land councils, community councils, legal services and housing associations, have raised Aboriginal self-esteem and restored, to many, a sense of control over important aspects of their lives.

One of the outstanding features of Aboriginal Community controlled Health Services has been their acceptability within the Aboriginal population. This acceptability is due largely to the fact that Aboriginal community controlled health services are, in the main, staffed by Aboriginal people. While the doctors and some of the trained nursing staff working in Aboriginal health services are non-Aboriginal, they are nevertheless accepted because they are perceived as having an empathy with Aboriginal people and a genuine interest in their well-being.

Aboriginal health care workers now play an increasingly important role in relation to primary health care, with training courses in each state seeking to provide Aboriginal health care workers with the professional development and career structure necessary to give them the status and recognition they deserve in the area of health care. While many work in Aboriginal community controlled health and health related services, others work as part of a multi-disciplinary team in mainstream health care settings.

Given the nature of Aboriginal community controlled health services, the distrust and discomfort so often experienced in main stream health services is no longer a barrier to accessing necessary health care.

Some of the larger health services, now provide a wide range of programs, including social/mental health and dental services as well as rehabilitation, welfare, public health and substance abuse programs. One innovative service established in the early 1990s was the Congress Alukura, a culturally appropriate birthing centre for Aboriginal women in Alice Springs.

Preventative health programs are a strong feature of Aboriginal Health Services, with specific programs directed at lifestyle factors including diet, exercise, smoking and alcohol and other substance misuse in an attempt to reduce the risk factors associated with obesity, diabetes, strokes, hypertension, heart disease, acute respiratory disease and alcoholism. Other programs target AIDS and other sexually transmitted diseases.

Alcohol misuse remains an area for grave concern and many attempts have been made by Aboriginal people over the years to combat the problem. There are in excess of 70 services funded by the Commonwealth Government throughout Australia, dealing with substance misuse. In addition an increasing number of remote communities have taken matters into their own hands and now ban the use of alcohol within their boundaries. Other communities in rural towns have taken action to limit the availability of alcohol within the town area.

Other Aboriginal health services have sought to address the range of problems arising from unhealthy living environments in an attempt to reduce the high rates of morbidity among Aboriginal infants and young children from illnesses such as gastroenteritis and pneumonia.

In the late 1980s, the Nganampa Health Council conducted a wide ranging survey of public and environmentally based health issues in the Pitjantjatjara homelands in the Northwest of South Australia. This project, the UPK (Uwankara Palyanku Kanyintjaku), provides an excellent model for developing an approach to environmental and public health in remote Aboriginal communities. It not only provides guidelines with respect to "healthy living practices and the health hardware necessary to achieve them" but also highlights the need for Aboriginal communities to be given the opportunity to acquire "the knowledge and skills to maintain healthy environments" (Saggers and Gray, 1991a:94).

Recent attention has been focussed on social and emotional health, and the need to provide Aboriginal health workers with the skills and knowledge necessary to cope with the high levels of depression and grief among Aboriginal community members.

The work being done by Aboriginal Health Services throughout Australia is of the utmost importance and has brought about a situation where more Aboriginal people now have access to culturally appropriate and acceptable health care services than at any time since white occupation began. However, as many Aboriginal communities are still without access to culturally appropriate health care, additional funding *must* be provided to allow all Aboriginal communities throughout Australia to have access to their own health services.

The National Aboriginal Health Strategy, formulated in 1989, provided for an "agreed national framework with the Aboriginal health sector and continues to be regarded as a robust document" (AHC and SAHC, 1995:13). It focussed, in particular, on the role of environmental factors in relation to Aboriginal ill health, the need for an Aboriginal definition of health and for a holistic approach to health care and emphasised the importance of community control.

In recommending that all Aboriginal primary health care services be transferred to Aboriginal community control, the NAHS recognised the critical importance of community participation and control and asserted the right of Aboriginal people to determine their own destiny in this and other aspects of their lives.

Improvements in health will not occur unless Aboriginal people throughout Australia are given the right and the responsibility to identify their own problems and to determine their own solutions. All governments—local, state/territory and Commonwealth—must make this their priority.

References

Abbie, AA (1976). *The Original Australians*. Sydney: Rigby.

Abbie, AA (1941). *Survey of the Half-caste Problem in South Australia*. Proceedings of the Royal Geographical Society of Australasia, SA, vol. XLII.

Aboriginal Health Council of SA Incorporated and South Australian Health Commission (1994). *Dreaming Beyond 2000: Our Future is in our History*. Adelaide: (typescript) .

AIHWJ (1991). "Appearance and reality: alcohol attitudes in Alice Springs". *Aboriginal and Islander Health Worker Journal*, vol. 15, no. 1.

Anderson, P, Bhatia, K, and Cunningham, J (1996). *Occasional Paper: Mortality of Indigenous Australians*. Australian Bureau of Statistics and Australian Institute of Health and Welfare. Cat. no. 3315.0. Canberra: ABS.

Australian Institute of Health and Welfare (1996). *Australian Health 1996: the Fifth Biennial Report of Australian Institute of Health and Welfare*. Canberra: AGPS.

Berndt, RM and CH (1988). *The World of the First Australians*. Canberra: Australian Studies Press.

Bhatia, K and Anderson, P (1995). *An Overview of Aboriginal and Torres Strait Islander Health: Present Status and Future Trends*. Canberra: Australian Institute of Health and Welfare.

Boyden, S (1987). *Western Civilisation in Biological Perspective*. Oxford: Clarendon Press.

Butlin, N (1983). *Our Original Aggression: Aboriginal Population in South Eastern Australia 1789-1856*. Sydney: Allen and Unwin.

Duguid, C (1972). *Doctor and the Aborigines*. Adelaide: Rigby.

Franklin, MA and White, I (1991). "The history of politics of Aboriginal health". In *The Health of Aboriginal Australians*, edited by J Reid and P Trompf. Sydney: Harcourt Brace Jovanovich.

Gatchel, RJ, Baum, A and Krantz, DS (1989). *An Introduction to Health Psychology*. New York: Random House.

Gould, RA (1980). *Living Archaeology*. Cambridge: CUP.

Hall, W, Hunter, E and Spargo, R (1993). "Alcohol-related problems among Aboriginal drinkers in the Kimberley region of Western Australia". *Addiction*, 88, pp 1091-1100.

Hollows, FC (1978). *Australian Aboriginal Eye Health—and What Must be Done*. Submission to the House of Representatives Standing Committee on Aboriginal Affairs—*Health Problems of Aboriginals*. Hansard:3602-11.

Human Rights and Equal Opportunity Commission (1997). *Bringing Them Home: a Guide to the Findings and Recommendations of the National Inquiry into the Separation of Aboriginal and Torres Strait Islander Children from Their Families*. Sydney: Human Rights and Equal Opportunity Commission.

Hunter, E, Hall, W and Spargo, R (1991). *The Distribution and Correlation of Alcohol Consumption in a Remote Aboriginal Population*. Monograph no. 12. Sydney: National Drug and Alcohol Research Centre, University of New South Wales.

Kamien, M (1993). "Aboriginal health: an overview". *Current Affairs Bulletin*, January 1993, 69 (8), pp 11-17.

Kunitz, SJ (1994). *Diseases and Social Diversity*. New York: Oxford University Press.

Lee, R and De Vore, I, editors (1968). *Man the Hunter*. Chicago: Aldine.

McEwan, M (1979). *Great Australian Explorers: the Courageous Exploits of the men who Challenged the New Land*. Kensington NSW: Bay Books.

Markus, A (1990). *Governing savages*. Sydney: Allen and Unwin.

Matthews, JD (1993). *Aboriginal Health Issues Report to Senator Graham Richardson from the Menzies School of Health Research*. Darwin, Northern Territory.

McLennan, W and Madden, R (1997). The health and welfare of Australias Aboriginal and Torres Strait Islander people. ABS Cat. no. 4704.0. Canberra: ABS.

Mobbs, R (1991). "In sickness and health : a socio-cultural context of Aboriginal well-being, illness and healing". In *The Health of Aboriginal Australians,* edited by J Reid and P Trompf. Sydney: Harcourt Brace Jovanovich.

Morice, R (1978, April). "Central Australian Aborigines, changes in lifestyle and the effect on health". *New Doctor,* no. 8.

Nathan, P and Japanangka, DL (1983). *Health Business.* Melbourne: Heinemann Educational Australia.

National Aboriginal Health Strategy Working Party (1989). *A National Aboriginal Health Strategy.* Canberra: AGPS.

Pollard, D (1988). *Give and Take: the Losing Partnership in Aboriginal Poverty.* Sydney: Hale and Ironmonger.

Powles, J (1979). "On the limitation of modern medicine". In *Ways of Healing,* edited by DS Sobel. New York: Harcourt Brace Jovanovich.

Reid, EJ and Lupton, D (1991). "Introduction". In *The Health of Aboriginal Australians,* edited by J Reid and P Trompf. Sydney: Harcourt Brace Jovanovich.

Reynolds, H (1982). *The Other Side of the Frontier.* Ringwood: Penguin..

Saggers, S and Gray, D (1991a). *Aboriginal Health and Society.* Sydney: Allen and Unwin.

Saggers, S and Gray, D (1991b). "Policy and practice in Aboriginal health". In *The Health of Aboriginal Australians,* edited by J Reid and P Trompf. Sydney: Harcourt Brace Jovanovich.

Senate Select Committee on Aboriginal and Torres Strait Islanders (1976). *The environmental conditions of Aboriginal and Torres Strait Islanders and the preservation of the sacred sites.* Canberra: AGPS.

Sibthorpe, G (1988). "All our people are dyin". *Diet and Stress in an Urban Aboriginal Community.* PhD thesis. Canberra: Australian National University.

Sobel, DS (1979). "Introduction". In *Ways of Healing,* edited by DS Sobel. New York: Harcourt Brace Jovanovich.

South Australian Health Commission (1993). "SA health statistics, chartbook, supplement 4". *Aboriginal Health.*

Stanner, WEH (1979). *White Man got no Dreaming.* Canberra: ANU Press.

Stevens, F (1974). *Aborigines in the Northern Territory Cattle Industry.* Canberra: ANU Press.

Swan, P and Raphael, B (1995). "Ways forward". *National Consultancy Report on Aboriginal and Torres Strait Islander Mental Health.* Part 2. Canberra: AGPS.

Taylor, SE (1986). *Health Psychology.* New York: Random House.

Thomson, N (1990). "A Review of Aboriginal Health Issues". In *The Health of Aboriginal Australians,* edited by J Reid and P Trompf. Sydney: Harcourt Brace Jovanovich.

Unwin, E, Thomson, N and Gracey, M (1994). *The Impact of Tobacco Smoking and Alcohol Consumption on Aboriginal Mortality and Hospitalisation in Western Australia: 1983-1991.* Perth: Health Department of Western Australia.

Western Australian Health Department (1992). *Mortality in Western Australia 1983-1989.* Perth: Health Department of Western Australia.

Endnotes

[1] It should be noted, however, that not all missions or reserves were like this and some Aborigines look back nostalgically to life on them as being happy and carefree (Dennis Ingram, May O'Brien and Denzal Humphries in Penny Taylor, editor (1988). After 200 years: photographic essays of Aboriginal and Islander Australia today. Canberra: Aboriginal Studies Press).

Chapter 11

Economics: Independence or Welfare

Colin Bourke

Background

Most people think of the economy as being involved with money, finance, banking, the stock exchange and business. Primary industry, mining and manufacturing are also considered to be integral to any discussion of the economy. Such institutions are not essential in economic systems. Some societies developed economic systems which were less complex, even though they had other intricate structures such as kinship obligations as their base.

The word economy is derived from two Greek words: *oikos* is a house or household while *nomos* is rule, law or custom. When combined as *oikonomos* they indicate the management of a house or household. An *oikonomos* then is the person involved, the manager. So, originally, *economics* involved the management of the resources of a household. It, therefore, involved the gathering, production, distribution, sharing and consuming of goods, products and services for the well-being of the household's members.

Today, economics has evolved into an academic discipline which is crucial to industry, finance and government. The modern concept of economics can be traced back to Adam Smith who in 1776 published *An enquiry into the nature and causes of the wealth of nations*. In this classic work Smith was as interested in the political as he was in the economic aspects of society.

Economics is not a separate entity. It involves large complex social and community realities, including personal relationships and expectations. It covers the processes of production, distribution, exchange and consumption and involves land, labour and capital.

Prior to 1788 Aboriginal people in Australia had a different economic system from that of the people who were to colonise Australia. Aborigines owned no valuable treasures that appealed to Europeans. Their economic life was based on sharing and cooperation. There were no individuals who possessed great wealth or land in European terms.

In most cases the people moved around their ancestral lands as hunters and gatherers, so many possessions would have been a hindrance. Their movements around their country were not haphazard but had a purpose. They were part of Aboriginal mastery over the resources of the land. This mastery gave individuals a great sense of assuredness.

Aborigines did not exhaust the resources of an area and:

> that very fact implies a process of deliberate resource management ... Spiritual attachment to the land, the sense of bonding with land, the protective myths and ritual, and attitudes that land ownership meant, in part, the right to share resources with others might be seen as modes of achieving, in the absence of market signals or governing direction, techniques of order in land/labour combinations that ensured an approximation of this style of rational behaviour or long term resource management (Butlin, 1993:92).

Due to environmental conditions and cultural practices there was great diversity in the economic activities of Aboriginal people.

As Professor Geoffrey Blainey (1975:v) noted:

> the various Aboriginal groups utilised the edible plants of their lands, worked their mines, developed the use of drugs and medicines, developed new manufacturing techniques and a large range of resources which ranged from raw materials for cosmetics and paints to hidden supplies of water.

Blainey (1975:v-vi) also observed:

> In one sense Aborigines resembled today's nations of Europe rather than Asia for the growth of their population was slow and their material standard of living was relatively high. Indeed, if an Aborigine in the 17th Century had been captured as a curiosity and taken in a Dutch ship to Europe, and if he had travelled all the way from Scotland to the Caucasus and had seen how the average European struggled to make a living, he might have said to himself that he had seen the third world and all its poverty and hardship.

Fire and smoke

The Aboriginal economy has been described as a *fire economy*. Fire was central to their way of life, affecting nearly every activity (Blainey, 1975:71). When Captain Cook sailed north up the Pacific Coast of Australia, he and his crew saw fires burning in the bush on most days. When the British arrived in 1788 they noticed Aborigines carrying lighted sticks. When they eventually ventured inland they were surprised to find large tracts of blackened country.

> Fire was used with limited areal burning both to capture game or to expose other foods, including eggs, slow-moving creatures and yam fields. It provided a short term abundance, it simplified all gathering tasks and it removed snakes and other dangerous creatures. Given the nature of many Australian shrubs and grasses, it removed physical injury and allowed unimpeded movement, further enhancing productivity (Butlin, 1993:78-79).

Although firesticks were carried, fire could be made with wood by friction generated through twirling or sawing. In some areas percussion was used by striking iron pyrite with flint to give sparks.

Fire was important in traditional life (Blainey, 1975:71). It affected most activity and was central to Aboriginal technology. Fire cooked meat, vegetables and damper. In some regions it cremated the dead. In others it was used to make body scars to adorn the living. Smoke was an insect repellent while flames were used to hunt animals. Along the Murray River hot ashes were used as a poultice.

Fire was the only light on moonless nights. In Arnhem Land burning a pandanus palm provided a beacon for canoes at sea. Around Botany Bay the early settlers noted the Eora people had small fires on clay hearths in their canoes while fishing at night.

Fire was used to straighten spears, shape wood, burn down trees for firewood, or to flush out animals. Most Aboriginal people had few clothes so fire was important for personal warmth. It was common practice to sleep between small fires at night and to carry a firestick during the day for warmth. An experienced person could enjoy the warmth of a firestick for hours.

Fire was also used for communication. Smoke signals could identify the location of groups and coordinate hunting and gathering activities. Early European colonists reported that in Queensland there was communication between the islanders and the natives of the mainland and that the rapid manner of carrying news from tribe to tribe for great distances was astonishing. Jack McLaren (1966:103) lived on an isolated property on Cape York and was informed of the outbreak of World War 1 by the local group who had received the information by smoke signals.

Through their use of fire Aborigines undoubtedly changed the environment of Australia (Butlin, 1993:94). Repeated burning over countless thousands of years resulted in the survival and flourishing of plants, animals, birds and insects which adapted best to the situation. Many Australian species of plant are relatively fire resistant and some need extreme temperatures for germination.

The use of fire enabled Aborigines to attain a high level of efficiency in the management of animals and plants to the mutual well being of human and other parts of the ecological system (Hallam, 1975:15).

Above all, however, the use of fire depended on control to prevent more than a limited area being burnt or even to ensure that special objects within the fired area were protected. That control depended on groups not individuals, effort. Failure of control could lead to destructive damage. At the extreme, this failure could damage neighbours' resources, creating intergroup or intertribal tensions (Butlin, 1993:79).

The lack of Aboriginal burning in some regions has resulted in damaging bushfires, especially in National Parks where there was an emphasis on minimal interference with nature. National Park Rangers are now looking at Aboriginal burning practices as a guide to effective control in such areas (Lewis, 1993:19-23).

Food and trade

Prior to 1788 agriculture was not practised on the Australian mainland, although Aborigines on Cape York Peninsula knew it was practised in the Torres Strait (Blainey, 1975:237). Instead, the women went out each day to gather edible roots, fruits and seeds. Some of these were eaten raw but some had to be treated and cooked in a fire. Women also collected small animals. If they lived near the sea they gathered shell fish. Men usually hunted for the larger animals or fished but women were also major providers of food—perhaps 50% to 70% of the daily diet (Hiatt, 1974:12). Aborigines have been criticised for not making gardens and domesticating animals. As the Berndts (1988:108) noted "before European settlers came to Australia there were no ... animals which could be domesticated". Later anthropologists such as Peter Sutton have suggested the lack of domestication and agriculture was cultural rather than ecological.

Although they were not a gardening people, the Aborigines were intimately concerned with the growth cycles of the plants they depended on for food. Their economy was a subsistence one, but it was not a matter of thoughtless, hand to mouth existence, or needless waste of natural resources.

It seems generally agreed that Aborigines achieved a large-scale alteration in the Australian environment through burning ... But areal burning was not the only form of resource management and change; much more intricate processes have to be considered, reaching a possible technological peak in the 'eel farming of Western Victoria' (Butlin, 1993:79).

The eel lands, ..., entailed a great deal of communal effort. This was required first to construct the system but also and very importantly to maintain it intact. The provision of this extensive asset not only increased the yield per person but also enhanced the supply (Butlin, 1993:78).

It is now clear that traditional Aboriginal people enjoyed a balanced diet of meat, fruit and vegetables. Most early historical records indicated that indigenous Australians were mainly meat eaters. However, Blainey (1975) noted that in a normal year Aborigines in many parts of the country ate a variety of plant foods that no present greengrocer or fruiterer in an Australian city would hope to display. He noted that on Cape York 73 different fruits and 46 different roots were eaten, while 19 kinds of seeds and nuts and 11 varieties of greens and shoots. In Arnhem Land at least 35 different fruits and 34 types of vegetables were available to Aborigines. While on Wilson's Promontory in Victoria about 120 edible plants existed. In 1979-80 Altman (1984) reported 170 species of flora and fauna being consumed. Edwards (1988:30-31) provides lists of food resources in Central Australia and North East Arnhem Land.

As well as plant food, meats, fish, shellfish and eggs of various types were popular. Aboriginal people also knew how to prepare their food, which to cook and which could be eaten raw. Some foods were poisonous unless properly prepared. For example, some tubers and the cycad palm nut require a preparation involving many processes over several days.

Given the concentration of activity within small bands, their separation from others for long periods, limited storage capacity for food stuffs and a broad similarity of supply conditions, the opportunity for sufficient differences in comparative advantage to generate flows was limited (Butlin, 1993:88). However, William Buckley, an escaped convict, reported that groups around Geelong traded fish for other goods (Morgan, 1967:38).

A system of trade by barter or exchange connected the people of Australia from one end of the continent to the other. Trading took place on the boundaries of the groups concerned, often at ceremonies and other gatherings. The method of exchange varied. If groups were hostile, a silent exchange took place. One group placed its products at a selected spot and then withdrew to provide an opportunity for the other group to place goods there. If both parties were satisfied, after separately examining the goods, the exchange was made. If not, other goods were included until a satisfactory conclusion was reached.

There were, however, special resource supply conditions in particular areas yielding valued objects that were traded over long distances. Thus axe heads from Gippsland were traded far into Australia (Butlin, 1993:85-86).

Goods frequently traded or exchanged included pigments, hairbelts, pearl shell, boomerangs, weapons, stone axes and knives, dilly bags and adhesive gums.

Trade between Aboriginal groups was not carried out for profit as it is in Australia today. In Arnhem Land a ceremonial exchange cycle was recorded by Professor Donald Thomson (1949). Goods passed continually from person to person along trade routes. In this way goods could end up hundreds of kilometres from their original location. The goods usually moved in one direction, thus ensuring they were never returned to the donors.

According to Thomson (1949:88) the Mildjingi clan of the Lower Glyde River in Eastern Arnhem Land were involved with a range of goods:

- From the east, iron-headed spears and a particular type of heavy stone used to crack cycad nuts.
- From the north, calico cloth, tobacco, blankets, glass, steel tomahawks and knives, belts and smoking pipes. All these goods and the iron spear heads were introduced into Arnhem Land by Macassans from Indonesia long before the Europeans arrived.
- From the north east, hooked spears and heavy clubs.
- From the south east, boomerangs, chain mesh dilly bags and possum fur aprons.
- From the south west, boomerangs (on another trade route), hooked spears and ceremonial human hair belts.

Trade routes criss-crossed Australia, many following the paths of The Dreaming Ancestors. Along these routes the totemic ancestors linked different people as brothers and sisters across group boundaries. The routes were often clearly marked tracks which followed rivers, valleys and skirted mountain ranges and coastal shores.

Various items have been followed along a chain of connecting exchanges. Red ochre from the quarry at Parachilna in the Flinders Ranges (SA) was traded throughout South Australia, the Lake Eyre Basin, western New South Wales and south-eastern Queensland. Pearl shell ornaments from the Kimberley coast were traded all over Western Australia and western Arnhem Land, south and Central Australia and western Queensland. Bailer shells from Cape York were exchanged all over Queensland and Western New South Wales, Central Australia and the Northern Territory. *Pitjuri* (native tobacco), grown in south-western Queensland and Central Australia, was traded as far as Western Australia.

Outside influences

Aborigines from Broome to Cape York exchanged goods with Indonesians (Macassans) for at least two hundred years before the European invasion (Butlin, 1993:103). The Indonesians travelled south using the prevailing winds, stayed for the dry season, bartering for *trepang* (dried sea-cucumber), pearl shell, tortoise shell and other items. Aborigines helped them and were paid with metal implements, food and clothing. Trepang had a reputation as an aphrodisiac and was traded right through to China.

> ... The arrival of trepang fishermen from Sulawese created a special condition on the northern shoreline of Australia. This was exceptional and recent. It led to new products, new imports (the dingo) and new ideas that might percolate throughout Australia (Butlin, 1993:85).

Aboriginal family histories record that some family members even travelled to Indonesia. This contact with the Macassans introduced new words, such as Balanda or Hollander, and ideas, techniques and concepts into Australia. The dugout canoe was probably introduced to Northern Australian by Macassans.

Until 1788 Aborigines had been able to choose what they wanted from other cultures. They didn't adopt agriculture apparently, because it wouldn't fit into their maintenance of sacred sites and attendance at ceremonies as they moved around their lands.

Ideas appear to have spread fairly slowly because hunting and gathering peoples really cannot afford to experiment boldly. A mistake can mean disaster. However, while it spread slowly change did occur. Aboriginal cultures were constantly changing. Ceremonies were exchanged, customs changed and new goods were introduced. But this was done slowly. Iron tools and macassan pipes had been in Arnhem Land for some 400 years before Cook, yet they hadn't reached south-eastern Australia by the 1830s.

Aboriginal economic life changed forever once the Europeans arrived. While it took nearly 100 years for the colonising encroachment of Aboriginal land to spread from Sydney to the Kimberleys, European diseases had disastrous effects on many Aborigines long before they knew a white man. Small pox, the common cold, measles and venereal disease were the frontline troops of European occupation. They wiped out countless indigenous people who had immune systems that were inadequate to counter European diseases.

> Given Aboriginal multi-resource use and seasonality of movements, British entry into Aboriginal areas could create major resource problems in a number of ways (Butlin, 1993:205).

Aborigines resisted the European invasion and hindered the spread of Europeans. They generally did not get involved in the European economic system. The European concepts of ownership, of private property and animals, were based on different values to those underlying Aboriginal economic life. With the exception of the pastoral industry Aboriginal skills were not valued by the colonisers since these did not seem to have an economic value in European terms.

> Habitats could be disturbed and strategic resources destroyed either by British persons or by livestock. Only a few such resources needed to be disturbed for a traditional 'equilibrium' to be upset or even for crisis to develop (Butlin, 1993:206).

Aboriginal employment

In the early years of the colony some Aborigines were used as house servants by the wealthy but the incompatibility of the differing value systems meant Aborigines saw few advantages in the European system of work. Aboriginal people were pushed to the fringes of settlements and generally remained fringe dwellers around Australia until the 1950s. Many found employment in the pastoral industry—the men as stockmen, the women in domestic work.

Non-acceptance by white society resulted in Aborigines not gaining the requisite education and skills to be useful employees. In 1986, 31% of Aboriginal males over 55 years reported they had received no schooling (Australian Bureau of Statistics, 1991). During the nineteenth century and the first half of the twentieth century Aborigines were generally offered seasonal work, picking fruit, cutting cane, casual employment in the rural areas and labouring jobs elsewhere. Children of mixed ancestry, who were forcibly removed from their families by government policy, were only trained to be domestics or semi-skilled farm workers. Large frontier landholders often appeared to accommodate Aborigines, to allow their presence on properties and to employ them in a variety of ways.

While Aborigines were able to maintain at least a substantial part of their resource supply to meet their needs which could be met within limited work hours. The balance of their time could be allocated in other ways such as ritual, education, and cultural activities. They had an intrinsic supply curve for labour in hunting and gathering. The evidence suggests that traditionally their diet exceeded those of the British so the only way they could become employees of pastoral properties was when their ecological conditions were significantly disrupted (Butlin, 1993:209).

Aborigines employed on stations across the north of Australia were not paid wages in most cases. Rations of dubious quality were given to them and their families. When the Federal Government legislated for equal wages in 1965 many station owners sacked their stockmen and evicted them from their land. But it was Aboriginal stockmen who had made the Australian cattle industry viable in the north of Australia. Their value was appreciated by leading pastoralists in the Gulf country according to Protector Galbraith in 1904 (Reynolds, 1977:47). Many thought they were superior to non-Aborigines. Traditional Aboriginal skills were useful in cattle station life, according to McGrath (1987:40). They were of course accustomed to outside activity and camping and had excellent orienteering skills. They knew the country intimately, which plants were poisonous and could always supplement the stock camp rations with bush tucker.

Aboriginal women were also widely used in stock work in North Queensland from the 1880's (May, 1994:51). Lawn Hill station near the Northern Territory border was being worked by thirteen Aboriginal women in 1892.

Aborigines had assisted European occupation of the country. Firstly, much of what Major Mitchell described as Australia Felix, vast grass lands, appears to have been the result of Aboriginal firestick farming. These grasslands were highly desired by the European squatters for their flocks of sheep.

Aborigines were used by many of the more successful European "explorers" to find their way over Aboriginal lands. One of the better known partnerships was Edward Eyre and Wylie. In many cases the name or value of the Aborigine was never mentioned in the journal of the explorer.

Socio-economic factors

In 1788 the Aboriginal population was spread across Australia. In the nineteenth century and early twentieth century the majority of Aborigines lived in rural areas. But the introduction of equal wages for Aborigines and increased mechanisation in the agricultural and pastoral industries quickly reduced Aboriginal employment in rural areas. Their role in the economy as cheap and convenient labour, always readily available and not unionised came to an end in the 1960s. The importance of Aboriginal people in the rural economy declined rapidly and the Aboriginal movement to the cities began to accelerate.

Since the 1960s Aborigines have endeavoured to improve their economic situation. They have struggled to have their rights to land recognised and have agitated for better education, health, employment and social justice.

Economic and social statistics are well-documented in Australia but it is difficult to isolate those which are Aboriginal. Aborigines still live in all parts of Australia and engage in a wide range of economic activities, as do other Australians.

At the risk of over simplification there is some justification in considering the Aboriginal economic situation according to the following groupings:

• outstations, homelands and other small groups
• Aboriginal towns
• small non-rural towns
• cities and large towns

Outstations, homelands and other small groups make an interesting category. The movement grew rapidly in the 1970s and 80s. It received encouragement and assistance from Governments. This benefited the communities socially and economically.

The homelands movement provides its member Aborigines with a refuge from the mainstream social and economic system. People can live in a way more in keeping with their cultural traditions and often on land with which they are culturally and emotionally associated.

Where the subsistence base is good, a judicious mixture of hunting and gathering using traditional skills and introduced technology such as guns, motor boats and motor vehicles allows a high level of subsistence. This is often augmented by cash income from the sale of arts and crafts and, in more recent years, by pensions, family allowance, JobStart allowance, NewStart and unemployment benefits or Community Development Employment Projects where communities agree to work for their unemployment money.

There are limitations and disadvantages to homelands life. Usually the remote location of the homeland adds to costs and restricts the choice of supplies from the market economy. This results in high prices and irregular supplies. The high prices are offset somewhat by lower housing rental costs in most of these areas.

Towns and settlements on Aboriginal lands differ considerably from the homelands in their economic and social structure, although most homelands have close ties with and are serviced by Aboriginal towns such as Ernabella, Yuendumu and Maningrida. The towns have a larger population as well as social and economic amenities not normally found at the homelands.

While the economic base of these towns is limited, there may be a certain amount of paid employment at schools, retail stores, council and other government institutions and perhaps a cattle station. Job opportunities are usually restricted, but such towns generally have reticulated water, some permanent housing and a health centre.

Most towns and settlements depend on the central government whether through social welfare payments, wage employment generated by public investment or government schemes where unemployment benefits are paid in full to the community and people work for their share.

In most states there are small non-rural towns with a significant Aboriginal population. They differ in several respects to Aboriginal towns. The chief economic difference is that some Aborigines in these situations are more fully integrated into the larger Australian economy as productive units. Indeed, in many such towns much of the non-Aboriginal employment is dependent on the presence of the Aboriginal population. Aboriginal employment in such towns is more likely to be integrated into the economy as a whole than is the case in Aboriginal towns. This happens simply because most country towns are sited to exploit some economic resource or opportunity. They have a substantial economic role in the total economy and do not exist solely to provide services to the residents as most Aboriginal towns do.

Although most Aboriginal employment is in unskilled areas, Aborigines have to compete for jobs against other ethnic groups whereas in Aboriginal towns they generally have the unskilled field to themselves.

Amenities in the country towns are generally good. Many Aborigines migrate into these townships from fringe camps and reserves where the level of amenities and of housing, in particular, is often poor. Those who do secure steady employment in these towns, who qualify for assistance with housing and who successfully adapt to town life do well. Those who do not are ultimately worse off than those in Aboriginal towns.

In cities and large towns the Aboriginal population is usually less differentiated from that of the rest of the population than in the other cases. Aboriginal people generally have more dependents, fewer marketable skills, less relevant work experience, less education than the majority of the population and are, thus, generally poorer with a higher unemployment rate.

The economic roles of Aborigines in the cities are basically similar in type to those of the majority of city dwellers, that is, they are either persons in paid employment, pensioners, unemployed or dependents. It is the proportion within each of these categories that they differ from the majority. They are rarely employers, managers, or highly paid professionals.

Aborigines in the economy today

Most economic discussions relating to Aborigines concentrate on Aborigines as consumers, employees or welfare recipients. The role of Aborigines as entrepreneurs in the private sector has generally been overlooked. Aboriginal individuals and organisations make important contributions in arts and crafts, the cattle industry and tourism. The proliferation of Aboriginal art shops in such centres as Darwin and Alice Springs suggests that this art makes a significant contribution to both the Aboriginal and non-Aboriginal economies of these regions.

As consumers Aborigines are an important component of the Australian economy, especially in those parts of Australia, such as the Northern Territory, where Aborigines are a significant proportion of the total population. Many towns depend on Aboriginal people for their existence. The 1991-92 Aboriginal and Torres Strait Islander Program totalled $1161 million, (*Social justice for indigenous Australians, 1992-93:*31). When added to earned incomes, social security payments, mining royalties and miscellaneous incomes, this results in a total of well over $1600 million of goods and services flowing into the Aboriginal sector of the economy (Altman J and Smith D). Refer to the diagram on the next page for more detail.

Little research has been done on the levels of Aboriginal savings. It is generally believed that savings are extremely low and, therefore, all income is spent almost immediately in the private sector in which there are few Aboriginal entrepreneurs. Traditional modes of production and distribution did not cultivate entrepreneurial endeavours. Today the Aboriginal sector of the economy does not benefit from a multiplier effect which would be achieved when Aborigines buy goods and services from one another.

Over the last two decades the Federal Government has provided additional funds for Aboriginal employment programs. Despite this, the unemployment rate is nearly three times that of other Australians. Aborigines have been employed by government bodies and government funded Aboriginal organisations but few have been employed in the private sector.

Figure 11.1: Commonwealth outlays by function Aboriginal and Torres Strait
Islander Programs 1991/92 ($million)

Source: *Social justice for Indigenous Australians*

Technological advances in the private sector, especially the pastoral
and agricultural industries, have lessened the demand for unskilled
labour, the location of much of the potential Aboriginal workforce.
Low levels of education and skills give few opportunities for
Aborigines in the private sector.

Aboriginal people and the mining industry have had difficult
relationships. Mining has grown rapidly but unevenly over the past
decade. It has had a large effect on the Australian economy. It has
directly affected some Aboriginal communities.

Mining constitutes about 20% of Australian exports. It is big
business. Many new towns, rail links and port facilities have been
constructed near Aboriginal communities. With the exception of the
Northern Territory, where some royalties are paid to the land
owners, there has been little benefit to Aboriginal people. In the rest
of Australia royalties are paid into State coffers. Very few
Aborigines are employed by mining companies. Less than 5% of
their total workforce is Aboriginal, even though many mines are in

areas where before mining the majority of the population was Aboriginal.

In 1973 Peter Rogers wrote "Australia has not done itself justice in the handling of the modern industry versus Aborigines conflict ... the lack of preparation ... is a disgrace to government, private organisations and unions alike" (Rogers, 1973).

The situation is beginning to look more hopeful. Mining companies such as Rio Tinto and Normandy are actively seeking to train Aboriginal workers and also develop Aboriginal entrepreneurs to provide goods and services to the mining companies and towns. In 1997 Rio Tinto received recognition for its efforts at the Reconciliation Convention in Melbourne.

Despite such developments the current Aboriginal economic structure is unsatisfactory. The sale of goods and services to the non-Aboriginal economy (private and public sector) is insignificant. Most Aboriginal income is still derived from transfers from the Australian economy such as age pensions, unemployment benefits and family allowances.

Policy

New policies in Aboriginal employment and economic development were announced by the Government in the 1986-87 Budget. The Aboriginal Employment Development Policy (AEDP) was the Government's response to the *Miller report on Aboriginal employment and training programs.*

The Prime Minister referred to a policy shift *away from the welfare dependency approach of the past towards measures to enhance Aboriginal economic independence.* A feature of the new policy was to be the development of strategies for improved Aboriginal access to the private sector and the creation of jobs in Aboriginal enterprises.

The Government anticipated that some two thirds of the employment growth required to achieve employment equality for Aborigines could be met through increased opportunities in the private sector. The private sector was seen as consisting of Aboriginal owned businesses and Aboriginal service organisations, as well as employment with non-Aboriginal employers. The target set was an extra 1,100 jobs per year for the remainder of this century. It could be argued that Aboriginal service organisations should not have been classified in the private sector while the bulk of their funds come from governments.

In the past, Government assistance to promote Aboriginal wage and salaried employment in the private sector has focussed almost exclusively on wage subsidies under the Training for Aboriginals Program (TAP).

The Aboriginal Employment Action (AEA) program was introduced in 1985 to develop group intake strategies for the recruitment of Aboriginals to the private sector. Activities funded included developing employment strategies and cross-cultural training.

However, by 1994 38% of Indigenous Australians remained unemployed (compared to 10% for all Australians) and of these, 77% had been looking for work for three months ore more, and over 50% had been unemployed for twelve months or more.

In 1996 ATSIC established a "Policy Framework for Future Directions" which set down four principles for economic development:

- respect for the diversity of circumstances of Aboriginal and Torres Strait Islander communities (in terms of cultures, values, needs, aspirations, strengths and weaknesses);
- empowerment of the people at all levels;
- increased responsiveness in the role of government agencies;
- realistic and sustainable outcomes.

ATSIC stated the real impetus for economic development must come from individuals wanting greater financial independence. While government policies and programs were seen as assisting in establishing a positive external environment.

Policies and strategies for achieving economic equality for indigenous Australians were launched by ATSIC in 1997. Three key action areas were identified for economic development: the development of indigenous businesses and entrepreneurs; increased employment and skill development; and, greater accumulation and utilisation of indigenous assets. Strategies attached to these action areas require successful implementation if there is to be any significant move towards economic equality for Indigenous

Australians. However, ATSIC believes such progress will take ten years to achieve incremental progress.

Entrepreneurial activity

The Hawke Government aimed to achieve equality in the self-employment of Aboriginal people in Aboriginal owned businesses by the year 2000. The Government's major program in this area was the Small Business Funding Scheme. This scheme involved either loans assistance to prospective Aboriginal entrepreneurs at concessional interest rates, or joint loans packages partly funded by Government at concessional interest rates and partly funded by commercial financial institutions at market interest rates, depending on individual circumstances.

The Government also established an Aboriginal Enterprise Incentive Scheme (AEIS) for unemployed people to assist them to establish businesses. This alternative approach to job creation for Aborigines required only small amounts of capital to establish sole trading businesses for self-employment. ATSIC allocated some $30 million in 1997/98 for the replacement Indigenous Business Incentive Program (IBIP). This program is to focus less on community based enterprises and place greater emphasis on assisting business opportunities for individuals, partnerships and joint ventures.

An Enterprise Employment Assistance program commenced in 1986. It provided assistance for labour costs in Aboriginal community enterprises and involved the payment of employment subsidies to Aboriginal community enterprises equivalent to the overall unemployment benefit payments that eligible Aboriginal participants would otherwise have received. This program was later extended to all Aboriginal businesses where the employment or self-employment of an eligible Aboriginal person was involved.

The Government's Aboriginal Employment Development Policy (AEDP) which has at last recognised that Aborigines must move into the private sector as employees and entrepreneurs. The AEDP has aimed to create an economic base which will generate jobs. However, according to Tesfaghiorghis and Altman (1991) "there is no concrete evidence to date that this strategy which incorporates a focus on enterprise development is having any success". But John Taylor (1993) reports that the CDEP scheme has increased from 6,000 participants in 1996/87 to more than 22,000 in 1993. By 1997 there were 26,000 employed under the program.

In 1993, the Arremte Council organised the first National Indigenous Business Economic Conference in Alice Springs. The Conference established the interim National Business and Economic Council (NIBEC) which consists of Indigenous business people from throughout Australia. NIBEC aims to promote the long-term growth of enterprise to enable Aboriginal and Torres Strait Islander business communities to achieve self-management and self-determination through financial independence.

A second NIBEC Conference was held in Brisbane in 1995. This conference had over 600 delegates and concentrated on business related issues and networking. The conference was organised by the Queensland Indigenous Business and Economic Corporation Limited (QIBEC) which had evolved from the Alice Springs Conference.

In 1997 an International Conference on Economic Development for Indigenous People was organised by the Department of Employment, Education, Training and Youth Affairs, and involved ATSIC and the DECO. The Conference received a report from the OECD on economic development from Aborigines and Torres Strait Islanders. Case histories of successful entrepreneurial activity by indigenous individuals and communities were described as "The Pathways to the Future".

Aboriginal and Torres Strait Islander Commercial Development Corporation (CDC)

Established in 1990 by Government to stimulate Indigenous involvement in business the CDC has concentrated on joint ventures with non-indigenous partners. The CDC is expected to be mainly a self-financing and commercial organisation. At the end of 1996 some 16 joint ventures had been established in a range of areas including retailing, mining, shipping and tourism with mainly non-Indigenous companies.

The CDC received seed funding from the government until 1994 but has since then financed its operations from loan repayments and financial investments.

Joint venturing has enabled the CDC and Indigenous people to receive business support from experienced non-Indigenous partners. This has also helped to break down barriers of negative perceptions and racial misunderstandings that have inhibited Indigenous efforts to gain economic self sufficiency.

Arthur (1996) has questioned the extent to which such joint venturing and other CDC initiatives are actually achieving Indigenous self-management and economic development which were the main aims of establishing the CDC.

Aboriginal and Torres Strait Islander Commission

The Commission has set itself three tasks to achieve in socio-economic development (ATSIC Report, 1990-91):

- to enable Aboriginal and Torres Strait Islander communities or groups to undertake community development activities (including community enterprises) designed and valued by the community or group and which involve the employment of community members;
- to provide training to the staff and executive Aboriginal and Torres Strait Islander community councils, organisations and community enterprises to enable them to perform their existing duties more efficiently and to achieve more effective self-management;
- to promote the number of self employment opportunities through Aboriginal and Torres Strait Islander enterprises.

ATSIC is one of several agencies involved in developing the Aboriginal Employment Development Policy (AEDP). It forms the basis of the Commission's approach to the economic development of Aboriginal and Torres Strait Islander people. In 1990-91 AEDP strategies related to community development employment projects ($194 million), business and enterprise development ($21 million) and training and planning ($9 million).

ATSIC realises that the AEDP depends on other programs which involve skill acquisition, employment and economic development opportunities. An AEDP Task Force has provided a forum for discussion and has had a coordinating, overseeing and monitoring role to increase the effectiveness of the program.

The Community Development Employment Projects (CDEP scheme) employed some 26,000 indigenous Australians in 1997 it offers an opportunity to replace unemployment with work on a variety of community projects and enterprises. It is commonly known as the *work for the dole scheme*. The Royal Commission into Aboriginal Deaths in Custody Report indicated that the scheme was a source of dramatic change in many communities. It highlighted social benefits and an improvement in race relations in some country towns. Critics of the scheme have questioned its effect on individual human rights, the concealing of unemployment numbers and the large number of non-Aboriginal administrators involved. A further fundamental criticism of CDEP has been its inability to achieve income equality between indigenous and non-indigenous Australians. Jon Altman, in a personal communication, states that income is a more significant measure of economic equality than employment. He also points out that income equality is a major plank of the AEDP.

The funding of enterprises and businesses is seen as essential if indigenous Australians are to participate in the full range of Australian economic activity. This part of the AEDP has had difficulty with the staff resources available, arrears control and the development of adequate management information systems. One inbuilt difficulty is that ATSIC officers are public servants with backgrounds, abilities and knowledge which may not be suitable for dealing with private enterprise.

AEDP also offered an enterprise incentive scheme, management advice and training for people desirous of establishing small businesses. Training was also available for staff and directors of Aboriginal organisations to increase effectiveness and achieve a higher degree of self management. For a statistical analysis of the AEDP based on the 1986 and 1991 Census data see Taylor (1993).

Community development planning has enabled communities to plan for an integrated framework of development and coordination of government services provision. These community plans are developed into regional plans but are centrally managed by ATSIC. At this stage, there appears to be some difficulty in coordinating community and regional needs into a national program.

By 1997 three industry strategies had been developed to focus on the economic aspects of participation in rural, tourism and cultural industries.

These strategies have a common bottom up approach from the community level and a realistic vision with an emphasis on building enterprise capacity at community level which is ecologically and economically sustainable.

However, significant government commitment is needed if these strategies are to bring meaningful economic outcomes to Indigenous communities.

In 1994 the Torres Strait Regional Authority (TSRA) was established under the Aboriginal and Torres Strait Islander Act 1989 following a review of that Act. Like ATSIC the TSRA has an elected and an administrative arm. Twenty elected representatives who are Torres Strait Islanders or Aborigines living in the Torres Strait region form the elected arm.

The functions and power of the TSRA are outlined in Section 142 C of the ATSIC Act. In essence the Authority has power to perform its functions, accept gifts and grants and act as a trustee which maintains island customs, implements and monitors programs, develops policy and advises communities.

The 1991 Census showed an indigenous population of 5,397 in the Torres Strait of whom 1,670 were employed under the CDEP scheme. In 1996 the TSRA had a budget of some $38 million for its operations. Its programs are aimed at increasing the economic power of Aboriginal people and Torres Strait Islanders and developing opportunities for enhancing employment, education, training and land ownership. Business funding and community economic activities are receiving high priority.

Conclusion

Since 1788 Indigenous Australians have ceased to be fully employed, self-sufficient individuals with high self-esteem. Today they are the poorest identifiable sector of the Australian community. Various government programs have been in place for many years, but progress is difficult to achieve.

Some 30% are officially recognised as being unemployed and Aborigines are not achieving equality in an increasingly technologically sophisticated Australia. Aboriginal society consists of many diverse groups. Consequently centralised policies do have difficulty meeting the needs of all Aborigines.

The Aboriginal Employment Development Policy Statement is a very optimistic document which, in some areas, has not come to grips with the private sector. A positive feature of the policy is that the government has at last recognised that Aboriginal people must move into the private sector as employees and entrepreneurs.

Government funded Aboriginal organisations are not in the private sector and should not be considered as such. The policy includes a gross over simplification of what it takes to succeed in small business (over 35% of all small businesses in Australia fail in the first year, this increases to over 50% by the second year). This over simplification is understandable because the policy was written by public servants with little background in business and a vested interest in maintaining Aboriginal people as a client group.

Despite this criticism there is a recognition of the importance of Aboriginal economic development and that Aboriginal people have to become involved in the private sector of the Australian economy to move out of the welfare sector.

The Miller Committee of Review of Aboriginal Employment and Training Programs (1985) found that Aboriginal people had low economic status. The Committee's recommendations resulted in the AEDP focussing on two broad policy goals:

- ensuring Aboriginal economic equality, using employment, income and education indicators, by the year 2000; and
- achieving a corresponding reduction in Aboriginal welfare dependency to the same level as other Australians.

Analysis of data indicates that the AEDP has not achieved its goals. The CDEP scheme, because it is based on unemployment benefits works against income equality, a goal of AEDP. The more Aborigines who go under CDEP, the more who will receive below average wages.

Measuring the success of AEDP will probably require dependence on census data because statistical data on Aboriginal people is very limited. Comparison between 1991 and 1996 census data is of immense policy interest when examined on an Australia wide basis. Any correlation between government expenditure on economic programs and improvement in social indices at a regional or community level is of great importance to the bureaucratic policymakers but, ultimately, crucial to improvement in Aboriginal economic well being. The economic development of Aboriginal people is vital to all Australians. Welfare dependence must be reduced and Aboriginal independence advanced through programs based on Aboriginal growth through self-determination.

References

Aboriginal and Torres Strait Islander Commission (1990-91). *Annual Report.*

Altman, Jon C and Nieuwenhuysen, John (1979). *The Economic Status of Australian Aborigines.* New York: Cambridge University Press.

Altman, Jon and Smith DE, *CAEPR Discussion Paper*, no. 47. Canberra: Centre for Applied Economic Policy Research, Australian National University.

Arthur, WS (1996). The Aboriginal and Torres Strait Islander Commercial Development Corporation, *CAEPR Discussion Paper*, no. 113. Canberra: Aboriginal and Torres Strait Islander Commission.

Berndt, Ronald M and Catherine H (1988). *The World of the First Australians: Aboriginal Traditional Life, Past and Present.* Canberra: Aboriginal Studies Press.

Blainey, Geoffrey (1982). *Triumph of the Nomads: a History of Ancient Australia.* South Melbourne: Macmillan.

Butlin, NG (1993). *Economics and the Dreamtime.* Melbourne: Cambridge University Press.

Committee of Review of Aboriginal Employment and Training Programs (1985). *Aboriginal Employment and Training Programs: Report of the Committee of Review.* Canberra: Australian Government Publishing Service.

Daylight, Phyllis and Johnstone, Mary (1986). *Women's Business: Report of the Aboriginal Women's Task Force.* Canberra: Australian Government Publishing Service.

Edwards, WH (1990). *An Introduction to Aboriginal Societies.* Wentworth Falls, NSW: Social Science Press.

Edwards, WH, editor (1987). *Traditional Aboriginal Society: a Reader*. South Melbourne: Macmillan.

Fisk, EK (1985). *The Aboriginal Economy in Town and Country*. Sydney: Allen and Unwin.

Hallam, Sylvia (1975). *Fire and Hearth*. Canberra: Australian Institute of Aboriginal Studies.

Hiatt, Betty (1974). "Woman the gatherer". In *Woman's Role in Aboriginal Society*. Second edition, edited by Fay Gale. Canberra: Australian Institute of Aboriginal Studies.

Lewis, Henry T (1993). "The technology and ecology of nature's custodians: anthropological perspectives on Aborigines and national parks". In *Aboriginal Involvement in Parks and Protected Areas*, edited by Jim Birckhead, Terry De Lacy and Laurajane Smith. Canberra: Aboriginal Studies Press.

May, D (1994). *Aboriginal Labour and the Cattle Industry*. Melbourne: Cambridge University Press.

McGrath, A (1988). *Born in the Cattle*. Sydney: Allen and Unwin.

McLaren, Jack (1966). *My Crowded Solitude*. Melbourne.

Morgan, John (1852, republished 1967). *The Life and Adventures of William Buckley*. Melbourne: Heinemann.

Reynolds, Henry (1972). *Aborigines and Settlers*. Australia: Cassell.

Rogers, Peter (1973). *The Industrialists and the Aborigines: a Study of Aboriginal Employment in the Australian Mining Industry*. Sydney: Angus and Robertson.

Rowse, Tim (1992). *Remote Possibilities: the Aboriginal Domain and the Administrative Imagination*. Darwin: Australian National University.

Social Justice for Indigenous Australians (1992-93). Budget related paper no. 7. Circulated by the Honourable Robert Tickner, Minister for Aboriginal and Torres Strait Islander Affairs and Minister assisting the Prime Minister for Aboriginal Reconciliation. Canberra: Australian Government Publishing Service.

Taylor, John (1993). *The Relative Economic Status of Indigenous Australians 1986-1991*. Canberra: Centre for Applied Economic Policy Research, Australian National University.

Tesfaghiorghis H and Altman J (1991). *Aboriginal Socio-economic Status: Are There any Evident Changes?* Canberra: Centre for Applied Economic Policy Research, Australian National University.

Thomson, DF (1949). *Economic Structure and the Ceremonial Exchange Cycle in Arnhem Land*. Melbourne: Macmillan.

Chapter 12

Art: Interpreting Reality

Franchesca Alberts and Christopher Anderson

Introduction

The art of Aboriginal Australia is one of the oldest, richest and most complex forms of creative expression in human history. In the earlier days of European occupation, it was mistakenly believed that Aboriginal people had no art, only basic craft and ritual-related decoration. Europeans found it incomprehensible that a people living in such a harsh environment and possessing such minimal material culture could have had more than a rudimentary notion of art. When the spectacular rock paintings in north western Australia, now known as Wandjina figures, were first described by Sir George Grey in 1837, it was assumed that they must have been done by alien visitors to Australia (Jones, 1988). Today Aboriginal art is recognised around the world as an exciting, major contribution to world art and an expression of deepest humanity and unity with nature.

In spite of this, there remain erroneous beliefs—for example, that bark paintings are the only real Aboriginal art form or that bark painting was done over the whole of Australia; that works made for sale today are somehow not genuine; or that modern written works, dance and music by Aboriginal artists are not "traditional" and hence not genuinely Aboriginal.

Aboriginal art is as much alive today as it was 40,000 years ago. As in that ancient past, the art is not easily separable from everyday life. It is a lively and positive art which describes and engages the world in a variety of guises—song, word, performance and paint, among others.

The art of Aboriginal Australians today takes on many forms. Despite significant change and diversity, the art retains an underlying unity of inspiration—the land and human relationships that are associated with it. It has solid links with the past but is firmly rooted as political, social and creative action in the present.

What is Aboriginal art?

Aboriginal art is the oldest continuous art tradition in the world. Recent scientific dating of engraved concentric circles on rocks in the Flinders Ranges of South Australia reveal them to be over 35,000 years old (Dorn and Nobbs, 1992).

While the meaning of the art and its symbolism have undoubtedly changed in this time, the *form* of the art—common to much of Aboriginal art today—has remained strikingly similar for thousands of years. This art, as an expression of Aboriginal people's relationship to the land and to each other, was being generated at a time when art and its association with a spiritual world were apparently unknown to the inhabitants of northern Europe.

The Aboriginal art of today has profound links with that of the past. The last several hundred years up to and including the present have seen a great variety of Aboriginal art forms around the country (See Berndt et al, 1982; Caruana, 1993; Isaacs, 1980, 1984; Sutton et al, 1988).

Across the continent, there are regional differences in artistic forms varying broadly in relation to the environment, with major differences between arid, tropical and temperate zones. In the visual arts and crafts, including ritual and everyday design, there are:

* concentric circles, dotting, tracks and meandering lines and use of more abstract imagery (Central Australia and much of the arid portions of Australia);
* the ubiquitous rock art of the Top End (of the Northern Territory), with heavy figurative emphasis, use of x-ray figures and cross-hatching in-fill;
* the use of heavy and broad white and red bands, a tradition of wood carving and beeswax sculpture in some areas (North Queensland);
* geometric, square incising, figures and forms incised on pearl shell (Kimberley);
* elaborate weaving and basketry tradition, finely incised wooden implements and weapons (Murray-Darling system).

The art of the Top End, the tropical region east of Darwin in northern Australia, is probably the best known. Here, people expressed themselves in body painting for ceremony, in rock painting and through decoration of everyday objects. In addition, at least in western and north-eastern Arnhem Land and on Groote Eylandt, people painted on sheets of bark. Sometimes bark sheets were used as parts of shelters and were occasionally painted (Edwards and Guerin, 1969). The sheets were taken from suitable trees, stripped, flattened and dried. Natural ochres were then applied with stick brushes. Dreaming stories were painted as a means of teaching novices and to "prove" the veracity of the stories' content.

Bark paintings, though, were confined to a limited area of the tropical north and generally were not found elsewhere in Australia. In other parts of the continent, Aboriginal people used other media for creative and spiritual expression.

In Central Australia, for instance, there were no trees suitable as bark "canvases". In addition, as Aboriginal people there say, "It is not part of our culture". In the arid and desert regions, people painted with a great variety of ochres, on their bodies, on rock surfaces, on their weapons, ceremonial objects and on everyday domestic implements. Using plant substances, ochres and sand, they also created elaborate ground sculptures for ceremony. Sometimes these covered hectares of ground and took many people months of preparation. Often these were secret and restricted only to initiated men. However, in some areas of Central Australia, women created ground paintings for public ceremonies (Anderson, 1993).

From the Lake Eyre region come *toas*, small, sculpted objects of wood, gypsum and ochre, often acting as bases for hair, plant material or feathers. Each one represents a Dreaming place and part of a related story, linking a particular group with the land and its Dreaming heritage. Although debate exists about their origin and function (Jones and Sutton, 1986), the toas are clearly an art form with real and long-standing roots in Lake Eyre Aboriginal culture.

Large-scale rock engravings and carvings were also produced in south eastern Australia by Aboriginal people, for example, in the Sydney area even fifty years after first European settlement. Large-scale wooden sculpture and fine line incising were another major tradition in the south eastern parts of the continent. The largest and most spectacular examples are the carved trees of New South Wales and inland Victoria.

In other parts of the country, such as west Cape York Peninsula in far north Queensland, sculpted animals and other beings in wood and beeswax depicted ancestral figures which were part of complex myth cycles and used in ceremonies.

The epic myth stories of Aboriginal Australia must also be seen as narrative, song and performance events equivalent to the best of European theatre, dance and literature. The unity of these forms in ceremony has tended to mask their artistic qualities for non-Aboriginal people.

Contrary to the common stereotypes, Aboriginal art took a multitude of forms and was manifest in different media right around the country. In terms of intent and inspiration, however, it shared a great deal.

In traditional Aboriginal society the distinctions between art and non-art, art and craft were meaningless. There was design inherent in both nature and in the manufacture and decoration of all human products. The designs were all "left" by the Ancestors; humans merely brought the religious force to visible form in different contexts.

All forms of art were not equal, however. There was a hierarchy of power, degrees of sacredness. In a sense, all art was sacred. But some was so sacred that it was kept secret from certain groups—the young, the untutored, men in some cases and women in others. This separation of different art for different situations and audiences still applies today in many Aboriginal societies.

Art was integral to traditional Aboriginal society. It was part of everyday life. Each person was expected to be able to depict in terms of the relevant art form their own place in the universe. Art was thus an integral part of religious life. Aboriginal people executed their ancestral stories in the various media: body painting during ritual, ceremonial ground designs and rock paintings or engravings, song, stories and performance.

Art gave people a means of describing their relationship to the land and to each other. It thus provided the bridge between nature and culture. It became a means for the affirmation of identity, an expression of individual creativity and feeling and a way of communicating with people, both living and dead. Through song, dance and painting people enacted and re-created their histories and affirmed their inalienable place in the landscape. Men and women each had their own artistic domains and particular means of fulfilling their social obligations to each other and to their Ancestors, to The Dreaming.

People shared rights in The Dreaming—that is, a man and his brother or sister would share the right to produce particular motifs and designs. They inherited these from one of their parents and they had the right, indeed the obligation, to produce their Dreaming designs in all possible media. Hence, today, as before, some Aboriginal art is produced by individuals and other art by groups of people who share similar rights. Artistic production is thus not only a function of individual creativity. It is also a social activity related to the web of kinship on which the society is based.

This is not to say, however, that "art" did not exist in Aboriginal society, that there were not people with special artistic skills and a desire to describe the world around them through art. However, this was always done through the filter of culture and people were limited by the media presented to them in their environment.

It is probable that the great variety of art existed at least at the time of first colonial settlement and probably before. Many of the forms still exist today, as integral parts of both everyday and religious life. In many cases, Aboriginal people now make a living in cash terms from their art.

Generating art, in any form, in pre-European days was seen as necessary to on-going life. The art of Aboriginal Australia was not static, however. It changed as fashion, trade and contact with other groups brought new ideas and innovations to local art.

The existence of change and of art as a reflection of particular circumstance, as part of a flexible and adaptive way of life, can be seen as far back as the first days of contact with non Aborigines.

Opportunity and adaptation

Many people believe that Aboriginal people once did "traditional" art and that now people do art that is somehow corrupted, either by the use of non-traditional materials or that they are doing it because of "outside" influences.

Contrary to this view, the art of Aboriginal Australia has always been dynamic and changing to reflect people's circumstances. Aboriginal people have seized opportunities to either express themselves artistically in new ways or to achieve their own ends via art in new situations. This adaptability was probably always the case. It may be that one of the forms now thought of as very "traditional", for example, rock painting, was once an innovation. In the post-contact era, one of the main factors influencing art was that Aboriginal people saw the political importance of teaching outsiders about their land and world view.

The view of the static, unchanging "traditional" is contradicted by a new and different look at the art history of Australia.

Bark paintings are often seen as the definitive Aboriginal art. However, in a sense, bark paintings are not "real". As we have seen, they were confined to one small part of Australia—Arnhem Land—and even here, painting on bark to produce portable art was probably not done prior to the early 20th century. Bark was used for shelter and it often happened to be decorated. As mentioned above, sheets of bark were also used for didactic purposes during ceremony. However, it was really only the demand created by missionaries, buffalo hunters and other key local Europeans, stimulated in turn by outsiders such as Professor Baldwin Spencer, NB Tindale and CP Mountford that created bark painting as an art form. This, however, does not make bark painting less authentic. Rather, it reflects, in content, northern Australian Aboriginal culture; in aim, the economic and political realities of Arnhem Land in the early 20th century.

In a similar way, the rock paintings of north Queensland contain many examples in which Aboriginal artists depicted the new objects, people and events around them, following the arrival of Europeans (see Walsh, 1988). In the Laura region of Cape York Peninsula for example, Aboriginal people were attempting to affect and alter with their art the events and forces which appeared in their country in terms of their own culture. The depiction in rock art of Europeans and Chinese on the Palmer River gold fields, for instance, was often part of the sorcery attempts by Aboriginal people to deal with these intruders. The native troopers and other police were also depicted, sometimes with horses and guns. Other north Australian examples include Macassan ships from Indonesia.

Elsewhere, Aboriginal artists made rapid use of new media and materials which seemed to appear out of nowhere. Just after the turn of the century, in the Gulf country of the Northern Territory, unknown Borroloola artists painted their Dreaming stories onto the boards of food packing crates which may have been washed up on the beach. We know little about these works, but it is apparent that artists were using the chance appearance of new materials to continue or elaborate an existing tradition.

In the Kimberley, Aboriginal artists of Karadjeri and Nyangamada descent, began from the early 1960s onwards to carve stone heads. This innovation came as a result of a dream-visitation experienced by a Karadjeri/Nyangamada man. In this visitation, a Dreaming being, Walkarurra, taught the man a new ceremonial sequence and insisted that human figures be carved. In similar fashion, the famous Nyangamada tin masks in the South Australian Museum are examples of introduced materials being used for "normal" Aboriginal religious practices (Kean et al, 1990).

In Central Australia, there are a number of significant examples of artistic opportunism which demonstrate the pre-existing Aboriginal tradition of art as education and political act, operating in a situation of radical change.

The first of these examples is crayon drawings. Aboriginal people from the desert regions of central Australia, many of whom had never seen Europeans, jumped at the chance to use introduced materials and media to portray their world view. With the arrival of South Australian Museum expeditions to Cockatoo Creek, Mt Liebig, Warburton Ranges, Mann Ranges and other parts of Central Australia in the 1920s and 30s, Aboriginal men drew un-prompted maps of their country, their Dreaming stories and the elements of their environment, in the same way they did with "traditional" body, rock and ground paintings.

The technique, developed by the anthropologist, Norman Tindale, consisted of giving Aboriginal people (usually men) crayons in colours normally available to them (red, yellow, white and black). They were then also given paper sheets, usually 50cm x

30cm. No suggestions were made as to what people should draw, only that they put "marks" on the paper.

In general, the iconography is the same as for that in other art forms of Aboriginal Central Australia: concentric circles represent mythic sites in the landscape (usually waterholes or campsites), with straight lines connecting the circles representing travelling paths. "U" shapes represent people sitting and domestic implements and weapons such as spears and boomerangs are often shown near them. The tracks of animals such as kangaroos, dingoes and birds are also common.

The fact that they were using crayons and brown paper and were drawing the paintings for Europeans is irrelevant. The artists were trying to teach the newcomers about their land, in the same way that they taught young Aboriginal people. The artists were also making statements about their affiliation to the land and their rights to it. These drawings are a unique and significant record, not only of the art of Central Australian Aborigines, but of a momentous encounter between two very different cultures.

The water-colours of Central Australia, the so-called Namatjira school, is another example of Aboriginal artistic opportunism and adaptability (Hardy et al, 1992). Albert Namatjira, an Aranda man from the western MacDonnell Ranges, took every possible opportunity for artistic expression. Having grown up within the classic Central Australian Aboriginal art traditions, his work as an artist included wood carvings and paintings. Through Namatjira's later work with artist Rex Battarbee, he and his family began a tradition of Aboriginal water-colour landscapes: once again, depicting the Central Australian landscape, not only because of its tourist appeal, but because it was familiar country containing particular sites of religious importance.

As one writer has put it:

> We now cannot but see Namatjira's paintings as a way of reaffirming his tribal territorial knowledge while simultaneously sharing with outsiders his pride in his land's great beauty. Further, we now perceive the repetition of similar rocks and similar ghost gums as a way of converting them from once-off observations to timeless symbols (Thomas, 1986:26).

The fact of showing their country and making statements about it is indisputable, despite the origin of the technique or the materials. The Namatjira movement, like the crayon drawings, can be seen as another Central Australian Aboriginal attempt to reaffirm to outsiders their interests and rights in land, a long-standing "traditional" function of art in this area as in other parts of Aboriginal Australia.

These earlier examples of crayon drawings and water-colours are sometimes obscured by what is probably now the most famous art form of Central Australia, acrylic dot paintings.

Acrylic painting has its origins in the community of Papunya, 200kms west of Alice Springs when, in the early 1970s a young school teacher, Geoff Bardon, attempted to get Luritja, Warlpiri and Pintupi school children to paint in terms of their own culture instead of from the point of view of an introduced one (Bardon, 1991). This perspective offered such serious and significant opportunities that the older men in the community took it over and began painting onto board, canvas and any other available material, the sacred stories of their origins. Over the years, and with the interest of the art market, a large scale movement spread to many other communities to the point where, now, hundreds of artists produce thousands of paintings a year. These vary from small canvases sold as souvenirs in Alice Springs to major works sold for large amounts of money to the art museums of the world.

Whether souvenir or fine art, the acrylic paintings of Central Australia depict The Dreaming stories and sites specific to particular artists and groups. The same rules which apply to the other more "traditional" art forms also apply to acrylic works. The aim in both is to state relations with and rights in land. Rock, body and ground paintings co-exist with acrylic painting in the Aboriginal communities of the Centre. In the former case the art is directed inwards. In the latter it is outward. The content, however, is the same (Anderson and Dussart, 1988).

Aboriginal artists have always interacted with the "outside" world in an active, opportunistic, adaptable, flexible way. Aboriginal people, at first contact and since, have always taken the opportunities presented to them via introduced media to express themselves and to achieve explicit aims vis-à-vis their position in the world.

Aboriginal arts today

It is a common view today that the world's interest in Aboriginal art is recent and a function of modern enlightened attitudes. However, the first exhibition of works done by Aboriginal people and exhibited as "art" occurred in Adelaide in the late 1880s. This exhibition, titled the "Dawn of Art", consisted of eighteen drawings of various animals and birds done by Aboriginal men who were inmates or workers at the Palmerston Gaol in Darwin.

Similarly, an exhibition called "Primitive Art" opened at the Museum of Victoria in Melbourne in 1929. This exhibition "presented a range of Aboriginal art: carved trees from New South Wales, spears and shields, painted ceremonial boards from Groote Eylandt, reproductions of rock paintings from Victoria, ... bark paintings ... and even the design for a wooden grave memorial" (Jones, 1988:167). Aboriginal craftsmen were brought to Melbourne from the Lake Eyre region to demonstrate the manufacture of artefact and ceremonial items.

These exhibitions, unlike the quite common museum displays of exotic "native" domestic paraphernalia, were billed as "art" and attracted considerable public interest. Such exhibitions played an important role in helping to change white attitudes and to bring about policy changes. It seems unlikely that Aboriginal artists were not active participants in this process.

Aboriginal art today

What is the Aboriginal art scene today? What are artists attempting to do and say about their contemporary position in the broader, European dominated Australian society? Does Aboriginal artist interaction with the commercial market affect the cultural integrity of the work?

Aboriginal art has been described by international art dealers and critics as the most exciting thing to happen in modern world art circles for many years. The Australian Aboriginal arts and crafts industry is thriving. A Government report (Altman et al, 1989:34) estimated that there were over 600 artists working in several hundred communities and locations across Australia. The effect on the Australian economy is significant with a total of $18.5 million generated in 1987-88. In addition, around 50% of this art was sold for export. The Australian Bureau of Statistics, states that the value of documented exports of Aboriginal visual art for the period 1994-95, totalled $22.4 million. As one writer notes the "total value to the Australian economy of all Aboriginal arts and crafts (not including imitations) is said to be at least $100 million a year" (Langsam, 1996:4-5). One in five of the 23 million visitors to museums and art galleries yearly in Australia come expressly to see Aboriginal art (Statistical Advisory Group of Cultural Ministers Council and Strategic Development Unit of Australia Council). Exhibitions of Aboriginal works now appear regularly in the United States, Europe and Asia.

Aboriginal writers, poets and playwrights such as Sally Morgan, Jack Davis and Kath Walker (Odgeroo Noonuccal) have met with success world-wide. Aboriginal-run art co-operatives and organisations such as Papunya Tula, Bula Bula, the Japukai and Sydney Dance Theatre groups and so on flourish. Festivals and conferences such as the National Black Playwrights and Aboriginal Writers Conference have been held by and for Aboriginal people. Many initiatives have come out of these forums and they demonstrate the vitality of Aboriginal arts today.

Despite the earlier European belief that there was no art originally in Australia and the not uncommon belief today that there is no "real" Aboriginal art left, artists have actively adapted and incorporated new elements presented to them, maintaining all the while the basically political thrust of their work in an attempt to alter their social and economic environments.

Aboriginal art today is a success story of the first order. Aboriginal artists demonstrate through their work that they are not victims of the "art machine" or of post-colonial exploitation. Rather they are actively dealing with their surroundings through means of their cultural heritage. They see their art as playing a critical role both in Aboriginal society today and in the broader Australian and world scene.

Aboriginal visual artists paint to make a living. If people stopped buying their paintings, the artists would stop painting. This does not diminish the "meaning" of the art for it comes out of a larger, more encompassing system. This demonstrates that the art is *directed*. Aboriginal artists are not passive victims of cultural commercialisation or of exploitation by a relentless art world. Exploitation obviously occurs. However, to portray the artists only as poor, helpless pawns is to present a distorted, object-oriented and racist view. Aboriginal art today should be viewed from a human-oriented perspective and as a positive force in Aboriginal communities and Aboriginal life. It is a wedge; it is subversive; it is explicitly political. It is active. The interaction is considerable, the blurring between black and white is the hallmark of Aboriginal art. The cultural interaction is both complex and typical.

There is substantial continuity in Aboriginal art past to present regardless of the nature and origin of the art. Aboriginal art today is a powerful example of the ability of Aboriginal society to adapt and to incorporate, or absorb, elements of the dominating, non-Aboriginal milieu. Art is a means, used actively by Aboriginal people, from first contact onwards, to challenge the European world view. Art is crucial to the attempt to alter the relationships between Europeans and Aboriginal people and to consciously and explicitly declare Aboriginal rights in land and to assert the validity of Aboriginal culture in the modern world.

Aboriginal art is thus an extremely positive force and a lively, complex and dynamic scene with implications for Australia as a whole, both overseas and in terms of how it sees itself. Aboriginal art, although ever dynamic and changing, continues today based on a fundamental continuity with the past, both in content and in aim. Many events today affirm the vitality of Aboriginal art and culture, its place on the world scene and its positive economic value in the lives of artists and their families: Central Australian artists in Paris at the "Magicians of the Earth" exhibition in 1990 interacting with artists from all over the world; the Aboriginal band, Yothu Yindi, on stage at the World Music Festival in Adelaide in 1993; the Stomping Ground Festival in the Kimberleys; international and national tours of the Aboriginal and Islander Dance Company; places such as the Eora Centre in Sydney and Tandanya in Adelaide; the international success of Aboriginal writers and the visual arts; the prominence of Aboriginal arts in the media. Aboriginal art is here to stay and it is the driving force of significant change in non-Aboriginal people's attitudes about Aboriginal culture.

References

Aboriginal Arts and Crafts Review Committee (1989). *The Aboriginal Arts and Crafts Industry: Report of the Review Committee.* Canberra: Australian Government Publishing Service.

Anderson, C (1993). "The art of the sacred and the art of art: Contemporary Aboriginal painting in Central Australia". In *Arts of the Pacific,* edited by Philip Dark. Honolulu, Hawaii. University of Hawaii Press.

Anderson, C and Dussart, F (1988). "Dreamings in acrylic: Western Desert art". In *Dreamings: the Art of Aboriginal Australia,* edited by Peter Sutton. Ringwood, Victoria: Viking, pp 89-143.

Altman, J (1989). *The Aboriginal Arts and Crafts Industry: Report of the Review Committee July 1989.* Canberra: AGPS.

Bardon, Geoffrey (1991). *Papunya Tula: Art of the Western Desert.* Ringwood, Victoria: McPhee Gribble.

Berndt, Ronald M and Berndt, Catherine H with John E Stanton (1982). *Aboriginal Australian Art: a Visual Perspective.* Sydney: Methuen.

Caruana, Wally (1993). *Aboriginal Art.* Melbourne: Thames and Hudson.

Dorn, RI and Nobbs, M (1992). "Further support for the antiquity of South Australian rock engravings". *Australian Aboriginal Studies,* 1992, no. 1, pp 56-60.

Edwards, Robert and Guerin, Bruce (1969). *Aboriginal Bark Paintings.* Adelaide: Rigby.

Hardy, J; Megaw, J V S and Megaw, M R, editors (1992). *The Heritage of Namatjira: the Watercolours of Central Australia.* Melbourne: Heinemann.

Isaacs, Jennifer, compiler and editor (1980). *Australian Dreaming: 40,000 Years of Aboriginal History.* Sydney: Landsdowne Press.

Isaacs, Jennifer (1984). *Arts of The Dreaming. Australia's Living Heritage.* Sydney: Lansdowne.

Jones, Philip (1988). "Perceptions of Aboriginal art: a history". In *Dreamings: the Art of Aboriginal Australia*, edited by Peter Sutton. Ringwood, Victoria: Viking, pp 143-179.

Jones Philip and Sutton, Peter (1986). *Art and Land: Aboriginal Sculptures of the Lake Eyre Region*. Adelaide: South Australian Museum in association with Wakefield Press.

Langsam, David (1996). "Aboriginal art: Australia's hidden resource". *Art Monthly* Australia, no. 87, pp 4-5.

National Conference of Aboriginal Writers—Perth, 1983 (1985). *Aboriginal Writing Today: Papers from the First National Conference of Aboriginal Writers, held in Perth WA, in 1983*. Canberra: Australian Institute of Aboriginal Studies.

Paper, Stone, Tin: Catalogue of an Exhibition at Tandanya, July 1990 (1990). Adelaide: Aboriginal Cultural Institute.

Smyth, Robert Brough (1972). *Aborigines of Victoria: With Notes Relating to the Habits of the Natives of Other Parts of Australia and Tasmania*. Melbourne: George Robertson.

Sutton, Peter, editor (1988). *Dreamings: the Art of Aboriginal Australia*. Ringwood, Victoria: Viking.

Thomas, D (1986). "Albert Namatjira and the worlds of art: a re-evaluation". In Amadio, Nadine et al. *Albert Namatjira: the Life and Work of an Australian Painter*. South Melbourne: Macmillan, pp 21-26.

Walsh, Grahame (1988). *Australia's Greatest Rock Art*. Bathurst, NSW: E J Brill/Robert Brown and Associates.

Chapter 13

Self-determination and the Struggle for Aboriginal Equality

David Roberts

Self-determination

Self-determination has been described as "the cornerstone of government policy" and "the central word" in Aboriginal affairs since the election of the Whitlam Government in 1972 (O'Donoghue, 1992:7). It was a significant departure from previous Government policies in that it recognised the demands of Aborigines and Torres Strait Islanders for social justice and equality and acknowledged their right to make decisions about matters affecting their own lives. Since 1972 successive governments have attempted to establish structures and processes that would facilitate Aboriginal and Torres Strait Islander self-determination and self-management within the Australian State.[1]

While there is no commonly agreed definition in Australia of self-determination, and its meaning is contested, there does appear to be general agreement that central to self-determination is the right of indigenous Australians to make decisions on issues relating to them and to manage their own affairs. There is no such agreement as to how this should be achieved nor has a framework within which this can occur been established.

The Government has defined self-determination as "Aboriginal communities deciding the pace and nature of their future development as significant components within a diverse Australia" (O'Donoghue, 1992:7). This in effect limits the exercise of self-determination to what is compatible with the interests of the Australian State. Successive Australian governments have rejected the view that self-determination includes the right of Aboriginal and Torres Strait Islander people to decide their political status and the exploration of political options such as self-government and sovereignty. Self-determination has been defined much more narrowly in Australia than it has been in international forums where, as part of the decolonisation process, it has been premised on the right of a people to decide their own political status and future.

The Australian Government indicated to the United Nations Working Group on Indigenous Peoples in July 1992 that it had great difficulty with interpretations of self-determination that included the possibility of independence when it stated:

> If self-determination in general means that each people has the option of full independence and forming their own state, it will be very difficult for states to accept the application of that right to many groups (Watson, 1993:8).

Indeed, the concept underlying the process of reconciliation that the Government set in motion in 1991 is for a "bringing together" of Aboriginal and Torres Strait Islander peoples with the rest of the Australian population into the one state, not their separation from it. In the Keating Labor Government, the Prime Minister and his Aboriginal Affairs Minister, Robert Tickner, consistently reinforced this purpose as a central objective of reconciliation. Likewise the Keating Government's "One Nation" policy reinforced the currency of its definition of self-determination in terms of Aboriginal and Torres Strait Islander incorporation within the Australian State.

For Aboriginal and Torres Strait Islander peoples self-determination has taken on different meanings and raises different possibilities to different groups. These meanings reflect the different situations and historical experiences of the diverse range of Indigenous communities across Australia.

The indigenous population of Australia is very heterogeneous and four broad categories of indigenous communities have been employed to categorise this diversity in Australia. Outstations, Aboriginal towns and settlements, small towns, and cities and towns of over 20,000 people comprise the four general categories of community settings in which Aboriginal people live. Almost 75% of Aborigines and Torres Strait Islanders live in minority situations in or around towns and cities, with the remainder living on outstations and Aboriginal settlements. Care, however, needs to be taken in the use of these categories as any more than general descriptors as no two communities are identical. Each reflects its own unique cultural background, historical experiences and local conditions. Communities differ in the degree to which they have been subjected to dispossession, dispersal and the destruction of their economies and law during the colonisation process.

The situations, needs and options for those living in remote areas are significantly different from those living in the urban areas. Land rights, for example, have been pursued with much more success in central and northern Australia and some communities such as those at Yirrkala, Uluru and Kakadu have engaged in successful commercial developments. Other groups have established pastoral enterprises which generate employment and income. Others have used the outstation movement and subsistence activities as a means of lessening their dependence on Government.

The options for those Aboriginal and Torres Strait Islander people living in more densely populated parts of Australia are more limited. Unless they are able to break into the employment market and gain jobs there is little alternative to welfare dependency. Likewise, in remote areas where opportunities for employment (as it is defined by Government agencies) are very limited, welfare dependency is the only option for most members of the community.

The diversity of situations, the varying impact of colonialism on communities and differential access to resources makes for different political agendas. Such differences render it difficult for any Aboriginal organisation to speak on behalf of the Aboriginal movement generally and can lead to apparent competing interests and priorities, a situation exacerbated by Government imposed structures. Attempts by activists to promote particular strategies for self-determination often run foul of localised interests trying to maximise their share of Government funds or of competing groups pursuing different agendas.

The diversity of positions and the difficulties involved in developing political programs that attract widespread support among Aborigines are illustrated in the comments of lawyer Darryl Cronin:

> Aboriginal people in this country are heading down a long road. This road leads to the proper recognition of our rights ... For us to be strong and fight for our rights all Aboriginal people have to go down that road together. My concern is some Aboriginal people are starting to go off the road onto little bush tracks. In the Northern Territory some Aboriginal people are following the Northern Territory Government and are accepting Community Government,

while some people are trying to move further away towards being part of the Government system.

Some Aboriginal people are just sitting on the side of the road, watching us fight for our rights. They don't want to get involved.

Some mob call us 'radicals' and say they don't want a part of the struggle for our rights. All these Aboriginal people going off the road ... are going to find it hard to get back ... when we begin negotiating a Treaty and developing our own form of Aboriginal Government. They have sold themselves short and have accepted things too early without looking at all the options (*Land Rights News*, July 1989:20).

Cronin's comments provide some insight into the range of different views among Aboriginal people. Some expect the Government to provide for them and fix their problems. Some identify equality within Australian society as their main goal. They want the opportunity to obtain employment and have equal access to facilities such as housing, health and education alongside other Australians. For others, the goal is a return of the land and recognition of Aboriginal lifestyles, while others seek new arrangements for political autonomy and even separate nationhood.

For Lois O'Donoghue, the inaugural Chairperson of the Aboriginal and Torres Strait Islander Commission, self-determination is summarised as "well-being" and social justice. It equals "full citizenship rights" and requires similar employment prospects, education opportunities, housing and municipal facilities and a life expectancy for indigenous Australians the same as for other Australians. Her approach has some congruence with the Government's definition of self-determination, although her demand for "appropriate recognition of our status as the First Australians" being enshrined in the Australian Constitution (O'Donoghue, 1992:15), her opposition to the Howard Government's proposed legislative response to the High Court's 1996 Wik decision, and her advocacy for more initiatives and funding to assist indigenous communities build a resource base and to reduce long term Aboriginal dependency on Government funding, have placed her at serious odds with it.

Some Aboriginal organisations and leaders have taken a more radical line on self-determination with the National Aboriginal and Islander Legal Service arguing that self-determination must involve a fundamental restructuring of power relations between indigenous and other Australians (NAILS, 1989:15). The Federal Land Council has taken the position that Aboriginal people have never ceded their sovereign rights as a nation and that negotiations on the future status of Aboriginal people should be not entered into with the Australian Government until Aboriginal sovereignty is recognised and Aboriginal people are accorded equal status.

Michael Mansell, representing the Aboriginal Provisional Government (APG), sees in sovereignty the opportunity for separation from the rest of Australia and in 1992 called on the Federal Government to conduct a referendum to enable Aborigines to choose "whether they wish to go down the track of sovereignty or whether they wish to stay in the Australian community" (The *Koori Mail*, 21/10/92:7). In his proposal Aboriginal communities would be granted Crown Land in rural areas of Australia and would become self-governing. The APG's use of sovereignty and self-government keeps the issue of Aboriginal autonomy firmly on the agenda. It also brings into sharp focus recognition that the difficulties being confronted in achieving self-determination remain embedded in colonialism.

The Aboriginal struggle

Throughout most of the history of Aboriginal-European relations Government policies and practices have been imposed. They have been characterised by a lack of consultation with the indigenous population. It has been Governments, together with their bureaucracies and advisers, that have controlled the situation for Aborigines and Torres Strait Islanders. They have imposed their will in a manner that serves to emphasise not only the powerlessness of Aborigines and Torres Strait Islanders in Australian society but also the failure to recognise the legitimacy of their ideas, views and aspirations.

Aborigines and Torres Strait Islanders have been involved in an ongoing struggle to improve their situation. Their campaign for social justice and equality was well in train by the time self-determination was adopted as Government policy. Their task has largely centred on finding ways to persuade other Australians to support their aims and the needs that they themselves identify. Their situation as a colonised people, small in population and widely dispersed across Australia, has forced them into working in and around a complex and foreign system of rules, structures, priorities and controls established by the dominant society.

Given the history of disempowerment and marginalisation of Aboriginal and Torres Strait Islander peoples, the small numbers and dispersal across Australia, indigenous Australians have been remarkably successful in bringing their issues to prominence in the national arena. O'Donoghue, believes that the political strength of the Aboriginal movement "lies in our weakness; our 1.5 per cent of the national population. We present no threat to mainstream Australia, as on the pastoral frontier we once did" (O'Donoghue, 1992:13). The Aboriginal movement has been able to gain influence largely by applying moral and political pressure on the Australian State to right wrongs of the past, for equality and for social justice. In so doing it has also made judicious use of international forums to publicise its situation and promote its agenda.

During the 1950s and 1960s organisations such as the Federal Council for the Advancement of Aborigines and Torres Strait Islanders (FCAATSI) were established and provided a national focus for political activity. Other organisations such as the Victorian Aboriginal Advancement League passed into the control and management of Aboriginal people. The 1965 Freedom Rides through northern New South Wales publicised the second class status of Aboriginal people and the blatant racism to which they were subjected. At Dagaragu (Wave Hill) the Gurundji Walk-off was to prove the beginning of a new movement for land rights and a secure resource base, while the establishment of the Tent Embassy in 1972 outside Parliament House in Canberra forced the major political parties to address Aboriginal demands.

The land rights campaign that has been waged by Aborigines and Torres Strait Islanders has been a significant element in their attempts to gain a secure base that will provide a social, cultural, economic and political basis for real autonomy. Its successes include the passage of the Northern Territory Land Rights Act in 1976, the granting of title in 1981 to large areas of land in the north west of South Australia to the Pitjantjatjara and the success of smaller land rights claims in other states such as New South Wales and Victoria. The land rights movement, however, received a major setback when the Hawke Labor Government withdrew its proposed national land rights legislation in 1986.

At the community level Aborigines and Torres Strait Islanders increasingly have taken the initiative in areas such as health, education and legal services. They have set up their own community-based organisations, such as the Aboriginal Medical Service in Redfern, and community organisations, to such an extent that there are now approximately 2,000 community organisations servicing the needs of Aboriginal and Torres Strait communities.

Three decades have passed since Australians voted overwhelmingly in the 1967 Referendum to give Aborigines and Torres Strait Islanders "a fair go", include them in the Census and give the Commonwealth Government the responsibility to legislate and provide funding in Aboriginal affairs. The referendum marked the beginning of a new era during which Aboriginal and Torres Strait Islander affairs have become predominantly a Commonwealth and, hence, national responsibility; funding for Indigenous affairs has increased dramatically; Aboriginal and Torres Strait Islander issues have become a significant part of the national agenda; anti racial discrimination legislation has been passed; land rights have become a reality for some Aboriginal communities; the principle of consultation has become acknowledged in Government processes; the administration of Aboriginal and Torres Strait Islander affairs has been placed under the direction of indigenous elected representatives with the establishment of the Aboriginal and Torres Strait Islander Commission; real gains have been made in increasing indigenous access to education and in reducing the high incidence of infant mortality, child health problems and trachoma; the Royal Commission into Aboriginal Deaths in Custody was conducted with additional funding made available to assist the implementation of its recommendations; and self-determination has become a key element within Government policy.

Commonwealth funding in Aboriginal affairs has increased significantly since the election of the Whitlam Labor Government in

1972. There was an almost four-fold increase in funding from $31 million in 1971/72 to $117 million in the 1973/74 financial year budgets (Howard, 1982:90). Succeeding governments continued to increase funding in Aboriginal and Torres Strait Islander Affairs with the budget outlays approaching $400 million by the mid-1980s and growing to $1,161 million in the 1992/93 financial year (ATSIC, 1993:158). These sums represent a considerable growth per capita over a period of two decades given an Aboriginal and Torres Strait Islander population of 115,951 in 1971 which had increased to 261,129 by 1991. These funds have been used for housing, education, health, community facilities, legal aid, welfare, employment and training initiatives and on the administration of Aboriginal affairs.

Despite these funding increases there has been little significant improvement in the overall socio-economic situation of Aboriginal and Torres Strait Islander people. In terms of health, education, income, housing and employment indicators, they remain significantly worse off than any other sector of the Australian community. In its paper *Social Justice for Indigenous Australians* the Commonwealth Government acknowledged that:

> The first Australians are now the most disadvantaged Australians. In every available measure of social and economic disadvantage, Aboriginal and Torres Strait Islander people record worse outcomes, face greater problems and enjoy fewer opportunities than the rest of the Australian population. The poverty and relative powerlessness of Australia's indigenous people is reflected in inferior education, employment, income and housing (Ministry of Aboriginal Affairs, 1992).

The level and extent of disadvantage, particularly in terms of incomes, employment and welfare, had already been documented extensively in the 1985 *Report of the committee of review of Aboriginal employment and training pro*grams (the *Miller Report*). The Miller Report had found that there had been little improvement in real economic status for Aborigines between the Census of 1971 and that of 1981 and that Aboriginal people who had employment continued to be concentrated in lower skilled or unskilled positions. Aboriginal employment opportunities had diminished rapidly as the economy restructured and the *Report* estimated that 50 per cent of the Aboriginal workforce was unemployed—an unemployment rate about six times the rate of all other Australians at the time. Moreover, the 1986 Census went on to reveal that Aboriginal median income remained at half the median income for other Australians.

The *Miller Report* also found an overwhelming dependence by Aboriginal and Torres Strait Islander people on Government funding. It identified 71 per cent of national Aboriginal income being provided by the Government, mainly in the form of social welfare payments. Only 16 per cent of Government funding was directed towards economic development. The Report pointed out that:

> This clearly demonstrates that current Aboriginal advancement policy is not positively directed towards the long-term economic prospects of Aboriginal people (Miller Report, 1985:40).

Essentially the *Miller Report* found that the Government was achieving little more than providing a minimum level of welfare and living standards for an alarmingly high proportion of the indigenous population. Far too little of the Government's funds were being used to enhance long term employment prospects or to assist Aborigines establish and develop viable economic bases for their communities.

The *Report* was highly critical of the failings in the Government's administration of its Aboriginal programs and emphasised the need for flexibility. It argued that policies needed to be designed to meet the needs of different Aboriginal situations and that responsibility for planning and use of programs should rest with Aboriginal people at the local level. It went on to:

> ... urge the government to adopt a policy of support to Aboriginal people which goes beyond welfare, housing and municipal services industries and which should be directed towards Aboriginal people becoming more independent by enabling them to provide for their livelihood. Programs to achieve this end will be longer term, involve real training and result in Aboriginal control of resources, as well as access to jobs in the regular labour market (Miller Report, 1985:10).

In 1991 the Academy of Social Sciences in Australia and the Centre for Aboriginal Economic Policy Research at the Australian National

University conducted a workshop entitled "Aboriginal Employment Equity by the Year 2000". The papers presented at the workshop portrayed a rather depressing picture which, six years on from the *Miller Report*, served to confirm its findings and to show that there had been little substantive improvement. Examination of the impact of greater opportunities in schooling, for example, had proved far less encouraging than had been expected. While education opportunities had increased and more educated Aborigines overall were gaining employment and higher incomes, for those who lived in rural or remote areas the opportunities for employment and higher income status were largely non-existent. Education alone was found insufficient to improve the socio-economic status of Aborigines (Sanders, 1991:15-16). Aborigines and Torres Strait Islanders remained overwhelmingly dependent on the welfare system for their incomes.

Charles Perkins has identified welfare as an instrument which has forced Aboriginal people into dependency and which maintains them in it. When giving the Frank Archibald Memorial Lecture in October 1990, he called for a total reorganisation and redirection of Aboriginal affairs in order to ... *project Aboriginal people out of this degrading, and self perpetuating dependency welfare system* (Perkins, 1990:1). He warned against the dangers of becoming resigned to and accepting of welfare dependency and exhorted Aborigines to *throw off the old social welfare system.*

> The time has come for our people to break out of this unworthy, enforced western dreamtime and charter a new course, not only for our people, and particularly for our children, but for our nation. We must throw off the yoke of welfare and the soul destroying concept of welfare and the subsequent dependency syndrome. It is destroying us and will continually do so ... .We are running out of time ... (Perkins, 1990:6).

Internal colonialism

Over the past two hundred years Australia has moved from colonial status to independence while Aboriginal and Torres Strait Islander peoples have remained in a situation described by Beckett (1987) as one of internal colonialism. Internal colonialism is characterised by relations of dominance and subordination, the expropriation of the land and natural resources of the colonised peoples, the exploitation of their labour and their marginalisation to the fringes of the majority society. It involves systematic discrimination of the subject peoples by the conquering group in a manner that serves to separate them and entrench inequality. Their subordination is justified and rationalised by the emergence of ideologies based on beliefs of racial and cultural superiority and becomes institutionalised throughout the structures of society. Some insight into its continued manifestation in contemporary Australia can be gleaned from the report of the Royal Commission into Aboriginal Deaths in Custody when the Royal Commissioner, Mr Elliott Johnston QC wrote:

> ... until I examined the files of the people who had died and the other materials which have come before the Commission and listened to Aboriginal people speaking, I had no conception of the degree of pin-pricking domination, abuse of personal power, utter paternalism, open contempt and total indifference with which so many Aboriginal people were visited on a day to day basis (cited in O'Donoghue, 1992:10).

Beckett's analysis is supported by Howard (1982) and Jennett (1987) who demonstrate that welfare has been a long standing government policy which has been used to order and control Aborigines, first under the reserve system and then, as that collapsed, through the social welfare system. They argue that the colonial structures that have been imposed and the forms of incorporation that have been forced upon Aboriginal and Torres Strait Islander peoples have served to obstruct their movement for greater autonomy and have continued to perpetuate their unemployment, inequality and powerlessness.

Given this context of internal colonialism it is hardly surprising that there has been so little progress in breaking out of welfare dependency over the past two decades for Aborigines and Torres Strait Islanders. As Howard points out the Government is not a neutral force which can improve the situation just by expanding funding and setting up new programs. For Aborigines the Government and its instrumentalities are part of the problem. It is through its actions and those of its predecessors that Aboriginal people have been denied the capacity and opportunity to be economically independent. Government agencies by their very nature seek to gain and maintain hegemonic control. They are not well placed to be agents of indigenous self-determination and their responses to Aboriginal and Torres Strait Islander demands have been essentially based on the provision of social welfare, thereby fostering continued dependency.

Government policies in general have reflected an inability to accommodate the interests of Aborigines and Torres Strait Islanders. The structures within which the latter have been obliged to operate have been imposed upon them by coercion, persuasion and welfare. Throughout their experience of colonisation their interests have not been protected by the State and where conflicts of interests exist, particularly over resource issues, they invariably lose out.

Governments, together with other vested interests have continued in recent years to go to great lengths to protect "the public interest" in order to set aside Aboriginal interests. Over the critical issue of land rights, a key economic resource and one of central spiritual significance, the mining lobby together with the Western Australian and Queensland Governments in the mid 1980s waged a relentless campaign against proposed national land rights legislation. They were instrumental in the Commonwealth Government's decision to first remove any reference to an Aboriginal right of veto on mining and then in its decision to withdraw and abandon the legislation altogether. Aboriginal bodies such as the National Aboriginal Conference and the Federation of Land Councils protested about the lack of consultation and against the changes that were "steamrolled" through, but to no effect.

While the abandonment of the national land rights legislation did not mean that the Federal Government had abandoned land rights altogether, and it did pass title over to the Mutitjulu people at Uluru in 1985, it does serve to emphasise the dependent status and lack of power of Aboriginal people in relation to the Australian State. This powerlessness is further illustrated by the Hawke Government's amendments to the *Northern Territory Land Rights Act 1976* which in effect enabled the Government to allow mining on Aboriginal owned land and the 1993 decision of the Keating Government to permit the Northern Territory to extinguish native title at McArthur River for the purpose of mining.

The state and territory governments also have operated to frustrate Aboriginal efforts to gain an economic base and control over their resources. In 1980 the Court Liberal Government in Western Australia conducted a military style operation to overcome Aboriginal resistance to oil drilling at Noonkanbah, even though the company concerned was prepared to drill elsewhere. The Government was determined to show that Aborigines had no control or rights over mining in Western Australia even on land they possessed. In the early 1980s, despite being reputedly more progressive, the South Australian Bannon Labor Government ignored Kokotha protests against the Roxby Downs uranium and gold mine which was situated on land they claimed. In the Northern Territory the government used an array of legal and administrative devices to frustrate Aboriginal land claims. In Darwin the town's area was increased to 4,350 square kilometres to defeat the Kuntai land claim on Cox Peninsula. Darwin is now the world's largest city in terms of area. A similar tactic was used to frustrate a Jawoyn land claim at Katherine and a Waramungu land claim at Tennant Creek. In Western Australia the Government even circumvented its own *Aboriginal Heritage Act* in its efforts in the late 1980s to permit the development of the Nyungar sacred Waugal (Swan Brewery) site.

Such actions have demonstrated very clearly to Aboriginal people how their rights are not guaranteed and protected by the Australian political and legal systems. In the case of the Nyungar struggle one commentator observed that:

> the hoops that the protesters have had to leap through in taking legal actions and making Heritage Act applications under both Federal and State legislation have convincingly demonstrated to them the ethnocentric nature of the whitefella Courts and the whitefella Acts (Ansara, 1989:12).

Government frameworks for self-determination

In pursuing their objectives Aboriginal and Torres Strait Islander people have had to operate within the constraints of the structures and processes imposed by the Australian State and its instrumentalities. Their capacity to effect the self-determination and self-management goals defined and determined for them by successive Australian governments, a contradiction in terms in itself, is further limited by the internal colonial framework within which they have been forced to operate.

Following its extensive investigation into indigenous management and community control the House of Representatives Standing Committee on Aboriginal Affairs described it as "ironic" that Aboriginal and Torres Strait Islander communities were being required to establish and use non-Aboriginal structures in order to have more control over their own affairs. The Committee found that:

> The imposition of council management structures on Aboriginal communities by and large has ignored the existence of traditional decision making processes (House of Representatives Standing Committee on Aboriginal Affairs, 1990:20).

Not only was the grafting of non-Aboriginal institutions onto Aboriginal communities and the continued failure to recognise the authority of Aboriginal organisations in the non-Aboriginal power structure seen as inappropriate, the Government was also criticised for not assisting Aboriginal people develop the instrumental capacity to manage their communities according to the requirements it stipulated.

The Committee was also very critical of the means by which policies of self-determination and self-management had been implemented, characterising them as "hurried" and lacking adequate consultation. The Committee found this to be a major contradiction, arguing that:

> the imposition of programs, policies and structures without adequate consultation is inconsistent with the notion of Aboriginal communities being self determining and having the ability to influence and control their own affairs (House of Representatives Standing Committee, 1990:8).

The Committee concluded that the policies of self-determination and self-management had been a failure "in many circumstances" with the Department of Aboriginal Affairs in its evidence to the Committee noting that:

> many Aboriginal communities have yet to make the transition to self-determination and that in some cases communities are just as dependent upon outside agencies as they have been in the past,

despite the implementation of the policy of self-determination (Quoted in House of Representatives Standing Committee Report, 1990:5).

The Committee found that there were two broad categories of reasons for this failure. The first group of reasons were located with the Government and its agencies and the second were located with the communities themselves. Government agencies needed to improve their performance, provide more appropriate and better coordinated services and develop more appropriate and sensitive executive management infrastructures. The Committee also found that there was often a lack of commitment and involvement in the Government's community management structures among community members which the Department of Aboriginal Affairs claimed placed "almost insuperable obstacles in the way of the transition of self-determination" (*House of Representatives Standing Committee Report,* 1990:7). The Department's position completely failed to recognise the contradictions involved in the imposition of alien structures on communities in the name of self-determination.

The determination of successive Governments to set up and control the frameworks for indigenous self-determination are also clearly evident in the national structures that were established for the representation of indigenous interests. In order to provide for a mechanism for consultation at the national level the Government established the National Aboriginal Consultative Committee (NACC) in 1973. Significantly, its existence, structure and functions were all government determined and the NACC had no decision making or policy making powers. Its function was advisory only. When the National Aboriginal Consultative Committee delegates, dissatisfied with their purely advisory role, voted to change their body into a National Aboriginal Congress with policy making powers and control over the budget of the Department of Aboriginal Affairs, the Government moved rapidly to quash the move, isolating those it identified as radicals and threatening to sack the delegates.

While the Government supported the establishment of Aboriginal organisations with funding, in so doing it ensured its own capacity to oversee and control activities. This it strengthened in 1975 with the introduction of a new set of administrative guidelines designed to increase administrative control over expenditure and to reduce the autonomy of Aboriginal communities and organisations. It also ruled that assets bought with government funds were to be vested in and owned by the Department of Aboriginal Affairs, the department it had set up in 1973 to administer Aboriginal affairs. Such actions served to undermine Aboriginal efforts to build an assets base and a measure of economic independence. They worked towards the maintenance of a colonial situation of dependency, rather than the declared purpose of self-determination.

With the election in 1975 of the Coalition Government under the leadership of Prime Minister Fraser the policy of self-determination was replaced with the more conservative policy of self-management and self-sufficiency. The Fraser Government was no more willing to hand over real control to Aborigines than its predecessor. It replaced the NACC with a new consultative body, whose role was advisory only, and which it named the National Aboriginal Conference (NAC).

Like the NACC, the NAC had a Government determined structure with delegates elected on the Westminster principle of representative democracy, a principle which bore no relation to Aboriginal community authority and decision making processes.

The NAC was a much criticised body and was tagged as being a "token". In 1984, following a formal review of its structure and function, it was found to have had little influence on the Government and its agencies, no capacity to deliver services or provide funding and tenuous links with the communities (Jennett, 1990:259). Such criticisms serve to expose some of the problems NAC delegates had in operating within such a structure, especially when the Minister for Aboriginal Affairs did not make significant use of his capacity to refer matters to the Conference for advice, and they also mask its efforts to provide a national voice for Aborigines on the issue of a treaty and on land rights.

When the NAC came to the end of its term in June 1985 it was not replaced. It was not until 1990 when the Aboriginal and Torres Strait Islander Commission (ATSIC) was established that a structure to enable broad representation of Aboriginal and Torres Strait Islanders was to re-emerge.

In ATSIC the Government attempted to amalgamate the representative functions of former bodies such as the NAC with the administrative functions of the Department of Aboriginal Affairs and the funding role of the Aboriginal Development Commission. In so doing the Government hoped to overcome the inter-bureaucratic rivalry that had characterised relations between the former bodies and to provide a more effective mechanism with which to pursue self-determination. Community representation in the management of ATSIC was incorporated initially through the establishment of sixty regional councils, organised into seventeen zones, across Australia. Each zone elected a commissioner to ATSIC with the remaining three commissioners, including the chairperson, being appointed by the Government.

The Government promoted ATSIC as a conduit that would facilitate Aboriginal self-determination and self-management with Prime Minister Hawke stating "via ATSIC we are going to have a better way of getting the views of the Aboriginal community" (Brennan, 1990:5). Lois O'Donoghue, on her appointment as the Chairperson of ATSIC, claimed that ATSIC was the "voice of Australia's Aboriginal and Torres Strait Islander peoples" and described its establishment as the commencement "of a unique and productive partnership with the Government" (Brennan, 1990:4). In an address to the National Press Club in May 1992 O'Donoghue argued that ATSIC's establishment was an acknowledgment that previous administrative and political arrangements had failed and that real progress in Aboriginal affairs was proving elusive. She described ATSIC "as the culmination of a long line of attempts to achieve Aboriginal self-determination at the governmental level and as a radical shift away from previous Aboriginal Affairs institutions" (O'Donoghue, 1992).

Organisations such as the Aboriginal Provisional Government and the Federation of Land Councils (FLC) were strongly critical of suggestions that ATSIC had the authority to speak on behalf of Aborigines and Torres Strait Islanders and that it was a vehicle for Aboriginal self-determination. The FLC viewed ATSIC as a body whose central function was to administer government services and argued that it did not have the capacity or authority to negotiate on behalf of Aborigines and Torres Strait Islanders on matters of significance such as a treaty, or even to provide a structure for consultation on such issues.

Indeed how well placed ATSIC is to actively foster self-determination is problematic. While its processes for representation and advice from communities and its attempts to decentralise and delegate decision making to regional and local levels have been welcomed, it remains a bureaucratic organisation operating within the confines of the *Public Service Act* and staffed accordingly. It is still a semi-government body subject to Government policy, funded by the Government and accountable to the Minister for Aboriginal Affairs who retains the power to direct the Commission. ATSIC has had to operate under so tight a regime of financial accountability that the Minister for Aboriginal Affairs informed Parliament:

> There is no other department or statutory authority in existence in the Commonwealth which will be as accountable as ATSIC. I defy Honourable Members opposite to find me any organisation under this Government or any other Government that will be as accountable as this structure (Brennan, 1990:5).

So restrictive are these requirements that Rowse (1992a) and the Foundation for Aboriginal and Islander Research Action (1991) argued that ATSIC lacked the capacity to devolve decision making and funding to the regional and local levels and, therefore, would be unable to give real substance to self-determination.

ATSIC also lacked the financial capacity to provide Aboriginal communities with the significant infrastructure and funds for capital development required for sustained economic development.

Despite her hopes for ATSIC, O'Donoghue pointed out in 1992:

> We remain very much dependent on the patronage and goodwill of governments—for recurrent funding of Aboriginal organisations, for special pieces of legislation such as the Northern Territory Land Rights Act and the ATSIC Act......Though the ultimate aim of self-determination is an end to this situation, Aboriginal people clearly have a long way to go (O'Donoghue, 1992:14).

O'Donoghue's words were prophetic and the vulnerability of ATSIC was sharply exposed by the Howard Government's slashing of

ATSIC's budget by over $400 million in 1996 and its tightening of controls over the ways in which these funds were to be expended. Not only did these actions sharply reduce funding for Aboriginal and Torres Strait Islander communities and organisations, including capital development, but they introduced new constraints that threatened to sabotage progress towards autonomy and self-determination.

Native Title: a chance for real progress?

The High Court's decision on native title in June 1992 provided a new basis upon which Aborigines and Torres Strait Islanders could pursue the return of land and compensation. The decision overthrew the doctrine of terra nullius, recognised indigenous prior ownership and provided an opportunity for Aborigines and Torres Strait Islanders to pursue their rights to the title of land with which they had maintained traditional ties and where native title had not already been extinguished.

Opening the International Year for the World's Indigenous Peoples at Redfern Park in December 1992 Prime Minister Keating described the High Court's decision as a *practical building block* for change adding that:

> By doing away with the bizarre concept that this continent had no owners prior to the settlement of Europeans, Mabo establishes a fundamental truth and lays the basis for justice ... Mabo is an historic decision—we can make it an historic turning point, the basis of a new relationship between indigenous and non-Aboriginal Australians (Keating, 1993:4).

The Council for Aboriginal Reconciliation also viewed the High Court's decision with optimism, describing it as an "... opportunity to set right the relationship [between Aborigines and other Australians] in a way that was not possible in the beginning" (Dodson, 1993:7). According to Dodson the decision not only provided a new basis for Aboriginal land tenure but also elevated into the forefront of the national political agenda issues of self-determination, self-government, recognition of customary law, protection of cultural and sacred sites and the rights of indigenous

Australians to choose the way of life that they want to follow. (Seminar, University of South Australia, 19/8/93).

The recognition of native title by the High Court led to many indigenous groups across Australia pursuing claims for land title. The economic and cultural significance of gaining ownership of land was emphasised by John Dalungdalu Jones of the Fraser Island Land Council when he explained the reasons for the Council's proclamation of ownership of Kgari (Fraser Island) and its claim to about $6 million a year in tourist levies to help fund education, social welfare, tourism and environmental management projects:

> Instead of our people having to have their hand out forever to get social welfare, we can use that money to establish economic and culturally viable jobs for our own young people for the future, just as Uluru does (The Australian, 21/7/93:2).

The High Court's decision proved a highly contentious issue throughout most of 1993 as different groups of powerful vested interests sought to protect their interests and resolve what they described as "uncertainty" over land title. The pastoral and mining industries in particular pursued a vigorous campaign aimed at securing the validation of their titles and the extinguishment of native title. The Australian Chamber of Commerce and Industry, the Australian Coal Association, the Australian Mining Industry Council, the Australian Petroleum Exploration Association, the Australian Tourism Industry Association, the National Association of Forest Industries and the National Fishing Industry Council joined forces to release a paper to give "the community a better understanding of the issues raised by Mabo". While the paper conceded that Aborigines may be entitled to some compensation, it argued that they should not have any right to veto development, asserting that experience in Western Australia and the Northern Territory had demonstrated that such powers have had quite dire consequences on industry. In some quarters the campaign against native title reached extreme heights with Hugh Morgan, managing director of Western Mining Corporation and longstanding opponent of land rights, arguing that the future of Australia had been put at risk, that its territorial integrity was under threat and that "all titles to property in Australia have been devalued as a result of Mabo"

(*The Australian* 1/7/93:1). He demanded that Prime Minister Keating retract from his "uncompromising" support for *Mabo* arguing that his position "could only lead to a very rapid economic decline and to a partitioning of the continent. Mabo directly threatens the unity of Australia" (*The Australian* 1/7/93:2).

As Social Justice Commissioner, Mick Dodson, was to observe, the campaign against a just settlement of native title poignantly captured the conflict and challenge that faced all Australians:

> Powerful vested interests have worked relentlessly to maintain the social and economic systems which structurally exclude other groups of peoples.
>
> They use their powerful voices to argue that human rights concerns must not be allowed to stand in the way of economic development. They use their powerful voices to induce paranoia in the attempt to convince the people of this country that their interest lay in supporting the status quo, regardless of its legal or moral basis. And there have been political figures who have been willing to support those interests and to ignore the voices of those seeking justice (cited in Roberts, 1993:20).

The Government sought to reassure non-Aboriginal Australians that they had nothing to fear from the native title decision and continued to link it with Reconciliation, stating that the High Court's judgment must be used to support the broader goal of reconciling Aboriginal and non-Aboriginal Australia and rectifying the dispossession of those Aborigines whose links with their traditional land have been broken.

The Government decided to resolve the "uncertainty" over native title through the means of legislation and, in September 1993 released its draft legislation for public comment. Aboriginal groups responded angrily to the draft legislation, denouncing it as an *empty promise* and for failing to safeguard their interests. Of particular concern was the Government's proposal to suspend the Racial Discrimination Act to extinguish native title in order to validate existing title, and the prime role given to the states in determining native title claims.

Confronted by trenchant criticism from Aboriginal leaders, the churches, human rights groups and members of its own backbench, the Government entered into further rounds of negotiations with Aboriginal and Islander representatives, state governments and mining and pastoral interests. It abandoned its proposal to suspend the Racial Discrimination Act and undertook to legislate to protect native title interests so that they could coexist with leasehold title. It also agreed to provide Aboriginal groups with the right to take their case for native title to a Commonwealth Tribunal. Alongside the legislation the Government also committed itself to providing a "social justice package" that would include a Land Acquisition Fund to enable Aboriginal communities to purchase land. The Prime Minister described the changes as a *win-win for everybody*, a position not endorsed by the Coalition which decided to oppose the legislation, nor the Western Australian Government which threatened to introduce its own legislation on native title.

Certainly the Government's changes to its legislation went some way towards addressing Aboriginal concerns but, just how many Aborigines would benefit and in what ways was uncertain. Estimates varied as to how many Aboriginal people could directly benefit from native title but the likelihood was that the number would be relatively small, probably no more than five per cent of the Aboriginal population. Even for the beneficiaries it was estimated that it would be quite some time, a matter of years rather than months, before native title claims could be heard and settled. Indeed, four years after the passage of the Native Title Act Aboriginal communities have yet to see much in the way of tangible benefits, with the first mainland native title claim only being confirmed in 1997 when a small parcel of land at Crescent Head, New South Wales, was awarded to the Dunghutti people. The New South Wales Aboriginal Land Council welcomed the decision as a positive example of what could be achieved when state and local governments, and Aboriginal communities worked together in a spirit of goodwill and reconciliation. The New South Wales Attorney General however was quick to dampen any rising expectations stating that the decision was unlikely to start a *flood* of native title determinations and he pointed to the *long struggle* of the

Dunghutti in proving a constant association with the Crescent Head Land.

While the processes for the preparation and hearing of native title claims have been lengthy and drawn out, the Howard Government's proposed legislative response to the High Court's judgement in the Wik case threatens to dramatically curtail the capacity of Indigenous Australians to mount native title claims. In 1996 the High Court, in a majority decision, ruled in favour of the Wik claim that native title had not been extinguished in the case of pastoral leases at Holroyd River. The judgement brought an immediate and strident reaction from pastoralists, the National Farmers Federation, the National Party, several State Governments (particularly those of Queensland and Western Australia), and some elements of the mining industry. Arguing that the High Court's decision had created an unsustainable level of uncertainty over the extent of native title rights and the security of land tenure under existing leases, the battle lines that had emerged in the lead up to the 1993 Native Title Act were rejoined.

In opposition the Coalition parties had been less than enthusiastic about the recognition of native title. Now in government they were quick to accept the argument that the Wik judgement had created a level of uncertainty that needed to be addressed urgently. The High Court was criticised strongly by the Deputy Prime Minister and the Queensland Premier for *judicial activism* while the Prime Minister made it clear that it was Parliament's responsibility to make law. Under intense pressure from the National Party to extinguish native title the Government set up a process of negotiation with and between all key stakeholders to find a solution to the "problem" that would be acceptable to all parties.

The attempt to establish "common ground", not surprisingly given the determination of indigenous negotiators to safeguard native title and of pastoralists and their supporters to extinguish it, proved to be largely unsuccessful and the Government drafted over 300 pages of legislative amendments to the Native Title Act, based on its own 10 Point Plan. While the Government's proposals did not extinguish native title outright, they aimed to limit its application as well as Aboriginal access to it, and rights of negotiation, and sought to provide security to pastoral leaseholders. In acknowledging these objectives Howard made his Government's position clear by stating:

> The fact is that the Wik decision pushed the pendulum too far in the Aboriginal direction. The ten point plan will return the pendulum to the centre (The Advertiser 8/5/97:6).

Aboriginal leaders reacted angrily to the Government's Wik response pointing out that it left them with few rights, with Pat Dodson arguing that it set back Aboriginal rights to the 1960s. In response to Aboriginal criticism that they were the only stakeholders whose interests had been ignored and that the draft legislation would result in minimal chance of success for any native title claim, the Deputy Prime Minister pointed out that vacant Crown Land remained unaffected and that native title claims could still be made. Even here, as Gatjil Djerrkura, chair of ATSIC has demonstrated, the proposed legislative changes would severely restrict native title and he described the Bill as an attack on indigenous rights that would only cause further uncertainty and division (*The Weekend Australian* 26-27/7/97:24).

The Government adopted an uncompromising stance in its determination to push its proposals through Parliament and signalled its preparedness to call a double dissolution if its draft legislation was rejected or amended in significant ways. Its hard-line position reflected the predominance of conservative views in its ranks and its reading of the response of the Australian electorate to the populist approach of Pauline Hanson and her One Nation Party. In terms of Aboriginal affairs, Hanson's attacks on what she termed the *Aboriginal industry*, her description of it as a *gravy train*, and her claims that $30 billion of tax payers' funds had been wasted on Aboriginal housing, education, welfare and ATSIC, were left unchallenged by the Government.

While the Government continued to hold that Aboriginal empowerment remained the cornerstone of its policy, it reduced its funding in Aboriginal affairs significantly and tightened up accountability requirements. The Aboriginal Affairs Minister conducted a sustained campaign against alleged *waste* and *mismanagement* in indigenous affairs. In addressing the Liberal

Party regional forum in Canberra he advised that mechanisms were now *in place* to ensure that funds were spent *correctly* and he foreshadowed a tougher Government stance and tightening up through new reviews of ATSIC, the Aboriginal Legal Services and the Aboriginal and Torres Strait Islander Heritage and Protection Act.

The Government professed to recognise the severity of Aboriginal disadvantage, but downplayed issues of race inequality, resource provision and Aboriginal autonomy in favour of "practical strategies" to resolve it. Arguing, with some justification, that despite the political rhetoric and injection of funds of preceding Labor Governments, Aborigines and Torres Strait Islanders remained the most disadvantaged groups in Australia, the Government claimed it was focussing on efficient and effective strategic action to address disadvantage. Any confidence that Aboriginal and Torres Strait Islander communities may have had in the Government's assurances of commitment to action was eroded significantly by its belated and arguably ineffectual response to the race debate inspired by Hanson; the response of its Health Minister to a departmental report that the gap between the health and welfare statistics between indigenous and other Australians was widening where he stated that he did not expect an improvement to be evident for another ten years (*The Advertiser* 3/4/97:6); the failure of the 1997 Ministerial Conference on Black Deaths in Custody to set targets or timeframes for reducing the incidence of deaths in custody despite evidence that it, along with indigenous rates of imprisonment, was increasing; and the Government's refusal to countenance the key recommendations of the Report of the Inquiry into the Separation of Aboriginal and Torres Strait Islander Children from their Families.

By failing to even consider compensation the Government put itself on an immediate collision course with Aboriginal communities for whom financial reparation was one of the keys to reconciliation. However it was in his refusal to issue a formal apology by the Government for the "stolen generations" that the Prime Minister lost a valuable opportunity to restore some faith with indigenous communities and offer a gesture of goodwill on behalf of all Australians to Aboriginal people and towards reconciliation. For indigenous Australians events since the election of the Howard Government have seen resources significantly reduced and the hard won gains promised by the recognition of native title under dire threat. Strategies designed to assist in overcoming inequity, such as the Abstudy scheme to support indigenous students, were abandoned while indigenous dispossession remained largely unaddressed. Instead of relinquishing control over indigenous affairs the Howard Government strengthened it, effectively reducing the scope for the exercise of meaningful autonomy.

While the response of the Australian public to the stolen generations report, reconciliation and the Hanson agenda exhibited the presence of considerable goodwill towards indigenous Australians, the actions of the Howard Government unequivocally have confirmed the view of many Aborigines and Torres Strait Islanders that ultimately self determination will only be achieved through their own endeavour and struggle. They cannot rely on governments to facilitate and support the achievement of their objectives. As Charles Perkins observed in 1993:

> The essential element in Aboriginal affairs that is most important and that a lot of Aboriginal people should never lose sight of, all the time, is that the only people who are going to make a change to Aboriginal affairs are Aboriginal people.

> White people will never change anything for you. Governments, good or bad, of whatever political colour, will never change anything for you.

> There's only one person that is going to do it, and that is that black face you see in the mirror when you wake up in the morning.

> That is the person that is going to change Aboriginal affairs for the better, and for your children (ABC Education TV 1993).

References

ABC Education TV (1993). "Towards the Future: Policies and Practice". *Windows on Aboriginal Australia*, OLAA Series, Melbourne, episode 13.

Altman, JC, editor (1991). *Aboriginal Employment Equity by the Year 2000*. Canberra: Centre for Aboriginal Economic Policy Research, Australian National University.

Ansara, M (1989). "Self determination". *Bulletin of the Olive Pink Society*, vol. 1, no. 2, pp 11-13.

Aboriginal and Torres Strait Islander Commission (1993). *Annual Report*.

Beckett, J (1987). *Torres Strait Islanders: Custom and Colonialism*. Sydney: Cambridge University Press.

Beckett, J (1988). "Aboriginality, citizenship and nation state". *Social Analysis*, vol. 24, pp 3-18.

Brennan, F (1990). "ATSIC: seeking a national mouthpiece for local voices". *Aboriginal Law Bulletin*, vol. 2, no. 43, pp 4-6.

Brennan, F (1991). *Sharing the Country: the Case for an Agreement Between Black and White Australians*. Ringwood, Victoria: Penguin.

Butt, PJ and Eagleson, R (1996). *Mabo: What the High Court said and What the Government did*, 2nd edition. Federation Press.

Cunneen, C (1992). "Aboriginal imprisonment during and since the Royal Commission into Aboriginal Deaths in Custody". *Aboriginal Law Bulletin*, vol. 2, no. 55, pp 13-14.

Cowlishaw, G and Kondos, V, editors (1995). *Mabo and Australia : On recognising Native Title After Two Hundred Years*. Anthropological Society of New South Wales.

Cowlishaw, G (1988). *Black, White or Brindle: Race in Rural Australia*. Cambridge: Cambridge University Press.

Department of Prime Minister and Cabinet (1992). *Council for Aboriginal Reconciliation: an Introduction*. Canberra: Australian Government Publishing Service.

Department of Prime Minister and Cabinet (1993). *Making Things Right: Reconciliation After the High Court's Decision on Native Title*. Canberra: Council for Aboriginal Reconciliation.

Department of Prime Minister and Cabinet (1992). *Aboriginal Reconciliation: an Historical Perspective*. Canberra: Australian Government Publishing Service.

Dodson, P (1993). "Reconciliation and the high court's decision on native title". *Aboriginal Law Bulletin*, vol. 3, no. 61, pp 6-9.

Dodson, P (1989). "Statehood for Northern Territory". *Aboriginal Law Bulletin*, vol. 2, no. 39, pp 14-16.

Foundation for Aboriginal and Islander Research Action (1991). "ATSIC: a limited step forward?" *Aboriginal Law Bulletin,* vol. 2, no. 43, pp 7-9.

Goot, M and Rowse, T, editors (1994). *Make a Better Offer: the Politics of Mabo.* New South Wales, Pluto Press.

Hiatt, LR (1987). "Treaty, compact or makarrata?" *Oceania,* vol., 58, no. 2.

Hiley, G, editor (1997). *The Wik Case: Issues and Implications.* Sydney, Butterworth.

House of Representatives Standing Committee on Aboriginal Affairs (1990). *Our Future Ourselves: Aboriginal and Torres Strait Islander Community Control, Management and Resources.* Canberra: Australian Government Publishing Service.

Howard, M (1982). "Australian Aboriginal politics and perpetuation of inequality". *Oceania,* vol. 53, no. 1, pp 82-101.

Jennett, C (1987). "Incorporation or independence? the struggle for Aboriginal equality". In *Three worlds of Inequality: Race, Class and Gender,* edited by C Jennett and R Stewart. South Melbourne: Macmillan, pp 57-93.

Jennett, C (1990). "Aboriginal affairs policy'" In *Hawke and Australian Public Policy,* edited by C Jennett and R Stewart. South Melbourne, Macmillan.

Johnston, E (1991). *National Report: Overview and Recommendations, Royal Commission into Aboriginal Deaths in Custody.* Canberra: Australian Government Publishing Service.

Jull, P (1993). "Political strategies for indigenous peoples: levels of practical action". Mimeo. Darwin: North Australian Research Unit, Australian National University.

Keating, P (1993). Australian Launch of the International Year for the World's Indigenous People, 10 December 1992. *Aboriginal Law Bulletin,* vol. 3, no. 61, pp 4-5.

Koori Mail.

Land Rights News.

Lavery, D (1992). "When the CAR Stops on reconciliation day will indigenous Australians have gone anywhere?" *Aboriginal Law Bulletin,* vol. 2, no.58, 7-8.

Mansell, M (1992). "Beyond 2001: the white man's dream may be an Aboriginal nightmare". Mimeo. Hobart: Aboriginal Provisional Government.

Miller Report of the Committee of Review of Aboriginal Employment and Training Programs (1985). *Aboriginal Employment and Training Programs: Report of the Committee of Review*. Canberra: Australian Government Publishing Service.

Ministry of Aboriginal Affairs (1992). *Social Justice for Indigenous Australians*. Budget paper no. 7. Canberra: Australian Government Publishing Service.

Moizo, B (1990). "Implementation of the community development employment scheme in Fitzroy Crossing: a preliminary report". *Australian Aboriginal Studies*, 1990, no. 1, pp 37-40.

Morris, B (1989). *Domesticating Resistance: the Dhan-gadi Aborigines and the Australian State*. London: Berg.

Mowbray, M (1990). "Mainstreaming as assimilation in the Northern Territory". *Australian Aboriginal Studies*, 1990, no. 2, pp 20-26.

National Aboriginal and Islander Legal Services (1989). "An interesting and informative chat was not what I had in mind ...". *Aboriginal Law Bulletin*, vol. 2, no. 36, pp 12-15.

O'Donoghue, L (1992). *One Nation: Promise or Paradox?* Speech at the National Press Club. Canberra: ATSIC.

Perkins, C (1989). "Governments and Aboriginal communities". *Australian Journal of Public Administration*, vol. 48, no. 1, pp 21-28.

Perkins, C (1990). "Welfare and Aboriginal people in Australia: time for a new direction". The Frank Archibald Memorial Lecture. NSW: University of New England.

Report of the National Inquiry into the Separation of Aboriginal and Torres Strait Islander Children From Their Families (1997). *Bringing Them Home*. Sterling Press.

Reynolds, H (1991). "Who is reconciling whom, and to what?" *Australian Society*, pp 3-4.

Roberts, D (1993). "Reconciliation and the Mabo Factor". *Kaurna Journal of Higher Education*, vol. 4, pp 16-24.

Rowse, T (1992a). "Can ATSIC really contribute to Aboriginal self-determination?" *Modern Times*, pp 22-23.

Rowse, T (1992b). *Remote Possibilities: the Aboriginal Domain and the Administrative Imagination*. Darwin: Northern Australia Research Unit, Australian National University.

Ryan, L (1989). "Aboriginals and Islanders". In *From Fraser to Hawke*, edited by Brian Head and A Patience. Longman Cheshire: Melbourne, pp 394-408.

Sanders, W (1991). "Destined to fail: the Hawke government's pursuit of statistical equality in employment and income status between Aborigines and other Australians by the year 2000". *Australian Aboriginal Studies*, 1991, no. 2, 13-17.

Stephenson, MA, editor (1995). *Mabo: the Native Title Legislation*. St Lucia, Queensland: University of Queensland Press.

Stephenson, MA and Ratnapala, S, editors (1993). *Mabo, a Judicial Revolution: the Aboriginal Land Rights Decision and the Impact on Australian Law*. St Lucia, Queensland: University of Queensland Press.

Tatz, C (1983). "Aborigines and the age of atonement". *The Australian Quarterly*, vol. 55, no. 3, pp 291-306.

Taylor, J (1993). "Industry segregation among employed Aborigines and Torres Strait Islanders". *ANZJS*, vol. 29, no. 3, pp 3-20.

The Advertiser.

The Australian.

Watson, I (1992). "International Year for Indigenous Peoples 1993: How far is there to travel in achieving indigenous rights?" Kaurna Lecture. Adelaide: University of South Australia.

Watson, I (1993). "Has *Mabo* turned the tide for justice?" *Social Alternatives*, vol. 12, no. 1, pp 5-9.

Wright, J (1988). "What became of that treaty?" *Australian Aboriginal Studies*, 1988, no. 1, pp 40-44.

Endnotes

[1] The State is defined here as the totality of institutions, structures and processes which together control and manage power in contemporary Australian society.

Index